Pocket Guide
BIRDS
OF BRITAIN AND IRELAND

JOHN GOODERS

LAROUSSE

KINGFISHER
Kingfisher Publications Plc
283–288 High Holborn
London WC1V 7HZ

This edition published by Kingfisher Publications Plc 1995
10 9 8 7 6 5
5TR (2BS) / 0399 / WKT / BA(BA) / 128KMA

Senior Editor : Michèle Byam
Assistant Editor : Mandy Cleeve
Design : Smiljka Surla

Colour separations : Newsele SRL, Milan
Printed in Hong Kong / China

Contents

Introduction

HOW TO USE THIS BOOK

Every one of the birds in this book is treated to a whole page. Each page has the same ingredients and a similar design. Like making a cake, each ingredient is an important contribution to the whole. If you miss an ingredient, an inaccurate identification or an inedible cake may result.

The first thing to do when you see an unfamiliar bird is to check the list of general types of bird (waders, birds of prey and so on) on page 16. Then turn to the appropriate pages and leaf through the illustrations to see if your bird is

there. If you spot it, or one that looks very similar, check the labels around the illustrations to see if your bird showed the same salient features. Then consult the text, map and monthly abundance chart to confirm your identification. It is unlikely however, that you will have noted each and every aspect of a bird's plumage and behaviour. This is where the checklist of features for each bird comes in. Use it to check details such as the bird's size, the colour of a particular part of the body or a distinctive piece of behaviour you may have noticed.

Accurate illustrations show major plumages (such as male, female, juvenile, summer and winter), and typical field postures (swimming, perching and so on).

Labels pick out the best clues to identification.

A text summarizes the most important points about the bird's appearance, behaviour and distribution and distinguishes it from similar species.

Abundance chart – from January to December.

0 = unknown, 1 = rare, 2 = must be definitely sought, 3 = needs a bit of searching, 4 = seen most days, 5 = regularly seen, 6 = impossible to miss

This colour shows which group of birds each species belongs to. Use it to help you find the different groups as you flick through the book. The colour code is explained on p.16.

A detailed checklist provides a 3-part summary of the bird's attributes, including its size, behaviour, voice, the colour of the different parts of its body and breeding characteristics.

A map shows breeding distribution (yellow) and wintering areas (blue). Where these colours overlap to make green, this indicates that the bird is resident.

Grey maps show the distribution of birds that occur only on migration.

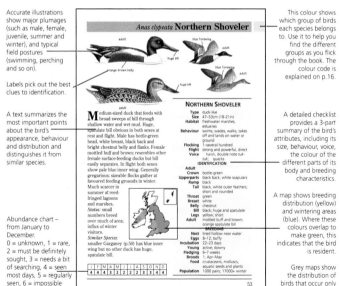

Anas clypeata **Northern Shoveler**

adult
adult
blue forewing
adult
huge bill
orange brown belly
blue forewing
adult
huge bill
adult

NORTHERN SHOVELER

Medium-sized duck that feeds with broad sweeps of bill through shallow water and wet mud. Huge, spatulate bill obvious in both sexes at rest and flight. Male has bottle-green head, white breast, black back and bright chestnut belly and flanks. Female mottled buff and brown; resembles other female surface-feeding ducks but bill easily separates. In flight both sexes show pale blue inner wing. Generally gregarious; sizeable flocks gather at favoured feeding grounds in winter. Much scarcer in summer at reed-fringed lagoons and marshes. *Status:* small numbers breed over much of area; influx of winter visitors. *Similar Species:* smaller Garganey (p.50) has blue inner wing but no other duck has huge, spatulate bill.

J	F	M	A	M	J	J	A	S	O	N	D
4	4	4	3	2	2	2	2	3	3	4	4

Type	duck-like
Size	47–53cm (18–21in)
Habitat	freshwater marshes, estuaries
Behaviour	swims, wades, walks, takes off and lands on water or ground
Flocking	1–several hundred
Flight	strong and powerful, direct
Voice	harsh, double note *tuk-tuk; quacks*

IDENTIFICATION

Adult

Crown	bottle-green
Upperparts	black back, white scapulars
Rump	black
Tail	black, white outer feathers; short and rounded
Throat	green
Breast	white
Belly	chestnut
Bill	black; huge and spatulate
Legs	yellow; short
Adult	mottled buff and brown; orange spatulate bill

BREEDING

Nest	lined hollow near water
Eggs	8–12; buffy
Incubation	22–23 days
Fledging	active; downy
Broods	6–7 weeks
Food	1; Apr–May
	crustaceans, molluscs, aquatic seeds and plants
Population	1000 pairs; 17000+ winter

53

6

The illustrations

The first reference points on each page are inevitably the illustrations. Each species is shown in its major plumages and in typical attitudes, as birds are generally seen in the field. Similar species appear on facing pages (wherever possible) and in the same postures to facilitate comparison. Some birds, such as several birds of prey, are treated more diagrammatically than others so that finer points of distinction can be picked out.

The labels

The labels around the illustrations are based on the sort of notes that most competent birders make in the field when they see an unfamiliar bird or a bird they do not recognize. We have used the labels to pick out the most important points to watch for and these may not necessarily be the most obvious. Indeed some are quite subtle. To become more competent at bird identification, it is a good idea to spend some time studying the illustrations and the labels so you know what to look for when you eventually see the bird in the field.

The text

The text is a total compliment to the illustrations and labels. It seeks to put the bird into the field as a living thing by painting a word picture of the appearance of the bird and the way it moves around the landscape it inhabits. Finally, the text describes where the bird usually occurs and in what numbers and points out how to distinguish it from similar species.

The maps

The maps show the usual distribution of almost all of our birds, using different colours to indicate breeding and wintering areas. Where these overlap, the two colours combine to produce a third. Some of these birds also pass through parts of the country where they neither breed nor winter. To keep our maps simple and understandable, we have omitted information about passage from them but mentioned the fact in the text instead. A small number of our regular birds do not breed or winter with us but pass through in spring or autumn, or both. The vast majority of these passage migrants are Arctic breeders, mainly waders. Grey coloured maps show where they regularly occur. The maps show what the birds regularly do. But occasionally, they may depart from their normal behaviour; a summer visitor may stay on through the winter for example. This brings them as much into the realms of rarity as the bird that occurs on our shores only once in a lifetime.

The abundance chart

The seasonal abundance chart uses a scale from 0–6 to indicate the likelihood of seeing the bird in each month of the year. The numbers are not so much a measure of the actual number of birds as a combination of number and visibility. The figures 0–6 have been defined in terms of a full day's birding in the right habitat by a competent birder.

Introduction

IDENTIFYING BIRDS

Let me say at the outset that bird identification is largely a matter of knowledge. Most birders acquire this from a combination of books and experience. Some people have a good eye for recognizing birds and others have a good ear for bird song but the lack of such attributes will certainly not prevent you from becoming a competent birdwatcher.

Reed Warbler

Habitat and appearance

Birds are creatures of habit. Each species has its own place in the world and exploits it in the same way generation after generation. Knowing when and where to look for a bird is half the battle in identification. Reed Warblers, for example, are summer visitors and there is no point in looking for them in January. They live among reeds and other aquatic vegetation and you will waste your time looking for

them in oakwoods. They range no further north than Lancashire and Yorkshire so don't arrange a special trip to Wester Ross to see them.

A knowledge of how birds behave is also a vital clue to their identity. So too is a knowledge of what to look for when a bird is seen. For example, you see a flock of black birds on the sea. They look like ducks and you put them down as Common Scoter without waiting patiently to see if any of them flap their wings to show a white speculum (patch on inner wings). Result? You missed a Velvet Scoter. A more obvious but more advanced example, is the separation of the small, olive-brown group of warblers. Here the differences are slight and points such as the length of eyebrow and bill, slope of the forehead, leg colour and tail shape are crucial to identification. If you don't know what to look for, then you won't see it.

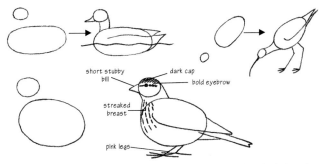

short stubby bill

dark cap

bold eyebrow

streaked breast

pink legs

Field descriptions

Perhaps the most important skill to learn when starting to identify birds is to watch, examine and note. Remembering a single feature will probably not be sufficient for an accurate identification. What is required is the patience to watch and note every part of a bird's body as well as when and where it was seen, how it moved, how it fed, how it flew, which other birds it associated with and so on. Such notes are called field descriptions.

Far and away the best form of note taking is to draw an outline of the bird and mark on it any particularly obvious features. I cannot draw birds but I have found that a couple of ovals works quite satisfactorily if I add on legs, bill and tail. This should preferably be done while the bird is still in view. If the bird flies, try to note the pattern on both the upperwing and underwing – if that is impossible, don't worry. An incomplete description is far better than an inaccurate one.

Armed with your field notes and little drawings, check through the guide to find the bird you have seen. If you have difficulty finding it, do not immediately jump to the conclusion that you have found either a bird new to Britain or even a major rarity. The chances are you haven't! Go back over the pages again and keep searching until you find it.

Velvet Scoter can be identified by a white patch (speculum) on the inner wing.

MAKING FIELD NOTES

On the next six pages are some of the points to consider when you are making your drawings of birds and compiling your field notes. The most important thing to remember is to note down as much information as you can – even seemingly trivial points may be significant when you come to identify the bird later.

finch-like

duck-like

wader-like

swallow-like

hawk-like

thrush-like

What type of bird is it

The division of birds into groups is not artificial; birds are different and these differences can be seen easily. Consult the list in page 16 to familiarize yourself with the major bird groups. If your bird does not fit into any of the categories you know, then say so.

What is the overall shape of the bird?

Is it, for instance, thin like a wagtail or plump like a Robin?

What shape are the wings?

Are they broad like a Buzzard?

Or pointed like a Kestrel?

Are they straight like a Fulmar?

Or sharply angled like a Swallow?

Are they rounded like a Partridge?

Or long and thin like a Swift?

What shape and size is the bill?

It is also useful to note how long the bill is compared to the length of the head. This is particularly important for waders.

Is it tiny like a Swallow?

Is it thin and pointed like a Robin?

Is it conical like a Greenfinch?

Is it long and thin like a Redshank?

Is it hooked like a Kestrel?

Is it decurved like a Curlew?

What shape is the tail?

There is a whole spectrum of shapes that takes in almost every British and Irish bird. Typical shapes are illustrated below, together with some examples of tail patterns.

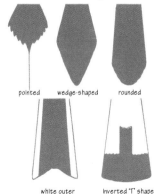

pointed   wedge-shaped   rounded   square   notched   forked

white outer tail feathers   inverted 'T' shape   black tip   white outer tips

Introduction

How does it fly?

Does it fly in a straight line like a Turtle Dove?

Or undulate like a Mistle Thrush?

Does it glide like a shearwater?

Or hang in the air like a gull?

Does it hover like a Kestrel?

Or dive like a Gannet?

Does it soar like a Buzzard?

Or flap and glide like a harrier?

How does it move?

Does it swim, walk, wade, dive, hop, run, climb or flit among vegetation? Different modes of locomotion offer valuable clues to a bird's identity. Treecreepers, Nuthatches and woodpeckers are most often seen climbing the trunks or major branches of trees. Flycatchers perch openly and dart out to catch flying insects. Warblers flit among vegetation but will also behave like flycatchers. Some ducks, such as Pochard, dive for their food, while others, such as Wigeon, do not. Swifts fly almost continuously, while other birds, such as Moorhens, seem to take to the air only under duress.

Movement during feeding varies enormously too. Some birds wade and probe into the mud; others pick food from the surface. Some walk, others hop or shuffle. Some are ever-active; others stand still and occasionally pounce.

When did you see the bird?

Note the date of every observation in your field notebook. Dates can be an important clue to identity.

Where did you see the bird?

Record the place in your notes; some birds simply do not occur in certain parts of the British Isles.

What sort of habitat was the bird using?

Note the type of countryside where the bird was seen. Was it, for instance, at sea, along the shoreline, on a coastal freshwater marsh, a pond or a lake? Was it among reeds or scrub, on heathland or in a wood? Was the wood coniferous, deciduous or mixed? It is impossible to go into too much detail and even identifying the trees and flowers growing in the area can be helpful.

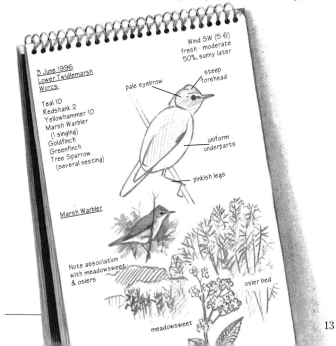

Wind SW (5-6) fresh - moderate 50%, sunny later

3 June 1996
Lower Twidlemarsh
Worcs.

Teal 10
Redshank 2
Yellowhammer 10
Marsh Warbler
(1 singing)
Goldfinch
Greenfinch
Tree Sparrow
(several nesting)

pale eyebrow

steep forehead

uniform underparts

pinkish legs

Marsh Warbler

Note association with meadowsweet & osiers

osier bed

meadowsweet

13

Introduction

What call or song did it make?
Most birders know the voices of the majority of our breeding birds and the most obvious calls of our visitors. The ability to recognize a bird from a brief twitter coming from the middle of a dense thicket saves a great deal of time and effort. If an unknown bird calls, try to write down a phonetic rendering or perhaps put it into words. It is not ideal, because each person tends to interpret a bird call in a different way, but it is better than nothing.

Alternatively, carry a tape recorder with you in the field and record calls and songs you don't know. Then, with the aid of a good set of bird recordings and much patience, try to find the owner. This is, incidentally, an excellent way of learning bird calls.

What size is it?
Size is notoriously misleading and everyone is prone to error. For this reason, I do not consider it of great importance nor do I think too much reliance should be placed on it. The best measure of size is to compare the unknown bird with a known species alongside it. Otherwise, stick to broad scales of size and compare the bird to familiar species, such as a Sparrow or a Blackbird.

What is its structure?
I have intentionally put structure at the end of the list because it is the most difficult feature to describe and appreciate – even though it is arguably the most important. Picking out a species by its structure must be based on experience although even the beginner should bear it in mind at all times.

Birds differ in structure even within quite closely related groups. The most common waders, for instance, are divided into two groups (the *Calidris* and the *Tringa* sandpipers) based on their structure. The generic names (the first scientific names) of the birds reflect these structural differences and are used to name the groups. Though there are differences within each group, their overall structure is similar.

A *Calidris* sandpiper – dumpy structure.

A *Tringa* sandpiper – elegant structure.

Little Stint

Wood Sandpiper

What are its field marks?
Field marks are nothing more than bold patches of plumage that stand out when the bird is seen. Head patterns, wingbars and tail and rump patterns are the most obvious and should be fully noted (and drawn) for every unknown bird. In the main, these marks are confined to a particular group of feathers and a sound knowledge of which feathers are which is an invaluable aid to identification. The main diagram below shows the names of each group of feathers and indicates in particular the complex structure of the feathers on a bird's folded wing. Separate diagrams show details of the field markings on the head and open wing. A full, working knowledge of a bird's anatomy is essential to producing an accurate field description.

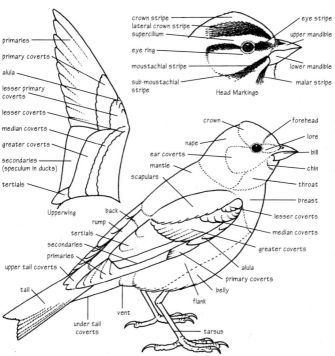

crown stripe
lateral crown stripe
supercilium
eye ring
moustachial stripe
sub-moustachial stripe
eye stripe
upper mandible
lower mandible
malar stripe

Head Markings

primaries
primary coverts
alula
lesser primary coverts
lesser coverts
median coverts
greater coverts
secondaries (speculum in ducks)
tertials

Upperwing

crown
nape
ear coverts
mantle
scapulars
forehead
lore
bill
chin
throat
breast
lesser coverts
median coverts
greater coverts
alula
primary coverts
belly

back
rump
tertials
secondaries
primaries
upper tail coverts
tail
under tail coverts
vent
flank
tarsus

Introduction

WHICH BIRDS?

Over 530 different species have been seen in Britain and Ireland at one time or another and new species are added to the list every year. Fortunately half the total are vagrants that occur once in a while from distant parts of Europe, Asia and America. They are in no sense 'British Birds'. Most tend to be young, lost birds in rather nondescript juvenile or first winter plumage. They are often difficult to identify and need a somewhat different approach from the normal field guide.

In this book, we cover the birds that are regular and most likely to be seen. These birds either breed regularly, winter regularly or regularly pass through on passage to and from their breeding areas. Of course things are never static; today's regular breeder may disappear and become a rarity. Conversely today's vagrant may become tomorrow's breeding species. Meanwhile there are over 230 species that one could reasonably expect to see and which most keen watchers would be pleased to see in a year.

Order of birds

The birds in this book are arranged in systematic order. This scientifically accepted system arranges birds in their approximate order of evolution. To the beginner, this order may seem chaotic compared with arranging the birds in say order of size, or by habitat, or particularly alphabetically. The systematic order does, however, have one great advantage – it generally groups similar birds together and

facilitates comparison. Where this does not happen, we have departed from the strict order to allow similar species to be grouped together.

Use the coloured square at the corner of the pages to help you find the different groups as you flick through the book.

Divers and Grebes

Shearwaters, Cormorants and Gannets

Herons

Wildfowl

Birds of Prey

Gamebirds, Crakes and Rails

Waders

Gulls, Terns and Auks

Pigeons and Cuckoos

Owls

Woodpeckers and Allies

Larks, Swallows and Pipits

Wrens and Allies

Chats and Thrushes

Warblers and Flycatchers

Tits, Nuthatches and Treecreepers

Shrikes and Crows

Sparrows, Finches and Buntings

BIRDS
OF BRITAIN AND IRELAND

Red-throated Diver *Gavia stellata*

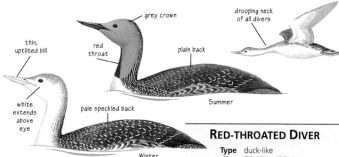

grey crown

drooping neck of all divers

thin, uptilted bill

red throat

plain back

white extends above eye

pale speckled back

Summer

Winter

Smallest of the divers and generally the most widespread and numerous throughout the year. Breeds on small lakes, usually within flighting distance of sea. Winters in coastal waters, often in loose flocks. Thin, uptilted bill. Pale grey crown and rust-red throat in summer. In winter pale grey or brown back, spotted white. Like other divers, flies fast on long, pointed wings with head and neck drooping.

Status: scarce but widespread breeder in northern and western Scotland and north-western Ireland. Winters along all shores.

Similar Species: Black-throated Diver (p.19) and Great Northern Diver (p.20). All divers similar in winter, though Red-throated paler; smaller size distinguishes throughout year.

RED-THROATED DIVER

Type	duck-like
Size	53–59cm (22in)
Habitat	freshwater, sea
Behaviour	swims, dives from surface, takes off and lands on water
Flocking	summer solitary; small flocks winter
Flight	strong and powerful; direct
Voice	harsh *kuk-kuk-kuk* in flight; wails and cackles in breeding season

IDENTIFICATION

Ad.summer	
Crown	pale grey
Upperparts	brown
Rump	brown
Tail	brown; short and pointed
Throat	rust-red
Breast	white
Belly	white
Bill	black; short, thin, uplifted
Legs	black; short
Ad.winter	white head and throat; grey cap; pale grey back spotted white; grey bill
Juvenile	as Ad.winter, darker back

BREEDING

Nest	scrape at water's edge
Eggs	2; olive buff-blotched black
Incubation	24–29 days, mainly ♂♀
Young	active; downy
Fledging	6 weeks
Broods	1: May–Sept
Food	fish, amphibians
Population	750+ pairs; 12,000+ winter

J	F	M	A	M	J	J	A	S	O	N	D
3	3	3	3	2	2	2	2	2	2	3	3

18

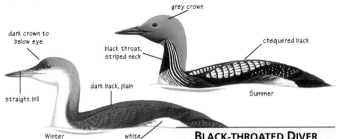

grey crown

dark crown to below eye

black throat, striped neck

chequered back

straight bill

dark back, plain

Summer

Winter

white flank patch

Intermediate in size between Red-throated and Great Northern Divers. Breeds on larger lakes and winters offshore. In summer, largely black and white with two chequered ovals on back. Neck striped black and white with black foreneck. In winter, upperparts plain slate-brown in adult; slightly mottled in juvenile. White patch on rear flanks often obvious. Dark of crown extends below eye giving masked effect.
Status: scarce breeder in north and west Scotland. Winters along all shores, mostly in west.
Similar Species:
Red-throated Diver (p.18) always paler and more slightly built. Great Northern Diver (p.20) has more massive head and bill and black, not grey, head in summer.

BLACK-THROATED DIVER

Type	duck-like
Size	56–69cm (25in)
Habitat	freshwater, sea
Behaviour	swims, dives from surface, takes off and land on water
Flocking	summer solitary; small flocks winter
Flight	strong and powerful; direct
Voice	grunts, croaks and loud wailing in breeding season

IDENTIFICATION

Ad.summer	
Crown	grey
Upperparts	black and white, with two chequered ovals
Rump	black
Tail	black; short and pointed
Throat	black
Breast	white
Belly	white
Bill	black; straight and pointed
Legs	black; short
Ad.winter	dark above, white below, white patch on rear flanks
Juvenile	as Ad.winter, speckly above

BREEDING

Nest	scrape at water's edge
Eggs	2; olive-brown, blotched black
Incubation	28–29 days ♂ ♀
Young	active; downy
Fledging	9 weeks
Broods	1; May–Sept
Food	fish, amphibians
Population	150 pairs; 1300 winter

J	F	M	A	M	J	J	A	S	O	N	D
3	3	3	3	2	2	2	2	2	3	3	3

Great Northern Diver *Gavia immer*

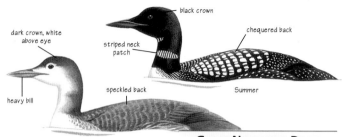

black crown

chequered back

dark crown, white
above eye

striped neck
patch

speckled back

heavy bill

Summer

Winter

L argest and generally least numerous
of the three divers. Size often
confusing at sea, but large, angular head
and heavy bill distinguish at all seasons.
In summer, black head and neck, broken
only by narrow oval of strips on neck.
Chequered back pattern more clear-cut
than Black-throated. In winter, darker
above than Red-throated, but scaly back
pattern produces paler effect than Black-
throated. Dark crown does not enclose
eye. In flight, wing beats slower than the
smaller divers.
Status: has bred
and regularly
summers in
northern Scotland.
Winter visitor to
most coasts; more
regular in north
and west.
Similar Species:
angular crown and mottled upperparts
distinguish from winter Black-throated
Diver (p.19).

GREAT NORTHERN DIVER

Type	duck-like goose-like
Size	69–81cm (30in)
Habitat	freshwater, sea
Behaviour	swims, dives from surface, takes off and lands on water
Flocking	summer solitary; small flocks winter
Flight	strong and powerful; direct
Voice	summer – loud wails, cackling laugh; winter – occasional croaks, moans
IDENTIFICATION	
Ad.summer	
Crown	black
Upperparts	black and white, two chequered ovals
Rump	black
Tail	black; short and pointed
Throat	black
Breast	white
Belly	white
Bill	black; straight and pointed
Legs	black; short
Ad.winter	brown above, white below
Juvenile	as Ad.winter, speckly back
BREEDING	
Nest	scrape at water's edge
Eggs	2; olive-brown, blackish spots
Incubation	29–30 days ♂ ♀
Young	active; downy
Fledging	12 weeks
Broods	1; May–Sept
Food	fish, amphibians
Population	3500+ winter

J	F	M	A	M	J	J	A	S	O	N	D
3	3	3	2	1	1	1	1	1	1	2	3	3

20

striped head

juvenile

Summer

ear tufts and crest

white above eye

white foreneck

Winter

L argest grebe; widespread resident and winter visitor to lakes, reservoirs and coastlines. In summer, black cap and prominent russet and black head plumes (erected in display) preclude confusion. In winter, black cap extends *above* eye forming prominent white eyebrow; foreneck white. Juveniles heavily streaked on head. Dives expertly; flies laboriously after lengthy pattering over water's surface. *Status:* widespread and quite numerous except in Scottish Highlands and Islands. In winter congregates at larger waters and sheltered coastlines. Some immigration from the Continent. *Similar Species:* large size, long neck and sharply pointed bill separate from all grebes except winter Red-necked (p.22), which has no eyebrow and dusky, not white, foreneck.

J	F	M	A	M	J	J	A	S	O	N	D
5	5	5	5	5	5	5	5	5	5	5	5

GREAT CRESTED GREBE

Type	duck-like
Size	45–51cm (19in)
Habitat	freshwater, sea
Behaviour	swims, dives from surface, takes off and lands on water
Flocking	summer solitary; small flocks winter
Flight	laboured; direct
Voice	harsh barking *ra-ra* and variety croaking sounds

IDENTIFICATION

Ad.summer	
Crown	black, crest
Upperparts	brown
Rump	brown
Tail	brown; short and rounded
Throat	white
Breast	white
Belly	white
Bill	red; straight and sharply pointed
Legs	green; short
Ad.winter	dark cap, white above eye, white neck
Juvenile	as Ad.winter, streaked head

BREEDING

Nest	floating mound in water
Eggs	4; white
Incubation	25–29 days ♂ ♀
Young	active; downy
Fledging	25–29 days
Broods	1 or 2; May–July
Food	fish
Population	3000 pairs; 7000+ winter

21

Red-necked Grebe *Podiceps grisegena*

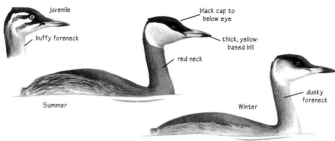

juvenile
buffy foreneck
Summer

black cap to below eye
thick, yellow-based bill
red neck

dusky foreneck
Winter

Mainly winter visitor and passage migrant to coastal waters. In summer, black cap extends to below eye; white cheeks and rust-red neck preclude confusion. In winter, overall pattern remains same but neck becomes dusky grey and cheeks less white. Yellow bill with dark tip. Often found in small groups in winter.

Status: scarce double passage migrant and winter visitor to east coast, extending westward along south coast to Dorset. Absent Ireland.

Similar Species: winter Great Crested Grebe (p.21). Red-necked slightly smaller with grey foreneck; shorter, thicker bill is yellow, not pink.

RED-NECKED GREBE

Type	duck-like
Size	40–46cm (17in)
Habitat	freshwater, sea
Behaviour	swims, dives from surface, takes off and lands on water
Flocking	1–10
Flight	laboured; direct
Voice	silent away from breeding grounds
IDENTIFICATION	
Ad.summer	
Crown	black
Upperparts	brown
Rump	brown
Tail	brown; short and rounded
Throat	rust-red
Breast	rust-red
Belly	white
Bill	yellow, dark tip; straight and pointed
Legs	black; short
Ad.winter	smudgy cap, grey foreneck
Juvenile	as Ad.winter; streaked head
BREEDING	
Nest	floating mount in water
Eggs	4–5; white
Incubation	22–25 days ♂♀
Young	active; downy
Fledging	?
Broods	1; May–June
Food	small fish, crustaceans, molluscs, insects
Population	1 pair, 120+ winter

J	F	M	A	M	J	J	A	S	O	N	D
2	2	2	1	1	1	1	1	2	2	2	2

22

clear-cut cap

thickish pointed bill

Winter

Winter

golden horns

Summer

red neck

Small grebe, only slightly larger than Little Grebe. In summer, black head marked by golden 'horns' extending through eye; neck and flanks rust-red. In winter, clear-cut black cap contrasts with white foreneck and flanks; back almost black. Generally gregarious all seasons. *Status:* rare breeder in northern Britain; scarce winter visitor, mainly to sheltered coasts and estuaries. *Similar Species:* Black-necked (p.24) is separated by black, not red, neck in summer and grey foreneck and less clear-cut cap in winter. At all times Slavonian has thicker, more symmetrical, bill.

J	F	M	A	M	J	J	A	S	O	N	D
2	2	1	2	2	2	2	1	1	1	2	2

SLAVONIAN GREBE

Type	duck–like
Size	31–36cm (13in)
Habitat	freshwater, sea
Behaviour	swims, dives from surface, takes off and lands on water
Flocking	colonial; small flocks (up to 15) winter
Flight	laboured; direct
Voice	trills when breeding

IDENTIFICATION

Ad.summer	
Crown	black, golden 'horns'
Upperparts	almost black
Rump	black
Tail	black; short and rounded
Throat	rust-red
Breast	rust-red
Belly	rust-red
Bill	black; short and pointed
Legs	black; short
Ad.winter	black cap, white throat
Juvenile	browner version of Ad.winter

BREEDING

Nest	floating mound in water
Eggs	4–5; white
Incubation	22–25 days ♂♀
Young	active; downy
Fledging	?
Broods	1; May–July
Food	small fish, crustaceans, molluscs, insects
Population	70+ pairs; 430 winter

Black-necked Grebe *Podiceps nigricollis*

dusky cap not clear-cut, pale hind crown

thin uptilted bill

dusky foreneck

Winter

golden fan

Summer

black neck

Winter

Small grebe, similar in size to Slavonian but head rounder and bill thinner and uptilted. Decidedly less maritime than Slavonian in winter, frequenting large reservoirs and gravel pits, usually within easy reach of coast. Winter plumage is dark cap with pale area extending to hind crown; neck smudgy grey. In summer, head, neck and breast black broken only by golden fan of plumes extending from eye. Back black; flanks rust-red.

Status: breeds central Scotland, western Ireland and occasionally elsewhere. Winter visitor to southern Scottish and English waters.

Similar Species: Slavonian Grebe (p.23), especially in winter when Slavonian has more clear-cup cap, white (not grey) neck, and appears more black and white.

BLACK-NECKED GREBE

Type	duck-like
Size	28–33cm (12in)
Habitat	freshwater
Behaviour	swims, dives from surface, takes off and lands on water
Flocking	colonial; small flocks winter
Flight	laboured; direct
Voice	quiet *poo-eep*; variety harsh notes

IDENTIFICATION

Ad.summer	
Crown	black, golden 'fan'
Upperparts	black
Rump	black
Tail	black; short and rounded
Throat	black
Breast	black
Belly	rust-red
Bill	black; short and uplifted
Legs	black; short
Ad.winter	black above, greyish white below, smudgy cap, smudgy grey throat
Juvenile	as Ad.winter but browner

BREEDING

Nest	floating mound in water
Eggs	3–4; white
Incubation	20–21 days ♂♀
Young	active; downy
Fledging	?
Broods	2; Apr–June
Food	insects, crustaceans, molluscs
Population	20+ pairs, 120 winter

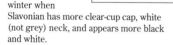

J	F	M	A	M	J	J	A	S	O	N	D
2	2	2	1	2	2	1	1	2	2	2	2

stubby bill

pale patch

red sides to head

Winter

Summer

sawn off tail

buffy neck

Smallest, most widespread and numerous of the grebes, found on variety of inland waters, mostly with plentiful vegetation emerging above water. In summer, rust-red cheeks, throat and neck with bold yellow spot at base of bill. In winter, dark cap and upperparts; buffy throat, neck and flanks.
Status: widespread breeding resident; often quite numerous (semi-colonial) at favoured waters both summer and winter.
Similar Species: can be confused with Slavonian Grebe (p.23) and Black-necked Grebe (p.24) in winter but short, square-cut tail distinguishes.

LITTLE GREBE

Type	duck-like
Size	25–29cm (10–11in)
Habitat	freshwater, estuaries
Behaviour	swims, dives from surface, takes off and lands on water
Flocking	colonial; small flocks winter
Flight	laborious; direct
Voice	brief *whit-whit*; loud, far-carrying whinnying song

IDENTIFICATION

Ad.summer	
Crown	black
Upperparts	black
Rump	brown
Tail	buff; short and rounded
Throat	rust-red
Breast	black
Belly	brown
Bill	black with yellow spot at base; short and stubby
Legs	green; short
Ad.winter & juvenile	brown above, buff below, dark cap

BREEDING

Nest	floating mound in water
Eggs	4–6 white
Incubation	19–25 days ♂♀
Young	active; downy
Fledging	44–48 days
Broods	2; Apr–July
Food	fish, insects, crustaceans
Population	9000–18,000 pairs; 11,000+ winter

J	F	M	A	M	J	J	A	S	O	N	D
5	5	5	5	5	5	5	5	5	5	5	5

Fulmar *Fulmarus glacialis*

short, stubby bill

thick neck

stiff wings

Stocky, heavily-built seabird; glides and skims water with typical stiff-winged shearwater flight. Flaps wings more frequently than shearwaters. Head, neck and body white; wings, back and tail grey. Lacks any distinctive black and white pattern on wingtips. Short yellow bill; tube-nose visible at close quarters. Thick 'bull-neck' quite unlike any similar species; particularly noticeable in flight. Often gathers in large numbers round trawlers; decidedly gregarious at cliff breeding colonies. *Status:* breeds along almost all coasts where suitable cliffs occur. In winter, widespread throughout Atlantic and North Sea. *Similar Species:* easily confused with gulls, especially when perched on cliffs. Only grey, stiff-winged species at sea.

FULMAR

Type	gull-like
Size	44–40cm (17–20in)
Habitat	sea and sea-cliffs
Behaviour	swims, perches on rocks, takes off and lands on water or cliffs
Flocking	colonial; sometimes huge flocks
Flight	strong and powerful; gliding
Voice	harsh crackle at breeding colonies

IDENTIFICATION

Adult	
Crown	white
Upperparts	grey
Rump	grey
Tail	grey; short and square
Throat	white
Breast	white
Belly	white
Bill	yellow; short, tube-nosed
Legs	yellow; short

BREEDING

Nest	bare ledge
Eggs	1; white
Incubation	55–57 days ♂♀
Young	helpless; downy
Fledging	46–51 days
Broods	1; May–Sept
Food	crustaceans, fish
Population	600,000 pairs

J	F	M	A	M	J	J	A	S	O	N	D
6	6	6	6	6	6	6	6	6	6	6	6

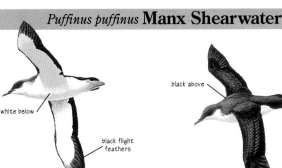

black above

white below

black flight
feathers

Most common and widespread of British shearwaters; usually seen in fast careering flight low over sea, or resting on sea awaiting cover of darkness to return to breeding colonies. Black above and white below, with broad black margins to underwing. In typical shearwater flight, flashes alternately black and white as turns low over waves on straight, stiff wings.
Status: breeds on islands in west and north; elsewhere passage migrant.
Similar Species: in some lights may resemble Mediterranean Shearwater.

MANX SHEARWATER

Type	gull-like
Size	30–38cm (11½–15in)
Habitat	sea and small islands
Behaviour	swims, takes off and lands on water and ground
Flocking	1–many thousands
Flight	strong and powerful; gliding; undulating
Voice	loud wails and screams at breeding colonies

IDENTIFICATION

Ad.N.Atlan

Crown	black
Upperparts	black
Rump	black
Tail	black; short and rounded
Throat	white
Breast	white
Belly	white
Bill	black; short and thin
Legs	grey; short

BREEDING

Nest	burrow, crevice
Eggs	1; white
Incubation	52–54 days ♂♀
Young	helpless, downy
Fledging	59–62 days
Broods	1; May–Sept
Food	fish, squid, crustaceans
Population	300,000 pairs +

J	F	M	A	M	J	J	A	S	O	N	D
0	1	2	2	3	4	3	3	2	2	1	1

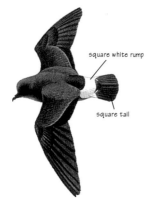

square white rump

square tail

fluttering flight

white extends
to sides

dangling legs

EUROPEAN STORM-PETREL

Type	swallow-like
Size	14–16cm (5–6in)
Habitat	sea and small offshore islets
Behaviour	swims, takes off and lands on water or ground
Flocking	1–several hundred
Flight	flitting, gliding, undulating
Voice	on nest, purr ending in hiccough; also high-pitched, repeated squeaks; silent at sea

IDENTIFICATION

Adult	
Crown	black
Upperparts	black
Rump	white
Tail	black; medium length and square
Throat	black
Breast	black
Belly	black
Bill	black; short and thin
Legs	black; medium length

BREEDING

Nest	burrow, crevice
Eggs	1; white
Incubation	38–40 days ♂ ♀
Young	helpless; downy
Fledging	56-64 days
Broods	1; May–July
Food	small fish, plankton
Population	50,000 pairs+

Tiny, black, bat-like seabird with prominent white rump. Usually seen at sea flying with non-stop wing action dipping to surface with feet dangling to pick up food. Wings straight, broad and rounded; white under wing bar. Tail square-cut, with broad white rump extending to sides of underparts. Feet do not project beyond tail. Often follows ships, picking up food from wake.
Status: highly localized breeder on small islands off coasts of Scotland, Wales and Ireland.
Elsewhere on passage or storm-driven.
Similar Species: Leach's Storm-petrel (p.29)

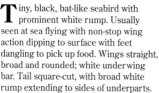

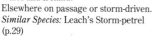

J	F	M	A	M	J	J	A	S	O	N	D
2	3	3	3	3	3	3	3	3	2	2	2

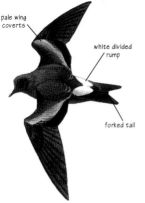

pale wing coverts

white divided rump

forked tail

longish wings

Usually black-brown bird with long, pointed, angled wings; pale edges to coverts form pale inner wing. Tail distinctly forked; white rump has dark central stripe. Feet do not extend beyond tail. Flight is shearwater-like; short glides between bouts of leisurely wing-flapping. Seldom follows ships. *Status:* confined to handful of remote islands off coast of Scotland and possibly Ireland. Otherwise scarce passage migrant and storm-driven waif. *Similar Species:* smaller European Storm-petrel (p.28) is blacker, has less angled wings and lacks forked tail and pale inner wing.

J	F	M	A	M	J	J	A	S	O	N	D
0	0	2	2	2	2	2	2	2	2	2	0

LEACH'S STORM-PETREL

Type	swallow-like
Size	19–22cm (7½–9in)
Habitat	sea and small offshore islets
Behaviour	swims, takes off and lands on water or ground
Flocking	1–20
Flight	hovers, glides; undulating
Voice	croons on nest; variety of screeches and repeated notes at colonies

IDENTIFICATION

Adult	
Crown	dark brown
Upperparts	dark brown
Rump	white, dark central stripe
Tail	dark brown; medium length and forked
Throat	dark brown
Breast	dark brown
Belly	dark brown
Bill	black; short and thin
Legs	black; medium length
BREEDING	
Nest	burrow, crevice
Eggs	1; white
Incubation	41–42 days ♂ ♀
Young	helpless; downy
Fledging	63–70 days
Broods	1; May–June
Food	fish, plankton
Population	several thousand pairs

29

Great Cormorant *Phalacrocorax carbo*

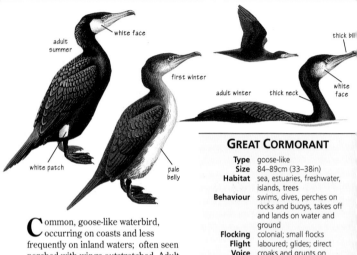

adult summer — white face

first winter

thick bill

adult winter — thick neck, white face

white patch

pale belly

Common, goose-like waterbird, occurring on coasts and less frequently on inland waters; often seen perched with wings outstretched. Adult glossy green-black with white face and round white flank patch in summer. Immature browner, with pale breast and belly. Swims low in water with uptilted head and heavy, yellow bill. Dives easily; often flies in 'V' formation like geese.
Status: found on all coasts, breeding mainly in north and west; also inland in lowland England and north and central Ireland.
Similar Species: Shag (p.31) is considerably smaller.

GREAT CORMORANT

Type	goose-like
Size	84–89cm (33–38in)
Habitat	sea, estuaries, freshwater, islands, trees
Behaviour	swims, dives, perches on rocks and buoys, takes off and lands on water and ground
Flocking	colonial; small flocks
Flight	laboured; glides; direct
Voice	croaks and grunts on breeding grounds

IDENTIFICATION

Adult	
Crown	black
Upperparts	black
Rump	black
Tail	black; medium length and rounded
Throat	white
Breast	black
Belly	black
Bill	yellow; straight and thick
Legs	black; short
Juvenile	brown above, buff below

BREEDING

Nest	mound of seaweed on cliff or tree
Eggs	3–4; pale blue
Incubation	28–29 days ♂ ♀
Young	helpless; naked
Fledging	50–60 days
Broods	1; Apr–June
Food	fish
Population	8000 pairs; 20,000+ winter

J	F	M	A	M	J	J	A	S	O	N	D
5	5	5	5	5	5	5	5	5	5	5	5

crest

greenish black

no white

thin bill

adult winter

thin neck

dark face

thin neck

adult summer

buffy

first winter

S maller version of Great Cormorant, though essentially marine along predominantly rocky coasts. Swims, dives and hangs out wings like Great Cormorant but seldom flies very high. Adult glossy green-black, with short tufted crest in summer. Bill black with yellow gape. Immature brownish with black scaling to feathers; underparts buffy, chin paler.
Status: widespread in north and west, scarce where does not breed.
Similar Species: separated from Great Cormorant (p.30) at all times by smaller size, steeper forehead, smaller, thinner bill and thinner neck.

J	F	M	A	M	J	J	A	S	O	N	D
3	3	3	4	4	4	4	4	3	3	3	3

SHAG

Type	goose-like
Size	72–80cm (28–31in)
Habitat	sea, sea-cliffs
Behaviour	swims, dives, perches on rocks and buoys, takes off and lands on water and ground
Flocking	colonial; 1–several thousand
Flight	laboured; glides; direct
Voice	grunts and hisses at breeding grounds

IDENTIFICATION

Crown	green-black; crest
Upperparts	green-black
Rump	green-black
Tail	green-black; medium length and rounded
Throat	green-black
Breast	green-black
Belly	green-black
Bill	black with yellow gape; straight and thinnish
Legs	grey; short
Ad.winter	no crest, dark face
Juvenile	brown above, buff below

BREEDING

Nest	mount of seaweed on cliff
Eggs	3; pale blue
Incubation	30 days ♂♀
Young	helpless; naked
Fledging	55 days
Broods	1; Mar–Apr
Food	fish
Population	32,000 pairs; 100,000+ winter

31

Northern Gannet *Morus bassanus*

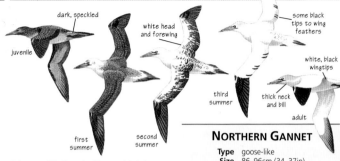

juvenile

dark, speckled

white head and forewing

some black tips to wing feathers

white, black wingtips

third summer

thick neck and bill

adult

first summer

second summer

Large black and white seabird that nests at a few colonies, mainly on remote islets. At sea, appears white and cigar-shaped with pointed head and tail. Wings long, straight and pointed with large black tips. Flies low over water on stiff, shearwater-like wings, before rising in series of flaps and starting another glide. Makes dramatic dives for fish, often from great height. Adult has yellow wash over head. Immatures share same basic shape, but are dark brown; gradually become whiter over period of four years.

Status: seen passing offshore, especially in north and west where main breeding colonies located; can be seen off all coasts during passage.

Similar Species: all-dark juveniles separated from Great Cormorant (p.30) by different flight and behaviour.

J	F	M	A	M	J	J	A	S	O	N	D
4	6	6	6	6	6	6	6	6	6	4	4

NORTHERN GANNET

Type	goose-like
Size	86–96cm (34–37in)
Habitat	sea, sea-cliffs
Behaviour	swims, dives from air, takes off and lands on water and ground
Flocking	colonial; 1–several thousand
Flight	strong and powerful; glides, dives; direct
Voice	variety grunts and cackles at breeding colonies

IDENTIFICATION

Adult

Crown	yellow
Upperparts	white, black wingtips
Rump	white
Tail	white; medium length and pointed
Throat	white
Breast	white
Belly	white
Bill	grey; straight and thickish
Legs	black; short
Juvenile	speckled dark brown, white rump
Second Year	dark brown, head and forewing becoming whiter

BREEDING

Nest	mound of seaweed
Eggs	1; white
Incubation	43–45 days ♂♀
Young	helpless; downy
Fledging	14 weeks
Broods	1; Apr–June
Food	fish
Population	150,000 pairs

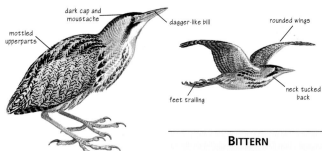

dark cap and moustache

dagger-like bill

rounded wings

mottled upperparts

feet trailing

neck tucked back

Large, secretive heron of dense reedbeds; more often heard than seen. Characteristic booming sounds more like distant foghorn than bird. Heavily camouflaged in shades of brown and buff; spends most of life hidden among reeds. Seen by chance during excursions across open areas, or in occasional flights with head tucked back and legs trailing behind. Close views reveal delicate plumage details as well as black crown and moustachial streak. Legs greenish-yellow.

Status: decidedly scarce, breeding regularly only in East Anglia and Lancashire. Some winter wandering and immigration from the Continent.

Similar Species: rare Purple Heron also appears brownish in flight.

BITTERN

Type	heron-like
Size	70–80cm (27–31in)
Habitat	freshwater marshes
Behaviour	wades, takes off and lands on ground
Flocking	solitary
Flight	laboured
Voice	deep, far-carrying *urrwoomp*, repeated

IDENTIFICATION

Adult	
Crown	black
Upperparts	brown and black, streaked
Rump	buff and brown, streaked
Tail	buff and brown, streaked; short and rounded
Throat	white
Breast	buff and brown, streaked
Belly	buff and brown, streaked
Bill	yellow; straight and thin
Legs	greenish yellow; medium length

BREEDING

Nest	platform of twigs, reeds on ground
Eggs	3–4; pale greenish blue
Incubation	21 days ♂ ♀
Young	helpless; downy
Fledging	6 weeks
Broods	1, sometimes 2; Apr–May
Food	fish, amphibians
Population	less than 20 pairs

J	F	M	A	M	J	J	A	S	O	N	D
1	1	1	1	1	1	1	1	1	1	1	1

Grey Heron *Ardea cinerea*

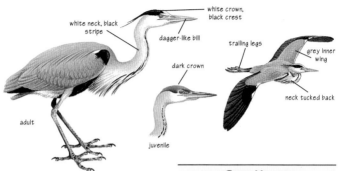

white neck, black stripe

white crown, black crest

dagger-like bill

trailing legs

grey inner wing

dark crown

neck tucked back

adult

juvenile

L arge, grey and white heron with long neck and dagger-like yellow bill. Flies with orange-yellow legs trailing behind and neck tucked into shoulders. Grey back; wings deeply bowed in flight. White head, neck and underparts; black crest and black streaking on neck. Frequents all wetlands. Nests colonially in heronries among tall trees; many have been used for more than a century.
Status: widespread resident throughout Britain and Ireland; population reduced by hard winters.
Similar Species: rare Purple Heron could possibly be confused.

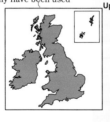

GREY HERON

Type	heron-like
Size	90–100cm (35–39in)
Habitat	freshwater margins and marshes
Behaviour	wades, walks, takes off and lands on ground
Flocking	1–50
Flight	laboured; glides; direct
Voice	harsh *snark*

IDENTIFICATION

Adult

Crown	black; crest
Upperparts	grey
Rump	grey
Tail	grey; short and square
Throat	white
Breast	white, streaked black
Belly	white, streaked black
Bill	yellow; straight and thin
Legs	orange-yellow; very long
Juvenile	greyer, lacks crest

BREEDING

Nest	platform of twigs high in trees
Eggs	3–5; pale greenish blue
Incubation	23–28 days ♂ ♀
Young	helpless; downy
Fledging	50–55 days
Broods	1; Feb–Apr
Food	fish, amphibians
Population	10,000 pairs

J	F	M	A	M	J	J	A	S	O	N	D
5	5	5	5	5	5	5	5	5	5	5	5

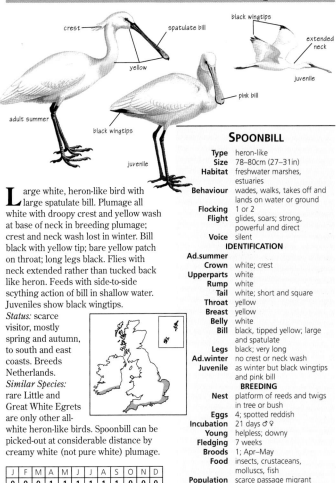

crest
spatulate bill
yellow
black wingtips
extended neck
juvenile
pink bill
adult summer
black wingtips
juvenile

Large white, heron-like bird with large spatulate bill. Plumage all white with droopy crest and yellow wash at base of neck in breeding plumage; crest and neck wash lost in winter. Bill black with yellow tip; bare yellow patch on throat; long legs black. Flies with neck extended rather than tucked back like heron. Feeds with side-to-side scything action of bill in shallow water. Juveniles show black wingtips.

Status: scarce visitor, mostly spring and autumn, to south and east coasts. Breeds Netherlands.

Similar Species: rare Little and Great White Egrets are only other all-white heron-like birds. Spoonbill can be picked-out at considerable distance by creamy white (not pure white) plumage.

SPOONBILL

Type	heron-like
Size	78–80cm (27–31in)
Habitat	freshwater marshes, estuaries
Behaviour	wades, walks, takes off and lands on water or ground
Flocking	1 or 2
Flight	glides, soars; strong, powerful and direct
Voice	silent

IDENTIFICATION

Ad.summer	
Crown	white; crest
Upperparts	white
Rump	white
Tail	white; short and square
Throat	yellow
Breast	yellow
Belly	white
Bill	black, tipped yellow; large and spatulate
Legs	black; very long
Ad.winter	no crest or neck wash
Juvenile	as winter but black wingtips and pink bill

BREEDING

Nest	platform of reeds and twigs in tree or bush
Eggs	4; spotted reddish
Incubation	21 days ♂ ♀
Young	helpless; downy
Fledging	7 weeks
Broods	1; Apr–May
Food	insects, crustaceans, molluscs, fish
Population	scarce passage migrant

J	F	M	A	M	J	J	A	S	O	N	D
0	0	0	1	1	1	1	1	1	1	0	0	0

Mute Swan *Cygnus olor*

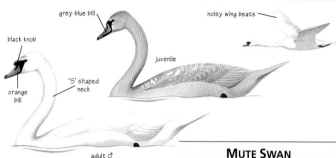

grey-blue bill

noisy wing beats

black knob

juvenile

orange bill

'S' shaped neck

adult ♂

Huge, familiar white waterbird found on all types of freshwater; also occurs on estuaries and occasionally the sea. Adult completely white; legs black; bill orange with large black knob at base. Juvenile grey-buff with grey bill. Swims easily and walks with rolling gait. At all times holds neck in gentle 'S' shape. Flies with noisy wing beats after laborious pattering take-off over water.
Status: widespread and numerous resident throughout lowland Britain; gathers in substantial flocks outside breeding season. Sometimes nests in colonies.
Similar Species: Bewick's Swan (p.37) and Whooper Swan (p.38) are winter visitors that often join Mute Swan flocks. Both have black and yellow bills and noisy calls in flight.

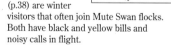

MUTE SWAN

Type	goose-like
Size	145–160cm (63in)
Habitat	freshwater, estuaries, fields
Behaviour	swims, up-ends, walks, takes off and lands on water
Flocking	1–30, exceptionally several hundred
Flight	laboured; direct
Voice	various hisses and grunts of aggression during breeding season; silent in flight

IDENTIFICATION

Adult	
Crown	white
Upperparts	white
Rump	white
Tail	white; short and square
Throat	white
Breast	white
Belly	white
Bill	orange with black knob at base; duck-like
Legs	black; short
Juvenile	grey-buff with grey-blue bill
BREEDING	
Nest	huge mound of vegetation, freshwater margins
Eggs	5–7; white, blue-grey wash
Incubation	34–38 days, mainly ♀
Young	active; downy
Fledging	4 months
Broods	1; Apr–May
Food	aquatic vegetation
Population	5000–6000 pairs

J	F	M	A	M	J	J	A	S	O	N	D
5	5	5	5	5	5	5	5	5	5	5	5

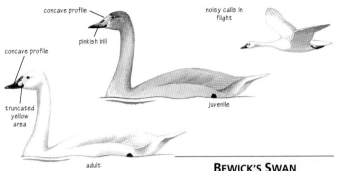

concave profile

pinkish bill

concave profile

truncated yellow area

adult

noisy calls in flight

juvenile

BEWICK'S SWAN

Type	goose-like
Size	116–128cm (45–50in)
Habitat	freshwater, estuaries, fields
Behaviour	swims, up-ends, walks, takes off and lands on water or ground
Flocking	gregarious, 1–several hundred
Flight	laboured; direct
Voice	goose-like honking flight call

IDENTIFICATION

Adult	
Crown	white
Upperparts	white
Rump	white
Tail	white; short and square
Throat	white
Breast	white
Belly	white
Bill	black with yellow base; duck-like
Legs	black; short
Juvenile	brownish grey, pinking bill

BREEDING

Nest	huge mound of vegetation
Eggs	4; creamy white
Incubation	29–30 days
Young	active; downy
Fledging	40-45 days
Broods	1; June–July
Food	grass, grain, roots
Population	16,000+ winter

S mallest of the three swans; size most apparent in flight when faster wing beats and noisy calls resemble goose. Black bill has truncated yellow area at base. Rounded crown with concave forehead and bill profile. Neck often held straight. Usually gregarious, forming large flocks at suitable feeding grounds; grazes in goose-like fashion. *Status:* localized winter visitor from Siberia to traditional feeding grounds, such as Ouse Washes and Slimbridge; most numerous in southern England. Late winter influxes due to hard weather in Germany and Holland. *Similar Species:* Whooper Swan (p.38) is much larger, has pointed yellow area on bill and flat crown and bill profile.

J	F	M	A	M	J	J	A	S	O	N	D
2	2	2	2	0	0	0	0	0	0	1	2

Whooper Swan *Cygnus cygnus*

straight profile

straight profile

pointed
yellow area

straight neck

juvenile

adult

Winter visitor forming medium-sized flocks, often in association with other swans. Neck usually held straight. Yellow base to black bill, which extends forward to form clear point, accentuating flat crown-bill profile. Generally noisy, especially in flight, when wing beats produce whistling noise.

Status: regular winter visitor mainly from Iceland; largest numbers in Scotland and Ireland.

Similar Species: Mute Swan (p.36) is same size but has orange bill and holds neck in 'S'. Smaller Bewick's Swan (p.37) has concave (not flat) crown-bill profile.

WHOOPER SWAN

Type	goose-like
Size	145–160cm (57–63in)
Habitat	freshwater, estuaries, fields
Behaviour	swims, up-ends, walks, takes off and lands on water or ground
Flocking	1–100
Flight	laboured; direct
Voice	loud, trumpeting *whoop*
IDENTIFICATION	
Adult	
Crown	white
Upperparts	white
Rump	white
Tail	white; short and square
Throat	white
Breast	white
Belly	white
Bill	black with yellow base; duck-like
Legs	black; short
Juvenile	brownish grey, pinkish bill
BREEDING	
Nest	mound of vegetation at water's edge, usually island
Eggs	5–6; creamy white
Incubation	35–42 days ♀
Young	active; downy
Fledging	?
Broods	1; May–June
Food	grass, grain, roots
Population	1 or 2 pairs; 5000+ winter

J	F	M	A	M	J	J	A	S	O	N	D
2	2	2	1	1	1	1	1	1	2	2	2

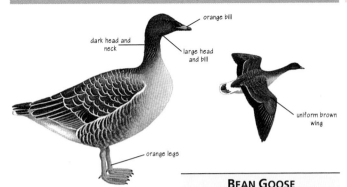

orange bill

dark head and neck

large head and bill

uniform brown wing

orange legs

BEAN GOOSE

Type	goose-like
Size	71–89cm (28–35in)
Habitat	freshwater marshes, grassland
Behaviour	swims, walks, takes off and lands on water and ground
Flocking	1–100
Flight	strong and powerful; direct
Voice	low *ung-unk*, generally less vocal than other geese

IDENTIFICATION

Adult	
Crown	brown
Upperparts	brown, barred buff
Rump	white
Tail	white with grey terminal band; short and square
Throat	brown
Breast	buff
Belly	buff, barred brown
Bill	orange, black base; duck-like
Legs	orange; medium length

BREEDING

Nest	lined scrape near water
Eggs	4–6; white
Incubation	27–29 days ♀
Young	active; downy
Fledging	8 weeks
Broods	1; June–July
Food	grass, grain
Population	200–300 winter

L arge, 'grey' goose with dark neck and dark head. Favours damp grassland habitat. Upperparts brown, closely barred buff. Underparts buffy, narrowly barred brown on flanks. Orange legs; bill orange with variable black base. Gregarious.
Status: scarce winter visitor with only small regular flocks in Solway and East Anglia. Elsewhere rare winter visitor after hard weather.
Similar Species: closely-related Pink-footed Goose (p.40) is smaller and prefers estuaries to damp grassland. Pink-footed and Greylag Goose (p.42) both show obvious pale forewing in flight, lacking in Bean Goose.

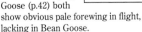

J	F	M	A	M	J	J	A	S	O	N	D
1	1	1	1	1	0	0	0	0	0	1	1

Pink-footed Goose *Anser brachyrhynchus*

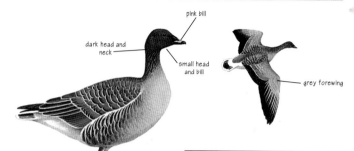

pink bill

dark head and neck

small head and bill

grey forewing

pink legs

S mall 'grey' goose; highly localized winter visitor to Scotland and northern Britain. Small dark head and small pink bill with variable dark base; legs pink. Upperparts greyish brown, closely barred buffy white. Shows bold grey forewing in flight.

Status: numerous winter visitor from Iceland and Greenland forming enormous roosting flocks at traditional sites, mainly Scotland and Lancashire. Elsewhere rather scarce visitor after hard weather.

Similar Species: dark head and neck separate from all other 'grey' geese except Bean Goose (p.39), which lacks grey forewing and has larger head and thicker neck.

J	F	M	A	M	J	J	A	S	O	N	D
3	3	3	2	0	0	0	0	1	2	3	3

PINK-FOOTED GOOSE

Type	goose-like
Size	61–76cm (24–30in)
Habitat	freshwater, estuaries, grassland
Behaviour	swims, walks, takes off and lands on water and ground
Flocking	1–many thousands
Flight	strong and powerful; direct
Voice	highly vocal; high-pitched *unk-unk* and *wink-wink-wink*

IDENTIFICATION
Adult

Crown	brown
Upperparts	grey-brown, barred buff
Rump	white
Tail	white with dark terminal band; short and square
Throat	brown
Breast	buff
Belly	buff, barred brown
Bill	pink, dark based; small and duck-like
Legs	pink; medium length

BREEDING

Nest	lines scrape, cliff-edge
Eggs	4–5; white
Incubation	25–28 days ♀
Young	active; downy
Fledging	8 weeks
Broods	1; June–July
Food	grass, grain, potatoes
Population	100,000 winter

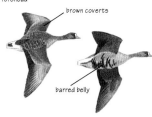

white forehead

brown coverts

barred belly

orange legs

barred belly

Most widespread of the 'grey' geese; found in variety of habitats throughout Britain and Ireland. Small size, broad white base to bill and bold smudgy bars on belly separate from similar geese. Pink or orange bill (see below); legs orange. In flight, lack of grey forewing distinguishes from other 'grey' geese, except Bean Goose (p.39). Juvenile lacks white face and black bars on belly.

Status: widespread winter visitor. Pink-billed (from Russia) visit England and Wales; orange-billed (from Greenland) visit Ireland, west Scotland and west Wales.

Similar Species: other 'grey' geese (pp. 39, 40, 42) and as above. Juvenile lacks white face and black bars on belly.

WHITE-FRONTED GOOSE

Type	goose-like
Size	65–76cm (26–30in)
Habitat	freshwater marshes, grassland
Behaviour	swims, walks, takes off and lands on water and ground
Flocking	1–6000
Flight	strong and powerful; direct
Voice	high-pitched *kow-yow* and *ryo-ryok*; more musical than other geese

IDENTIFICATION

Ad.Russian	
Crown	brown
Upperparts	brown; barred
Rump	white
Tail	white with grey terminal band; short and square
Throat	brown
Breast	buff
Belly	brown, barred black
Bill	pink; duck-like
Legs	orange; medium length
Ad.Greenland	
	bill orange

BREEDING

Nest	lined scrape in bog or thicket
Eggs	5–6; white
Incubation	27–28 days ♀
Young	active; downy
Fledging	?
Broods	1; June–July
Food	grass, cereals, potatoes
Population	5000 Russian; 16,000+ Greenland winter

J	F	M	A	M	J	J	A	S	O	N	D
3	3	3	2	0	0	0	0	1	2	3	3

Greylag Goose *Anser anser*

large head and bill

orange bill

grey forewing

pink legs

Largest and most frequently seen 'grey' goose; ancestor of most domestic geese. Upperparts dark brown, closely barred buff. Underparts, head and neck buff; some faint barring on flanks. Pink legs; orange bill (pink in eastern sub-species). In flight shows prominent pale grey forewing. Eastern sub-species has orange legs.
Status: native birds breed only in Outer Hebrides and nearby Scottish mainland, but many successful re-introductions in various parts of the country. Widespread visitor, mainly from Iceland.
Similar Species: overall size, large pale head and neck with large bill separate from all other 'grey' geese.

GREYLAG GOOSE

Type	goose-like
Size	76–89cm (30–35in)
Habitat	freshwater, estuaries, grassland
Behaviour	swims, walks, takes off and lands on water or ground.
Flocking	1–several hundred
Flight	strong and powerful; direct
Voice	deep *aahng-ung-ung*; highly vocal

IDENTIFICATION

Adult	
Upperparts	brown
Crown	brown, barred buff
Rump	white
Tail	white with grey terminal band, short and square
Throat	brown
Breast	buff
Belly	buff
Bill	orange; large and duck-like
Legs	pink; medium length

BREEDING

Nest	scrape near water
Eggs	4–6; white
Incubation	27–28 days ♀
Young	active; downy
Fledging	1; Apr–May
Broods	1; Apr–May
Food	grass, grain, roots
Population	700–800 pairs; 100,000 winter

J	F	M	A	M	J	J	A	S	O	N	D
3	3	3	3	2	2	2	2	2	3	3	3

Branta canadensis **Canada Goose**

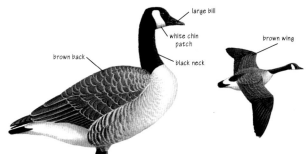

large bill

white chin patch

brown wing

brown back

black neck

Largest of the 'black' geese; about same size as bulkier Greylag. Familiar inhabitant of ponds, lakes, reservoirs and other freshwater habitats; generally tame and often aggressive. Buffy brown above and buff below; long black head and neck broken only by white chin patch. Forms large flocks at end of breeding season (for moulting), otherwise in pairs and family parties.

Status: prospering after introduction from native North America, where is long distance migrant. Widespread in Britain but highly local in Ireland. Most birds resident, but with some long distance migrations (for moulting) developing.

Similar Species: Barnacle Goose (p.44) has white face, grey back and is much smaller.

CANADA GOOSE

Type	goose-like
Size	90–100cm (36–40in)
Habitat	freshwater, marshes and margins, grassland
Behaviour	swims, walks, takes off and lands on water or ground
Flocking	1–1000
Flight	strong and powerful; direct
Voice	loud *wagh-onk* repeated

IDENTIFICATION

Adult	
Crown	black
Upperparts	brown, barred buff
Rump	white
Tail	white with black terminal band; short and square
Throat	black and white
Breast	buff
Belly	brown
Bill	black; large and duck-like
Legs	black; medium length
BREEDING	
Nest	lined hollow beside water, often on island
Eggs	5–6; white
Incubation	28–30 days ♀
Young	active; downy
Fledging	9 weeks
Broods	1; Apr–May
Food	grass, aquatic vegetation, cereals, grain
Population	34,000 individuals

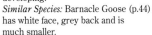

J	F	M	A	M	J	J	A	S	O	N	D
4	4	4	4	4	4	4	4	4	4	4	4

Barnacle Goose *Branta leucopsis*

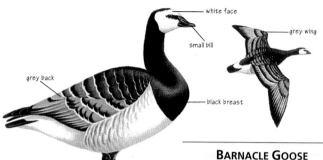

white face

grey wing

small bill

grey back

black breast

Strikingly attractive 'black' goose; highly localized winter visitor, forming large flocks in favoured areas. Back grey, heavily barred black and white. Neck and breast black. White face and black crown. Underparts white. In flight shows grey wings with black trailing edge. Small, black bill and black feet.
Status: largest numbers in western Scotland and western Ireland, but has prospered under careful conservation and now occurs irregularly in small numbers at other, mainly coastal, sites.
Similar Species: Canada Goose (p.43) and Brent Goose (p.45).

BARNACLE GOOSE

Type	goose-like
Size	58–69cm (23–27in)
Habitat	grassland, estuaries
Behaviour	swims, walks, takes off and lands on water and ground
Flocking	1–several thousand
Flight	strong and powerful, direct
Voice	barking, puppy-like yaps with deeper growls

IDENTIFICATION

Adult	
Crown	black
Upperparts	grey, barred black and white
Rump	white
Tail	white with black terminal band; short and square
Throat	black and white
Breast	black
Belly	white
Bill	black; small and duck-like
Legs	black; medium length

BREEDING

Nest	lined depression, ledges of cliffs
Eggs	3–5; white
Incubation	24–25 days ♀
Young	active; downy
Fledging	7 weeks
Broods	1; June–July
Food	grass
Population	33,000 winter

J	F	M	A	M	J	J	A	S	O	N	D
3	3	3	2	1	0	0	0	1	3	3	3

white flash

belly almost as
dark as breast

dark-bellied

black breast
and neck, pale
belly

pale-bellied

Smallest, darkest 'black'
goose; predominantly
estuarine species regularly found
feeding amongst coastal fields. Two sub-
species occur: Pale-bellied *B.b. hrota*
brown above and pale below; black head
and neck ends in clear-cut breast band.
Adults have small white neck flash.
Dark-bellied *B.b. bernicla* similar, but
lacks contrast
between breast and
belly. Juveniles
lack neck flash.
Status: has
prospered with
protection. Dark-
bellied mostly
southern and
eastern England;
Pale-bellied in Ireland and N.E. England.
Similar Species: Barnacle Goose (p.44)
and Canada Goose (p.43).

BRENT GOOSE

Type	goose-like
Size	56–61cm (22–24in)
Habitat	estuaries, grassland
Behaviour	swims, walks, takes off and lands on water or ground
Flocking	1–several thousand
Flight	strong and powerful; direct
Voice	grumbling *krook*, garrulous in flocks

IDENTIFICATION

Ad.dark	
Crown	black
Upperparts	brown
Rump	white
Tail	white with black terminal band; short and square
Throat	black
Breast	black
Belly	brown
Bill	black; duck-like
Legs	pale; medium length
Ad.pale	as above but belly buff
Juveniles	white wingbars; no neck flash

BREEDING

Nest	lined scrape near water, mostly near sea
Eggs	3–5; white-yellow
Incubation	24–26 days ♀
Young	active; downy
Fledging	?
Broods	1; June–July
Food	eelgrass, salting plants, growing cereals, grass
Population	Dark-bellied 92,000+ winter; Pale-bellied 13,000+ winter

J	F	M	A	M	J	J	A	S	O	N	D
3	3	3	2	0	0	0	0	0	1	2	3

Common Shelduck *Tadorna tadorna*

green-black head

red knob

black 'shoulder-straps'

adult ♀

juvenile

chestnut breast band

adult ♂

L arge, goose-like duck showing bold black and white pattern. Head and neck dark bottle-green; rest of plumage white with broad, chestnut breast band and black stripe along folded wing. Bill bright red in adult male with bulbous knob at base. Females and immatures have pinkish red bills (without knob) and less clear-cut breast and wing markings. In flight, main wing feathers are black and contrast with white forewing. Generally gregarious, forming large flocks in winter and for moulting. Mainly coastal; favours estuaries and muddy shores.

Status: resident along most coasts; most migrate N. Germany to moult.

Similar Species: none.

COMMON SHELDUCK

Type	duck-like, goose-like
Size	58–64cm (22–25in)
Habitat	shorelines, estuaries, freshwater marshes
Behaviour	swims, wades, walks, takes off and lands on water or ground
Flocking	1–several hundred
Flight	strong and powerful; direct
Voice	whistling and growling

IDENTIFICATION

Adult ♂	
Crown	bottle-green
Upperparts	white and black
Rump	white
Tail	white with black terminal band; short and square
Throat	bottle-green
Breast	chestnut
Belly	white
Bill	red with knob; duck-like
Legs	pink; medium length
Adult ♀	as ♂ but less clear-cut markings and pink-red knobless bill
Juvenile	as ♀ but lacks breast band; grey-brown crown

BREEDING

Nest	down-lined cup in burrow, hollow tree
Eggs	8–15; cream
Incubation	28–30 days ♀
Young	active; downy
Fledging	8 weeks
Broods	1; May–June
Food	crustaceans, molluscs
Population	12,000 pairs; 66,000 winter

J	F	M	A	M	J	J	A	S	O	N	D
4	4	4	3	3	3	3	4	4	4	4	4

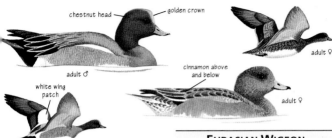

chestnut head · golden crown

adult ♂

cinnamon above and below

adult ♀

adult ♀

white wing patch

adult ♂

A bundant winter visitor; often forming large flocks in favoured areas. Male has golden blase extending from forehead over crown. Rest of head and neck chestnut; body grey with white flash along flanks. Rear flanks white with black end to body. In flight, shows white patch on inner wing; lacking in female and first winter male. Small silver-grey bill. Female cinnamon-brown with delicate rounded head. Largest flocks feed on coastal grassland and most roost on estuaries. Often found alongside geese; also occurs at inland reservoirs and flooded ground.
Status: widespread and numerous winter visitor; small numbers breed, mainly in north of Britain.
Similar Species: female more cinnamon than other surface-feeding ducks.

EURASIAN WIGEON

Type	duck-like
Size	43–48cm (16–19in)
Habitat	estuaries, shores, marshes, grassland
Behaviour	swims, wades, walks, takes off and lands on water or ground
Flocking	1–several thousand
Flight	strong and powerful; direct
Voice	♂ high pitched whistle; ♀ growls

IDENTIFICATION

Adult ♂	
Crown	yellow and chestnut
Upperparts	grey
Rump	grey
Tail	black and white; short and pointed
Throat	chestnut
Breast	buff
Belly	white
Bill	silver-grey; duck-like
Legs	grey; short
Adult ♀	rufous; barred above and below

BREEDING

Nest	lined hollow near water
Eggs	7–8; creamy
Incubation	22-25 days ♀
Young	active; downy
Fledging	6 weeks
Broods	1; May–June
Food	grass, eelgrass
Population	300–500 pairs; up to 300,000 winter

J	F	M	A	M	J	J	A	S	O	N	D
4	4	4	3	2	1	1	1	2	3	4	4

Northern Pintail *Anas acuta*

long tail

chocolate head

pale forewing

adult ♂

adult ♂

adult ♂

heavily spotted

adult ♀

pointed tail

adult ♀

base of neck low in water

Slim elegant duck; characteristic swimming attitude with foreparts lower in water than hindparts. Male has chocolate-brown head with vertical white stripe up back of long neck. Upperparts grey; long drooping black and white scapulars. Grey underparts; pale rear flank patch and black rear end. Long tail has pointed central tail feathers. Bill silver-blue. Female grey-buff, boldly blotched brown above and below – the palest surface-feeding duck. In flight, male shows pale inner forewing; female virtually featureless. Pointed rear end more obvious in male than female. *Status:* scarce, very localized breeder. Winter visitor everywhere, but only common at favoured areas. *Similar Species:* Eurasian Wigeon (p.47) also has pointed tail in flight.

NORTHERN PINTAIL

Type	duck-like
Size	♂ 63–70cm (25–27in)
	♀ 53–59cm (21–23in)
Habitat	marshes, estuaries
Behaviour	swims, up-ends, takes off and lands on water or ground
Flocking	1–several thousand
Flight	strong and powerful; direct
Voice	♂ growls and whistles; ♀ quacks

IDENTIFICATION

Adult ♂

Crown	brown
Upperparts	grey; black and cream scapulars
Rump	grey
Tail	black; long and pointed
Throat	brown
Breast	white
Belly	white
Bill	silver-blue; duck-like
Legs	black; short
Adult ♀	buff and brown with spotting; pointed tail

BREEDING

Nest	lined hollow in vegetation
Eggs	7–9; yellowish white
Incubation	21–23 days ♀
Young	active; downy
Fledging	7 weeks
Broods	1; Apr–June
Food	aquatic vegetation, invertebrates
Population	50 pairs; c25,000 winter

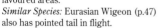

J	F	M	A	M	J	J	A	S	O	N	D
3	3	3	3	1	1	1	1	2	3	3	3

white flank stripe

chestnut and green head

white wingbar

adult ♂

yellow patch

adult ♂

white bar

green speculum

adult ♀

adult ♀

Small, fast-flying, highly gregarious duck. Often forms compact flocks that fly in twisting, turning formation, like waders. Male's chestnut head has bottle-green, yellow-edged area round eye. At any distance appears simply dark headed. Breast buff, spotted brown. Grey back and flanks separated by narrow black and white 'lateral line'. Black rear end encloses large yellow patch. In flight, shows inconspicuous bottle-green speculum and clearer white wingbar. Female brown and buff. *Status:* uncommon but widespread breeder; huge winter influx. *Similar Species:* similar to, but smaller than, all female surface-feeding ducks except Garganey (p.50), from which separated by green speculum and different face pattern.

COMMON TEAL

Type	duck-like
Size	34–38cm (13–15in)
Habitat	freshwater, estuaries
Behaviour	swims, wades, walks, takes off and lands on water or ground
Flocking	1–several hundred
Flight	strong and powerful
Voice	♂ whistles; ♀ quacks
IDENTIFICATION	
Adult ♂	
Crown	chestnut-brown
Upperparts	grey
Rump	black
Tail	grey; short and rounded
Breast	buff, spotted brown
Belly	buff
Bill	grey; duck-like
Legs	black; short
Adult ♀	mottled brown and buff
BREEDING	
Nest	lined hollow in marsh
Eggs	8–12; creamy buff
Incubation	21–28 days ♀
Young	active; downy
Fledging	44 days
Broods	1; Apr–May
Food	aquatic vegetation, seeds
Population	3500–6000 pairs; 150,000+ winter

J	F	M	A	M	J	J	A	S	O	N	D
4	4	4	4	3	3	3	3	3	5	5	5

49

Garganey *Anas querquedula*

white eyebrow

adult ♂

blue-grey forewing

adult ♂

blue-grey forewing

adult ♀

striped faced pattern

adult ♀

adult ♀

Dainty, Teal-sized duck easily overlooked in eclipse and female plumages. Male has maroon-brown head with bold white eyebrow, drooping black and white scapulars and grey underparts. Female has striped face pattern. In flight, shows pale blue inner wing like Northern Shoveler.

Status: scarce summer visitor, mainly to south and east England; winters in Africa.

Similar Species: female and eclipse male like similar plumages of Common Teal (p.49) and much larger Mallard (p.52). Female similar to other female surface-feeding ducks but separated by pronounced face pattern. Some female and eclipse Common Teal, and many Mallard, show similar pattern.

J	F	M	A	M	J	J	A	S	O	N	D
0	0	1	2	2	2	2	2	1	1	0	0

GARGANEY

Type	duck-like
Size	37–41cm (14–16in)
Habitat	freshwater and marshes
Behaviour	swims, up-ends, takes off and lands on water or ground
Flocking	1–10
Flight	strong and powerful; direct
Voice	♂ crackling rattle; ♀ quacks

IDENTIFICATION

Adult ♂	
Crown	maroon-brown
Upperparts	buff and brown
Rump	buff and brown
Tail	buff; short and square
Throat	brown
Breast	buff and brown
Belly	grey
Bill	grey; duck-like
Legs	grey; short
Adult ♀	spotted buff and brown with distinctive striped face pattern

BREEDING

Nest	lined hollow, well-hidden near water
Eggs	8–11; buffy
Incubation	21–23 days ♀
Young	active; downy
Fledging	5–6 weeks
Broods	1; Apr–May
Food	aquatic invertebrates and plants
Population	less than 100 pairs

grey back and flanks

adult ♂

white in wing

adult ♂

black rear end

adult ♀

orange-yellow bill edges

adult ♀

white in wing

adult ♀

Rather nondescript grey and brown duck, slightly smaller than Mallard. Resident at marshes and waters with growth of reeds. Male has mottled brown head and upperparts with dark eye stripe, similar to females of other surface-feeding ducks. Flanks finely barred grey. Best field mark is black rear end and white speculum, particularly in flight. Female has white speculum and yellow sides to bill. *Status:* nowhere numerous, mostly introduced and resident. Some Scottish birds migrate from northern Europe. *Similar Species:* only adult male Wigeon (p.47) show white in dark wing in flight. Female Northern Pintail, Common Teal (pp.48-49), Mallard and Northern Shoveler (pp.52-53), resemble both sexes adult Gadwall but all lack Gadwall's white in wing.

GADWALL

Type	duck-like
Size	48–54cm (18–21in)
Habitat	freshwater marshes, estuaries
Behaviour	swims, walks, takes off and lands on water or ground
Flocking	1–15
Flight	strong and powerful; direct
Voice	♂ whistles; ♀ quacks

IDENTIFICATION

Adult ♂	
Crown	brown
Upperparts	grey
Rump	black
Tail	black; short and square
Throat	brown
Breast	grey, spotted
Belly	grey, barred
Bill	black; duck-like
Legs	yellow; short
Adult ♀	mottled buff and brown with white speculum (as ♂) and yellow sides to bill

BREEDING

Nest	lined hollow by water
Eggs	8–12; creamy
Incubation	25–27 days ♀
Young	active; downy
Fledging	7 weeks
Broods	1; May–June
Food	aquatic vegetation
Population	250 pairs; 4000 winter

J	F	M	A	M	J	J	A	S	O	N	D
3	3	3	3	2	2	2	2	2	2	3	3

Mallard *Anas platyrhynchos*

bottle-green crown

blue and white speculum

adult ♂

brown breast band

adult ♂

black rear end

adult ♂

blue and white speculum

adult ♀

orange-yellow bill

adult ♀

Common and widespread throughout year in wide variety of aquatic habitats, from wild marshes and floods to city-centre ponds. Male's bottle-green head separated from chocolate-brown breast by narrow white neck ring. Back and wings pale grey; underparts paler grey. Black rear end with two upward-curling feathers. In flight head appears dark; dark blue speculum bordered fore and aft by white bars. Female resembles other female surface-feeding ducks; dark cap, dark eye stripe and orange-yellow bill aid separation. Generally gregarious.
Status: mainly resident; breeds throughout area. Large winter influx from the Continent.
Similar Species: female and eclipse male often show similar face pattern to much smaller Garganey (p.50).

MALLARD

Type	duck-like
Size	55–62cm (22–24in)
Habitat	freshwater, marshes, estuaries
Behaviour	swims, up-ends, takes off and lands on water or ground
Flocking	1–several thousand
Flight	strong and powerful; direct
Voice	♂ whistles and grunts; ♀ familiar quack

IDENTIFICATION

Adult ♂

Crown	bottle-green
Upperparts	pale grey
Rump	black
Tail	white; short and rounded
Throat	bottle-green
Breast	chocolate-brown
Belly	very pale grey
Bill	yellow; duck-like
Legs	orange; short
Adult ♀	mottled buffs and browns, orange-yellow bill, blue and white speculum

BREEDING

Nest	lined hollow on ground
Eggs	10–12; creamy
Incubation	28–29 days ♀
Young	active; downy
Fledging	7–8 weeks
Broods	1; Mar–July
Food	omnivorous
Population	70,000–150,000 pairs; 500,000 winter

J	F	M	A	M	J	J	A	S	O	N	D
6	6	6	6	6	6	6	6	6	6	6	6

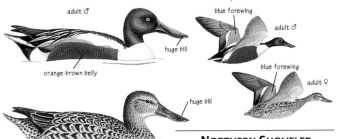

adult ♂

blue forewing

adult ♂

huge bill

orange-brown belly

blue forewing

adult ♀

adult ♀

huge bill

adult ♀

Medium-sized duck that feeds with broad sweeps of bill through shallow water and wet mud. Huge, spatulate bill obvious in both sexes at rest and flight. Male has bottle-green head, white breast, black back and bright chestnut belly and flanks. Female mottled buff and brown; resembles other female surface-feeding ducks but bill easily separates. In flight both sexes show pale blue inner wing. Generally gregarious; sizeable flocks gather at favoured feeding grounds in winter.

Much scarcer in summer at reed-fringed lagoons and marshes.
Status: small numbers breed over much of area; influx of winter visitors.
Similar Species: smaller Garganey (p.50) has blue inner wing but no other duck has huge, spatulate bill.

NORTHERN SHOVELER

Type	duck-like
Size	47–53cm (18-21in)
Habitat	freshwater marshes, estuaries
Behaviour	swims, wades, walks, takes off and lands on water or ground
Flocking	1–several hundred
Flight	strong and powerful, direct
Voice	♂ harsh, double note *tuk-tuk*; ♀ quacks

IDENTIFICATION

Adult ♂	
Crown	bottle-green
Upperparts	black back, white scapulars
Rump	black
Tail	black, white outer feathers; short and rounded
Throat	green
Breast	white
Belly	chestnut
Bill	black; huge and spatulate
Legs	yellow; short
Adult ♀	mottled buff and brown; orange spatulate bill

BREEDING

Nest	lined hollow near water
Eggs	8–12; buffy
Incubation	22–23 days ♀
Young	active; downy
Fledging	6–7 weeks
Broods	1; Apr–May
Food	crustaceans, molluscs, aquatic seeds and plants
Population	1000 pairs; 17000+ winter

J	F	M	A	M	J	J	A	S	O	N	D
4	4	4	3	2	2	2	2	3	3	4	4

Common Pochard *Aythya ferina*

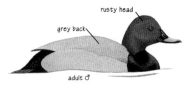

rusty head
grey back

adult ♂

grey wings

adult ♂

pale eye ring
and line

adult ♀

buff-grey wings

adult ♀

Compact diving duck with prominent sloping forehead and large bill. Male has grey body, chestnut head and black breast. At any distance whole of foreparts appear dark; body pale grey with dark rear end. Female greyish-brown, darker on head and neck. In flight shows inconspicuous pale grey wingbar. Highly gregarious, forming huge rafts at suitable waters. Flocks generally spend much time sleeping during the day. Dives mainly for aquatic vegetation. *Status:* widespread, but not a common breeder, often abundant winter visitor.
Similar Species: none.

COMMON POCHARD

Type	duck-like
Size	44–48cm (17–19in)
Habitat	freshwater, sea, estuaries
Behaviour	swims, dives from surface, walks, takes off and lands on water
Flocking	1–2000
Flight	strong and powerful; direct
Voice	generally quite; ♀ growls in flight

IDENTIFICATION

Adult ♂	
Crown	chestnut
Upperparts	grey
Rump	black
Tail	grey; short and rounded
Throat	chestnut
Breast	black
Belly	grey
Bill	grey; large and duck-like
Legs	black; short
Adult ♀	greyish brown with darker head and breast and dark rear end

BREEDING

Nest	mound of vegetation at or near water's edge
Eggs	6–11; greenish
Incubation	24–26 days ♀
Young	active; downy
Fledging	7–8 weeks
Broods	1; Apr–June
Food	aquatic plants, invertebrates
Population	400 pairs; 80,000 winter

J	F	M	A	M	J	J	A	S	O	N	D
4	4	4	3	2	2	2	2	2	3	4	4

crest
black back
rounded head

adult ♂

white wingbar

adult ♂

hint of crest

adult ♀

white wingbar

adult ♀

Dainty diving duck, with round head, drooping crest and short neck. Male has all-black breast, back and tail; black head has purple sheen; white flanks and underparts. Inconspicuous crest extends from hind crown. Female sooty brown, with paler barred flanks and less obvious crest. Grey bill often has white base in female. In flight both sexes show prominent, broad, white wingbar. Gregarious, often gathering in large winter flocks, frequently in company of Common Pochard. Dives easily, mainly for invertebrates *Status:* widespread breeding bird in small numbers; abundant winter visitor.

Similar Species: Goldeneye (p.61) is similarly black and white. White-faced females resemble female Greater Scaup.

TUFTED DUCK

Type	duck-like
Size	41–45cm (16–17in)
Habitat	freshwater, estuaries
Behaviour	swims, dives from surface, takes off and lands on water or ground
Flocking	1–2000
Flight	strong and powerful; direct
Voice	generally silent; ♀ growls

IDENTIFICATION

Adult ♂

Crown	black, glossed purple; crest
Upperparts	black
Rump	black
Tail	black; short and rounded
Throat	black
Breast	black
Belly	white
Bill	grey; duck-like
Legs	black; short
Adult ♀	brown above, buffy on flanks; reduced crest

BREEDING

Nest	lined hollow near water; well-hidden
Eggs	5–12; greenish
Incubation	23–25 days ♀
Young	active; downy
Fledging	6 weeks
Broods	1; Apr–June
Food	aquatic invertebrates, plants
Population	9000 pairs; 90,000 winter

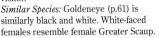

J	F	M	A	M	J	J	A	S	O	N	D
5	5	5	5	4	4	4	4	4	4	5	5

Greater Scaup *Aythya marila*

sloping hind crown

grey back

large bill

adult ♂

white wingbar

adult ♂

clear-cut white at base of bill

adult ♀

adult ♀

adult ♀

Marine equivalent of Tufted Duck and generally similar. Male has black, green-glossed head, black breast and rear end; grey back and white flanks and belly. Female has large, clear-cut white area at base of bill. In all plumages, steep forehead and backward-sloping crown create distinct head shape. Essentially coastal, gathering in large, sometimes huge, flocks at favoured feeding grounds; small numbers storm-driven inland.
Status: occasional rare breeder in extreme north; common winter visitor but large flocks localized, mainly in north.
Similar Species: female usually separated from female Tufted Duck (p.55) by white on face, but beware white-faced female Tufted inland. Male like male Tufted, but grey-backed.

GREATER SCAUP

Type	duck-like
Size	46–51cm (18–20in)
Habitat	freshwater marshes, sea, estuaries
Behaviour	swims, dives from surface, takes off and lands on water or ground
Flocking	1–10,000
Flight	strong and powerful; direct
Voice	generally silent, ♀ growls

IDENTIFICATION

Adult ♂	
Crown	black, green-glossed
Upperparts	grey
Rump	black
Tail	black; short and rounded
Throat	black
Breast	black
Belly	white
Bill	grey; duck-like
Legs	black; short
Adult ♀	brown above, buffy on flanks, white face

BREEDING

Nest	lined hollow near water; open sites
Eggs	6–15; greenish
Incubation	24–28 days ♀
Young	active; downy
Fledging	5–6 weeks
Broods	1; May–June
Food	molluscs, aquatic vegetation
Population	c5 pairs; 5000–10,000 winter

J	F	M	A	M	J	J	A	S	O	N	D
3	3	3	2	1	1	1	1	1	1	2	3

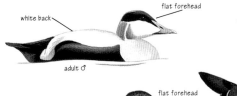

white back

flat forehead

adult ♂

white back and inner wings

adult ♂

flat forehead

adult ♀

adult ♀

L arge, stocky seaduck. Male mainly white above and black below with pink tinge to white breast. Bold black mark extends over each side of crown. Pale green nape visible at close range. Female warm buff and brown, finely barred. Long, sloping forehead and longish bill form continuous line, creating wedge-shaped head with feathering reaching half way to bill tip. Immature male like female, but white developing from breast to back over first summer creates patchy effect. Forms small flocks in coastal waters; breeds colonially. *Status:* resident along coasts of Scotland, northern Ireland and north-east England. Winter visitor elsewhere. *Similar Species:* none.

COMMON EIDER

Type	duck-like
Size	55–61cm (21–24in)
Habitat	sea, estuaries
Behaviour	swims, dives from surface, takes off and lands on water
Flocking	1–several thousand
Flight	strong and powerful; direct
Voice	♂ dove-like cooing ♀ repeated *gok-gok-gok*

IDENTIFICATION

Adult ♂	
Crown	white, black sides
Upperparts	white
Rump	black
Tail	black; short and rounded
Throat	white
Breast	white, pink-tinge
Belly	black
Bill	grey; duck-like
Legs	brown; short
Adult ♀	barred buff and brown above and below

BREEDING

Nest	lined hollow on island, coast or nearby river
Eggs	4–6; greenish
Incubation	27–28 days ♀
Young	active; downy
Fledging	60–75 days
Broods	1; May–June
Food	molluscs, crustaceans, other invertebrates
Population	15,000–25,000 pairs; 70,000 winter

J	F	M	A	M	J	J	A	S	O	N	D
4	4	4	4	4	4	4	4	4	4	4	4

Long-tailed Duck *Clangula hyemalis*

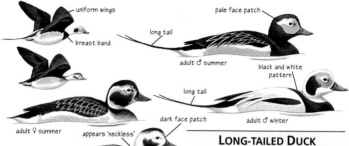

uniform wings

breast band

long tail

pale face patch

adult ♂ summer

long tail

black and white pattern

dark face patch

adult ♂ winter

adult ♀ summer

appears 'neckless'

adult ♀ winter

Small, stocky seaduck. Large head, small bill and pointed tail; male has extended central tail feathers. Variable plumage always includes face patch. Summer male has dark brown head and neck; face silvery grey. Winter male has white head with grey patch on side of face. Female always has pale patch around eye; remaining upperparts broadly edged buff in summer, browner in winter. In flight, wings uniform brown in all plumages. Gregarious around coasts.
Status: winter visitor; most numerous on inshore waters in north and east where flocks amount to half of British population.
Similar Species: none.

J	F	M	A	M	J	J	A	S	O	N	D
3	3	3	2	1	1	1	1	1	2	3	3

LONG-TAILED DUCK

Type	duck-like
Size	♂ 54–58cm (21–23in)
	♀ 41–45cm (16–17in)
Habitat	sea, estuaries
Behaviour	swims, dives from surface, takes off and lands on water
Flocking	1–1000
Flight	strong and powerful; direct
Voice	♂ yodelling call, ♀ quacks

IDENTIFICATION

Ad. ♂ summer

Crown	blackish brown
Upperparts	brown and black, edged buff
Rump	blackish brown
Tail	dark brown, white outer feathers; long and pointed
Throat	blackish brown
Breast	blackish brown
Belly	buff-grey
Bill	pink; small and duck-like
Legs	black; short

Ad. ♂ winter

	black and white back
Adult ♀	brown above with distinctive pale face patch

BREEDING

Nest	lined hollow hidden in vegetation
Eggs	5–9; yellow
Incubation	23–25 days ♀
Young	active; downy
Fledging	5 weeks
Broods	1; May–July
Food	molluscs, crustaceans
Population	20,000 winter

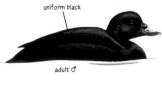

uniform black

adult ♂

adult ♂

adult ♀

pale sides
to face

adult ♀

A ll-black seaduck most often seen as small dark blobs bouncing among waves, or as all-dark birds flying fast and low over sea. Male black with yellow bill and black knob at base. Female brown with pale cheeks that may be picked out at considerable distances. Gregarious, usually forming flocks 10-100 strong. *Status:* scarce breeder in extreme north and north-west; winter visitor to most coasts; non-breeders in summer. *Similar Species:* Velvet Scoter (p.60)

COMMON SCOTER

Type	duck-like
Size	46–51cm (18–20in)
Habitat	sea
Behaviour	swims, dives from surface, takes off and lands on water
Flocking	1–several hundred
Flight	strong and powerful; low; direct
Voice	often silent; occasional harsh whistles

IDENTIFICATION

Adult ♂	
Crown	black
Upperparts	black
Rump	black
Tail	black; short and rounded
Throat	black
Breast	black
Belly	black
Bill	yellow, black knob at base; duck-like
Legs	grey; short
Adult ♀	brown with creamy cheeks; black bill with smaller knob

BREEDING

Nest	lined hollow near water
Eggs	6–9; creamy
Incubation	27–31 days ♀
Young	active; downy
Fledging	6–7 weeks
Broods	1; June–July
Food	cockles, mussels, crustaceans
Population	160–190 pairs; 25,000–30,000 winter

J	F	M	A	M	J	J	A	S	O	N	D
3	3	3	3	3	2	2	3	3	3	3	3

Velvet Scoter *Melanitta fusca*

white in wing — adult ♂

adult ♂

white in wing

adult ♀

dark face
pale patches

adult ♀

S imilar to Common Scoter, but generally scarcer; often forms mixed flocks. Male black with larger yellow bill. Female brown with two pale face patches. Both sexes show white in wing in flight; may also be visible at rest. When observing all-dark ducks on the sea at a distance, Velvet Scoter may betray their presence by flapping wings to reveal white patches.
Status: less numerous than Common Scoter. Winter visitor to inshore waters, except western Ireland.
Similar Species Common Scoter (p.59) has no white in wing.

VELVET SCOTER

Type	duck-like
Size	53–59cm (20–23in)
Habitat	sea
Behaviour	swims, dives from surface, takes off and lands on water
Flocking	small flocks
Flight	strong and powerful; low; direct
Voice	mostly silent; some croaking

IDENTIFICATION

Adult ♂	
Crown	black
Upperparts	black
Rump	black
Tail	black; short and rounded
Throat	black
Breast	black
Belly	black
Bill	yellow; large and duck-like
Legs	red; short
Adult ♀	dark brown; pale face patches, grey bill

BREEDING

Nest	lined hollow in open country, near water
Eggs	7–10; creamy
Incubation	27–28 days ♀
Young	active; downy
Fledging	6–7 weeks
Broods	1; June–July
Food	mussels, crabs, shrimps
Population	2500–5000 winter

J	F	M	A	M	J	J	A	S	O	N	D
2	2	2	1	1	0	0	0	1	2	2	2

Bucephala clangula **Goldeneye**

white back, black lines

bottle-green head

white spot

white inner wing

adult ♂

adult ♂

brown triangular head

white in wing

adult ♀

white flank line

adult ♀

Medium-sized diving duck found on freshwater as often as on sea. Both sexes marked by steep forehead, peaked crown and sloping hind crown, giving head uniquely characteristic shape. Male has black, green-glossed head with white patch between bill and eye; upperparts black with transverse streaks across folded wing. Flanks and underparts white; rear end black. Female has chocolate-brown head, white neck band and grey body. In flight, both sexes have white inner wing with narrow, dark, central band(s). Generally gregarious, forming small, loose flocks. *Status:* small numbers breed in Scotland; widespread winter visitor. *Similar Species:* male Tufted Duck (p.55) also black and white.

GOLDENEYE

Type	duck-like
Size	40–48cm (16–19in)
Habitat	freshwater, sea, estuaries
Behaviour	swims, dives from surface, takes off and lands on water
Flocking	1–15
Flight	strong and powerful; direct
Voice	silent except in courtship

IDENTIFICATION

Adult ♂	
Crown	black, glossed green
Upperparts	black; white wing streaked black
Rump	black
Tail	black; short and rounded
Throat	black
Breast	white
Belly	white
Bill	black; duck-like
Legs	yellow; short
Adult ♀	mottled grey with dark brown head and white neck-ring

BREEDING

Nest	unlined tree hole
Eggs	6–11; blue-green
Incubation	27–32 days ♀
Young	active; downy
Fledging	51–60 days
Broods	1; Apr–June
Food	molluscs, crustaceans
Population	27–57 pairs; 10,000–15,000 winter

J	F	M	A	M	J	J	A	S	O	N	D
4	4	2	2	1	1	1	1	1	1	2	3	4

Smew *Mergus albellus*

black and white

black eye-patch

white striped inner wing

adult ♂

adult ♂

red crown

small bill

adult ♀/juvenile

adult ♀/juvenile

Compact little duck and scarce winter visitor. Male white with narrow black lines on crown, back and flanks. Steep forehead and hint of crest create large-headed appearance; small bill, black facial mask. Female and first winter male – 'redheads' – have chestnut crown extending to below eye, white face, grey back and pale grey underparts. Mostly found in small flocks on inland waters, with 'redheads' predominating.

Status: scarce late winter visitor in variable numbers in south and east England; regular at a few favoured waters. Hard weather may bring larger numbers from the Continent.

Similar Species: male none; at distance, 'redheads' could be confused with Slavonian Grebe (p.23),

SMEW

Type	duck-like
Size	36–43cm (14–17in)
Habitat	freshwater, estuaries
Behaviour	swims, dives from surface, takes off and lands on water
Flocking	1–25
Flight	strong and powerful; direct
Voice	usually silent

IDENTIFICATION

Adult ♂	
Crown	white, black lines
Upperparts	white, black lines
Rump	grey
Tail	grey; short and rounded
Throat	white
Breast	white
Belly	white
Bill	grey; small and duck-like
Legs	grey; short
Adult ♀	grey above, paler grey below; white cheeks, chestnut crown

BREEDING

Nest	unlined tree hole
Eggs	6–9; creamy
Incubation	30 days ♀
Young	active; downy
Fledging	10 weeks
Broods	1; May–June
Food	fish
Population	100 winter

J	F	M	A	M	J	J	A	S	O	N	D
2	2	2	0	0	0	0	0	0	0	1	2

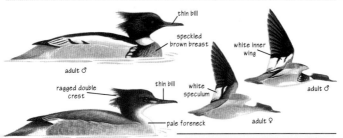

thin bill
speckled brown breast
white inner wing
adult ♂
ragged double crest
thin bill
white speculum
pale foreneck
adult ♀
adult ♂
adult ♀
adult ♀

Long, slim duck with long, thin bill – a typical 'sawbill'. Male has dark bottle-green head with double crest extending from hind crown. Breast rufous brown, spotted black; forms breast band in flight. Head and breast separated by broad white collar. Upperparts black; flanks and underparts pale grey. Female has rusty head with similar double crest; foreneck and chin white. In flight, male shows black and white inner wing; female white speculum. Mergansers dive well to catch fish.

Status: breeds along rivers in north and west; large flocks in north-east in autumn, more widespread along most coasts in winter.

Similar Species:
female Goosander (p.64); Red-breasted Merganser has thinner, horizontal-pointing crest and white foreneck.

RED-BREASTED MERGANSER

Type	duck-like
Size	51–61cm (20–24in)
Habitat	freshwater, sea, estuaries
Behaviour	swims, dives from surface, takes off and lands on water
Flocking	1–several hundred
Flight	strong and powerful; direct
Voice	mostly silent; purrs and croaks in display

IDENTIFICATION

Adult ♂	
Crown	green; double crest
Upperparts	black
Rump	grey
Tail	white
Breast	brown, spotted black
Belly	pale grey
Bill	red; long, straight and thin
Legs	red; short
Adult ♀	grey with reddish head and similar double crest

BREEDING

Nest	lines hollow, well hidden among rocks or tree roots
Eggs	7–12; buffy
Incubation	29–35 days ♀
Young	active; downy
Fledging	59 days
Broods	1; May–June
Food	fish
Population	2000–3000 pairs; 11,000 winter

J	F	M	A	M	J	J	A	S	O	N	D
3	3	3	3	3	3	3	3	3	3	3	3

Goosander *Mergus merganser*

bottle-green head

thin bill

adult ♂

adult ♂

adult ♂

pinkish cream underparts

rounded head

thin bill

white chin
dark neck

adult ♀

adult ♀

Typical 'sawbill' duck, found mainly on freshwater throughout year. Larger and bulkier than Red-breasted Merganser but with similar long, thin, serrated bill. Male has green-glossed, black head with rounded crest, giving head unique shape. Back black; flanks and underparts white with warm, pinkish flush. White inner wing shows in flight. Female has white chin, rusty foreneck and hint of crest. Generally found on inland waters, occasionally larger flocks on sheltered estuaries.
Status: breeds on lakes, mostly in forested country in north.
Similar Species: Red-breasted Merganser (p.63); females most similar but Goosander has less ragged crest angled sharply downwards towards back.

GOOSANDER

Type	duck-like
Size	57–59cm (22–27in)
Habitat	freshwater
Behaviour	swims, dives from surface, takes off and lands on water
Flocking	1–50
Flight	strong and powerful; direct
Voice	generally silent; various courtship croaks and cackles.

IDENTIFICATION

Adult ♂	
Crown	black, green gloss; crest
Upperparts	black, white sides
Rump	grey
Tail	grey; short and rounded
Throat	green
Breast	pinkish white
Bill	red; long, straight and thin
Legs	red; short
Adult ♀	grey with reddish head and rounded crest

BREEDING

Nest	lined tree hole or similar cavity
Eggs	7–14; creamy
Incubation	32-35 days ♀
Young	active; downy
Fledging	5 weeks
Broods	1; Mar–June
Food	fish
Population	900–1250 pairs; 5000 winter

J	F	M	A	M	J	J	A	S	O	N	D
3	3	3	3	3	3	3	3	3	3	3	3

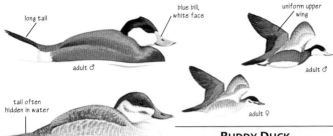

long tail

blue bill, white face

uniform upper wing

adult ♂

adult ♂

tail often hidden in water

adult ♀

adult ♀

Dumpy little duck of strangely 'weight forward' appearance; stiff tail often held cocked upright but equally often horizontal and invisible. Male russet, with dark cap and hind crown enclosing white face. Brilliant blue bill. Female brown above, barred buff and brown below; dark cap and distinctive dark line across face. Bill greyer blue than male.
Status: introduced from North America to West Midlands where now common breeder; spreading eastwards through south-east England and adjacent Continent. Poses a threat to White-headed Duck in Spain.
Similar Species: none.

RUDDY DUCK

Type	duck-like
Size	36–43cm (14–17in)
Habitat	freshwater
Behaviour	swims, dives from surface, takes off and lands on water
Flocking	1–15
Flight	strong and powerful; direct
Voice	generally silent; quiet courtship grunts and hisses

IDENTIFICATION

Adult ♂	
Crown	black
Upperparts	russet
Rump	russet
Tail	brown; long and pointed
Throat	russet
Breast	russet
Belly	russet
Bill	bright blue; duck-like
Legs	blue; short
Adult ♀	buff-brown, barred below; dark cap and pale cheek with distinctive line; greyer bill than ♂

BREEDING

Nest	floating mound
Eggs	6–10; white
Incubation	20–21 days ♀
Young	active; downy
Fledging	?
Broods	1; May–June
Food	larvae; seeds
Population	2000+ individuals

J	F	M	A	M	J	J	A	S	O	N	D
2	2	2	2	2	2	2	2	2	2	2	2

Honey Buzzard *Pernis apivorus*

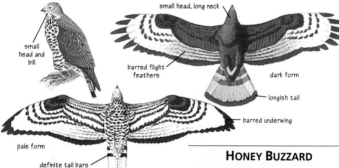

small head, long neck

small head and bill

barred flight feathers

dark form

longish tail

barred underwing

pale form

definite tail bars

Rare summer visitor to large areas of woodland in southern England. Slimmer and more angular than similar Common Buzzard. Small head, thin neck and waisted, 'wasp-like' wings. Tail longer than Common Buzzard; wings droop when soaring. Plumage highly variable but carpals always dark and underwing has regularly spaced barring. Tail with terminal band and two other similar bands.
Unique 'butterfly-like' display flight of male involves wings high above back and fluttering before diving.
Status: very scarce summer visitor and passage migrant.
Similar Species: Common Buzzard (p.75)

HONEY BUZZARD

Type	hawk-like
Size	50–59cm (20–23in)
Habitat	forests and woods
Behaviour	takes off and lands on vegetation and ground
Flight	soars, glides; strong and powerful
Voice	high-pitched *kee-a*
IDENTIFICATION	
Adult	
Crown	brown
Upperparts	brown
Rump	brown
Tail	buff with brown bands; longish and square
Throat	white
Breast	brown, buff and brown barred or white
Belly	varies (as breast)
Bill	brown; hooked
Legs	yellow; medium length
BREEDING	
Nest	sticks high in tree
Eggs	1–3; white, speckled reddish
Incubation	30–35 days, mainly ♀
Young	helpless; downy
Fledging	40–44 days
Broods	1; June
Food	larvae and adult wasps and bees; also amphibians, birds
Population	c20 pairs

J	F	M	A	M	J	J	A	S	O	N	D
0	0	0	0	2	2	2	2	2	1	0	0

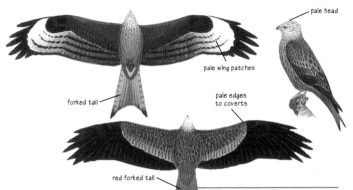

pale head

pale wing patches

forked tail

pale edges
to coverts

red forked tail

Uncommon raptor, similar in size to Common Buzzard, but much more angular and less bulky with longer wings and tail. Rufous above and below with pale, almost whitish, head. In flight, upperwing brown with rufous coverts; underwing brown with prominent whitish patches on outer wing. Tail rufous and deeply forked, almost translucent against light. Often hangs on rising air; circles and weaves in slow, effortless flight on bowed wings with tail twisting as rudder. Mostly found over hillside woods. *Status:* resident in Wales; reintroduced Scotland and England; scarce passage migrant elsewhere. *Similar Species:* none.

RED KITE

Type	hawk-like
Size	58–64cm (22–25in)
Habitat	forests and woods
Behaviour	perches openly, takes off from vegetation and ground
Flocking	usually solitary
Flight	soars, glides; strong and powerful
Voice	repeated *he-he-heea*

IDENTIFICATION

Adult	
Crown	white
Upperparts	rufous
Rump	rufous
Tail	rufous; long and forked
Throat	white
Breast	rufous, streaked
Belly	rufous, streaked
Bill	yellow; hooked
Legs	yellow; medium length

BREEDING

Nest	twigs, plus rubbish in tree
Eggs	2–3; white, spotted red
Incubation	28-30 days ♀
Young	helpless; downy
Fledging	45–50 days
Broods	1; Mar–May
Food	mammals, birds, carrion
Population	c100 pairs

J	F	M	A	M	J	J	A	S	O	N	D
2	2	2	2	2	2	2	2	2	2	2	2

White-tailed Eagle *Haliaeetus albicilla*

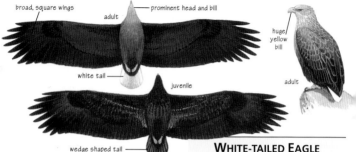

broad, square wings — prominent head and bill

adult

huge yellow bill

white tail

adult

juvenile

wedge shaped tail

Huge, bulky eagle with enormous broad wings and prominent head and bill. Adult mostly dark brown with pure white tail; large pale head with very large yellow bill. In flight, prominent head and bill and short white tail contrast with huge, square-cut dark wings. Juveniles share this shape, but have dark tails or only white centres to tail feathers, depending on age. Found by sea or near freshwater.

Status: exterminated as breeding bird in Scotland in 1916 but re-introduced to Rhum since 1975; first bred in 1985. Otherwise rare winter visitor.

Similar Species: immatures superficially similar to adult Golden Eagle (p.72); adult similar to immature Golden Eagle, which also has white tail but with black terminal band.

WHITE-TAILED EAGLE

Type	hawk-like
Size	69–91cm (27–36in)
Habitat	moors, sea
Behaviour	dives from air, perches openly, takes off from vegetation or ground
Flocking	usually solitary
Flight	soars, glides, aerial dive; strong and powerful
Voice	laughing *kok-kok-kok* while courting

IDENTIFICATION

Adult	
Crown	buff
Upperparts	dark brown
Rump	dark brown
Tail	white; short and rounded
Throat	dark brown
Breast	brown, streaked
Belly	brown
Bill	yellow; large and hooked
Legs	yellow; medium length
Juvenile	all brown but with white centres to tail feathers

BREEDING

Nest	huge mass of twigs on cliff or tree
Eggs	2; white
Incubation	34–45 days ♂♀
Young	helpless; downy
Fledging	70 days
Broods	1; Mar–May
Food	fish, carrion
Population	8 pairs re-introduced

J	F	M	A	M	J	J	A	S	O	N	D
2	2	2	2	2	2	2	2	2	2	2	2

broader wings
than Montagu's

adult ♂

adult ♀

white rump

pale collar

adult ♀

broad white
rump

adult ♀

adult ♀

M edium-sized harrier, between Montagu's and Marsh Harrier in size and bulk. Male pale grey above with white rump and black wingtips; breast grey, remaining underparts white. Female and juvenile brown above with bold white rump; streaked brown or buff below. Hunts low over moors and young conifer plantations in summer.

Status: scarce resident; breeds in hill districts. Regular passage migrant and winter visitor, mainly to coasts. *Similar Species:* Montagu's Harrier (p.70). Females and juveniles especially similar – often jointly called 'ring-tail' harriers.

HEN HARRIER

Type	hawk-like
Size	43–51cm (17–20in)
Habitat	marshes, moors and heaths
Behaviour	perches openly, takes off and lands on ground
Flocking	1 or 2
Flight	hovers, soars, glides; laboured; undulating
Voice	mostly silent, cackles and squeals in courtship

IDENTIFICATION

Adult ♂	
Crown	grey
Upperparts	grey
Rump	white
Tail	grey; long and square
Throat	grey
Breast	grey
Belly	white
Bill	black; hooked
Legs	yellow; medium length
Ad. ♀ and juv.	
	all brown with white rump, streaked below

BREEDING

Nest	platform of sticks and twigs hidden in low vegetation
Eggs	4–6; pale blue
Incubation	29-39 days ♀
Young	helpless; downy
Fledging	37 days
Broods	1; Apr–June
Food	small birds and mammals
Population	500-600 pairs; 1000 winter

J	F	M	A	M	J	J	A	S	O	N	D
3	3	3	3	3	3	3	3	3	3	3	3

69

Montagu's Harrier *Circus pygargus*

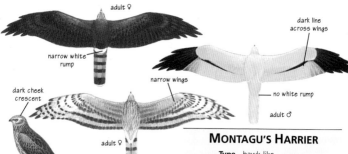

adult ♀

dark line across wings

narrow white rump

narrow wings

no white rump

adult ♂

dark cheek crescent

adult ♀

adult ♀

Smaller and slimmer than Hen Harrier and much less common. Male pale grey above with black wingtips and black line across upperwing. Underwing has several lines of bars. Tail and rump grey with no more than hint of white on rump. Underparts white, streaked chestnut. Female brown like female Hen Harrier but more lightly built, with narrower rump and more boldly marked 'face'. Juvenile more uniformly rufous below.
Status: passage migrant and rare summer visitor to England, Wales and southern Ireland.
Similar Species: Hen Harrier (p.69).

J	F	M	A	M	J	J	A	S	O	N	D
0	0	0	1	1	1	1	1	1	1	0	0

MONTAGU'S HARRIER

Type	hawk-like
Size	39–46cm (15–18in)
Habitat	freshwater marshes, heaths, fields and hedges
Behaviour	perches openly, takes off and lands on vegetation or ground
Flocking	1 or 2
Flight	hovers, soars, glides; laboured; undulating
Voice	shrill courtship *kek-kek-kek*

IDENTIFICATION

Adult ♂

Crown	grey
Upperparts	grey
Rump	grey
Tail	grey; long and square
Throat	grey
Breast	grey
Belly	white, streaked chestnut
Bill	black; hooked
Legs	yellow; medium length
Ad. ♀ and juv.	all brown, buffy and streaked below with white rump

BREEDING

Nest	platform of reds, twigs, grass on ground
Eggs	4–5; bluish
Incubation	27–40 days ♀
Young	helpless; downy
Fledging	35–40 days
Broods	1; May–June
Food	small birds and mammals
Population	7–14 pairs

creamy head and forewing

grey flight feathers

adult ♀

adult ♂

pale head

grey tail

juvenile

pale head

grey in wing

adult ♂

Largest of the harriers with typical slow, flap-and-glide flight creating lumbering appearance. Long wings, long tail and gliding flight near ground with wings held in 'V' identify as a harrier. Male brown with pale brown head and forewing edges. In flight, grey tail and large grey area on inner wing contrasts with dark wingtips and brown wing coverts. Female all brown with creamy head and forewing. Juveniles all brown with creamy head similar to female. Found mostly over large reedbeds and marshes.
Status: scarce breeder, mostly in East Anglia; scarce passage migrant and winter visitor, mostly east coasts.
Similar Species: Hen Harrier (p.69) and Montagu's Harrier (p.70). Bulkier and broader-winged than other harriers.

MARSH HARRIER

Type	hawk-like
Size	48–56cm (19–22in)
Habitat	freshwater marshes, moors, heaths, estuaries, shores
Behaviour	perches openly, takes off from vegetation or ground
Flocking	1 or 2
Flight	hovers, soars, glides; laboured; undulating
Voice	high-pitched *kee-a*

IDENTIFICATION

Adult ♂	
Crown	buff
Upperparts	brown, dark wingtips
Rump	brown
Tail	grey; long and square
Throat	buff
Breast	brown, streaked
Belly	brown
Bill	black; hooked
Legs	yellow; medium length
Adult ♀	all brown with creamy head and forewing
Juvenile	all brown or similar to female

BREEDING

Nest	platform of reeds in large reedbed
Eggs	4–5; blue–white
Incubation	33–38 days ♀
Young	helpless; downy
Fledging	35–40 days
Broods	1; Apr–May
Food	birds, eggs, small mammals, carrion
Population	92–111 pairs

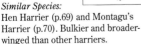

J	F	M	A	M	J	J	A	S	O	N	D
1	1	1	2	3	3	3	2	2	2	2	1

Golden Eagle *Aquila chrysaetos*

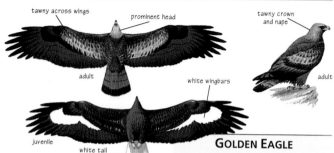

tawny across wings

prominent head

tawny crown and nape

adult

adult

white wingbars

juvenile

white tail
black band

L arge eagle of mountains and moorlands; virtually confined to Scotland. Adult dark brown with pale tawny crown and forewing. In flight, appears all dark from below. Juvenile has white tail with broad black terminal band and white base to outer primaries. From below, white tail less noticeable, but bold white line extends along all flight feathers. Flight powerful with deep wing beats; quarters hillsides like huge harrier. Long, broad wings held in shallow 'V' when soaring; dives on folded wings.

Status: sedentary in Scottish Highlands and Lake District.

Similar Species: White-tailed Eagle (p.68). Often confused with much smaller buzzards (pp.75–76) but proportions of head, wings and tail quite different.

J	F	M	A	M	J	J	A	S	O	N	D
3	3	3	3	3	3	3	3	3	3	3	3

GOLDEN EAGLE

Type	hawk-like
Size	76–90cm (30–35in)
Habitat	moors and heaths, forests and woods
Behaviour	perches openly, takes off from vegetation or ground
Flocking	solitary
Flight	soars, glides; strong and powerful; laboured
Voice	yelping *kaa*; generally silent

IDENTIFICATION

Adult

Crown	tawny-buff
Upperparts	brown
Rump	brown
Tail	brown; medium length, square
Throat	brown
Breast	brown
Belly	brown
Bill	yellow; hooked
Legs	yellow; medium length
Juvenile	brown with white wing flashes above and below; white tail with black band

BREEDING

Nest	massive structure of twigs on cliff or tree
Eggs	2; white, blotched brown
Incubation	43–45 days, usually ♀
Young	helpless; downy
Fledging	63–70 days
Broods	1; Feb–May
Food	small mammals, large birds
Population	420+ pairs

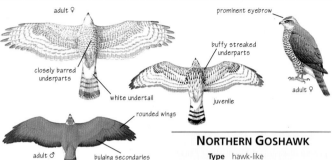

prominent eyebrow

buffy streaked
underparts

closely barred
underparts

white undertail

juvenile

adult ♀

rounded wings

adult ♂

bulging secondaries

long tail

L ike large European Sparrowhawk
with rounded wings and long,
banded tail. Adult brownish grey with
darker cap and bold white eyebrow.
Closely barred pale grey below, with
particularly prominent white undertail
coverts. Female about Common
Buzzard-sized; much larger than male,
which is only a little larger than female
European Sparrowhawk. Juvenile
browner; streaked
below. Dives in
spectacular display,
with white undertail
coverts spread.
Status: scarce but
increasing resident.
Similar Species:
European
Sparrowhawk
(p.74); Northern Goshawk is larger,
bulkier and has slower wing beats and
bulging secondaries.

NORTHERN GOSHAWK

Type	hawk-like
Size	48–58cm (19–23in)
Habitat	forests and woods, fields and hedgerows
Behaviour	perches openly, takes off from vegetation or ground
Flocking	solitary
Flight	soars, glides, aerial dive; strong and powerful; direct
Voice	chattering *gek-gek-gek*

IDENTIFICATION

Adult

Crown	grey, dark cap
Upperparts	brownish grey
Rump	grey
Tail	grey; long and square
Throat	white
Breast	white, barred grey
Belly	white, barred grey
Bill	black; hooked
Legs	yellow; medium length
Juvenile	browner; streaked below where adult finely barred

BREEDING

Nest	twigs in tree
Eggs	2–3; pale blue
Incubation	36–41 days ♀
Young	helpless; downy
Fledging	45 days
Broods	1; Apr–June
Food	bird and mammals
Population	150–230 pairs

J	F	M	A	M	J	J	A	S	O	N	D
2	2	2	2	2	2	2	2	2	2	2	2

European Sparrowhawk *Accipiter nisus*

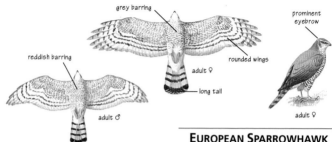

grey barring

prominent
eyebrow

reddish barring

rounded wings

adult ♀

long tail

adult ♂

adult ♀

Fast-flying, agile hawk of woodlands
and fields. Grey or grey-brown
above, with clear, pale eyebrow in
female. Male barred russet below;
female barred grey. Both have long tails
with at least four distinct bars showing.
Dashing flight in pursuit of small birds
makes confusion with Common Kestrel
impossible. When soaring or travelling,
shape is similar but European
Sparrowhawk flaps rounded wings
quickly for a few beats before gliding.
Status: widespread; increasing after
1960s pesticide
disaster.
Similar Species:
Common Kestrel
(p.77) has longer,
more pointed wings
and often hovers in
flight. Northern
Goshawk (p.73) is
larger and more
bulky, although large female European
Sparrowhawk may be confused with
small male Northern Goshawk.

EUROPEAN SPARROWHAWK

Type	hawk-like
Size	28–38cm (11–15in)
Habitat	forests and woods, fields and hedgerows, heaths
Behaviour	perches openly, takes off and lands on vegetation or ground
Flocking	solitary
Flight	soars, glides, aerial dive; strong and powerful; direct
Voice	loud *kek-kek-kek*
IDENTIFICATION	
Adult ♂	
Crown	grey
Upperparts	grey or grey-brown
Rump	grey
Tail	grey and white, banded; long and square
Throat	white
Breast	whitish, reddish barring
Belly	whitish, reddish barring
Bill	black; hooked
Legs	yellow; medium length
Adult ♀	larger than ♂, brown above, pale eyebrow; heavily barred grey below
BREEDING	
Nest	twigs in trees
Eggs	4–5; white, blotched brown
Incubation	42 days ♀
Young	helpless; downy
Fledging	32 days
Broods	1; Apr–June
Food	small birds
Population	33,000+ pairs

J	F	M	A	M	J	J	A	S	O	N	D
4	4	4	4	4	4	4	4	4	4	4	4

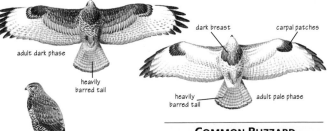

dark breast   carpal patches

adult dark phase

heavily
barred tail

heavily
barred tail   adult pale phase

adult

Most common of the larger raptors;
prefers wooded areas with open
fields as well as moorland and heath.
Highly variable plumage from dark
brown with pale wing linings to pure
creamy white with dark wing edges. Tail
heavily barred or almost pure creamy
white. Always shows dark patches at
carpal joint and at sides of breast. Soars
on broad wings held forward in shallow
'V'; small head and short tail.

Status: common
resident of hilly
districts in north of
Ireland and west of
Britain, also in West
Midlands. In the
south, occurs as far
east as Hampshire.
Scarce passage
migrant and winter
visitor elsewhere.

Similar Species: Rough-legged Buzzard
(p.76).

J	F	M	A	M	J	J	A	S	O	N	D
4	4	4	4	4	4	4	4	4	4	4	4

COMMON BUZZARD

Type	hawk-like
Size	50–56cm (20–22in)
Habitat	moors and heaths, forests and woods, fields and hedgerows
Behaviour	perches openly, takes off and lands on vegetation or ground
Flight	soars, glides; laboured
Voice	mewing *pee-oo*

IDENTIFICATION
Ad.dark

Crown	brown
Upperparts	brown
Rump	brown
Tail	brown, barred; short and square
Throat	brown
Breast	buff, dark patches on sides
Belly	brown
Bill	black; hooked
Legs	yellow; medium length
Ad.pale	variable, often almost white below, especially in flight

BREEDING

Nest	bulky sticks and twigs in tree, on cliff, rock outcrop, occasionally ground
Eggs	3–4; white, blotched
Incubation	42 days; mainly ♀
Young	helpless; downy
Fledging	40-45 days
Broods	1; Mar–May
Food	small mammals
Population	8000–10,000 pairs

Rough-legged Buzzard *Buteo lagopus*

adult

adult

dark carpal patch

pale head

white tail
black band

dark belly

white tail
black band

adult

adult

Similar to Common Buzzard, but with less variable plumage pattern. Flight feathers always very pale, mostly white with a few indistinct bars. Underwing coverts vary from brown to white; carpal patch always black and prominent. Tail white with broad black sub-terminal band and up to four narrow, less distinct, bars towards tip. Dark belly or flank patches more obvious than Common Buzzard. Always pale headed. Soars on flat wings and frequently hangs on wind or hovers.
Status: scarce winter visitor, mainly to east coasts; numbers vary from year to year.
Similar Species: Common Buzzard (p.75) and see above.

ROUGH-LEGGED BUZZARD

Type	hawk-like
Size	50–61cm (20–24in)
Habitat	freshwater marshes, moors, estuaries
Behaviour	perches openly, takes off and lands on vegetation or ground
Flocking	1–4
Flight	hovers, soars, glides; laboured
Voice	mostly silent
IDENTIFICATION	
Adult	
Crown	white
Upperparts	brown
Rump	brown
Tail	white with black band and narrow bars near tip; medium length, square
Throat	buff
Breast	white, streaked brown
Belly	brown, blackish patches on sides
Bill	black; hooked
Legs	yellow; medium length
BREEDING	
Nest	twigs on rock outcrop
Eggs	2–3; white, blotched brown
Incubation	28 days, mainly ♀
Young	helpless, downy
Fledging	40–42 days
Broods	1; May–June
Food	small mammals
Population	c20 winter

J	F	M	A	M	J	J	A	S	O	N	D
2	2	2	2	0	0	0	0	1	2	2	2

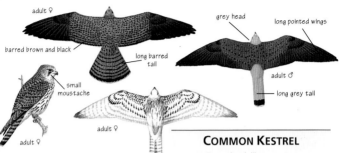

adult ♀

grey head

long pointed wings

barred brown and black

long barred tail

small moustache

adult ♂

long grey tail

adult ♀

adult ♀

M ost common raptor frequenting farmland, moors, parks, heaths, coastlines, marshes and city-centres. Often seen hovering, especially over motorway verges. Male has grey head with thin black moustachial streak; grey tail with broad black sub-terminal band. Upperparts rufous brown spotted black with dark brown flight feathers. Underparts tawny with spotted streaks; underwing pale. Female all brown above with dark streaking on head, heavily barred back, and multiple dark tail bands. In flight, long tail and shallow beats of long, pointed wings distinctive. *Status:* common and widespread resident.

Similar Species: European Sparrowhawk (p.74) has rounded wings and distinctive flight.

J	F	M	A	M	J	J	A	S	O	N	D
5	5	5	5	5	5	5	5	5	5	5	5

COMMON KESTREL

Type	hawk-like
Size	33–36cm (13–14in)
Habitat	towns, marshes, moors, heaths, cliffs, forests, fields
Behaviour	perches openly, takes off and lands on vegetation or ground
Flocking	solitary
Flight	hovers, soars, aerial dive; strong and powerful; direct
Voice	high-pitched *kee-kee-kee*

IDENTIFICATION

Adult ♂

Crown	grey
Upperparts	brown, spotted black
Rump	grey
Tail	grey, black terminal band; long and square
Throat	buff
Breast	buff, spotted black
Belly	buff, streaked on flanks
Bill	black; hooked
Legs	yellow; long

Ad. ♀ and juv.

	heavily barred back; lacks grey on head and tail

BREEDING

Nest	bare ledge or hole
Eggs	4–5; white, heavily speckled
Incubation	27–29 days, mainly ♀
Young	helpless; downy
Fledging	27–39 days
Broods	1; Apr–June
Food	small mammals and birds
Population	30,000–80,000 pairs

Merlin *Falco columbarius*

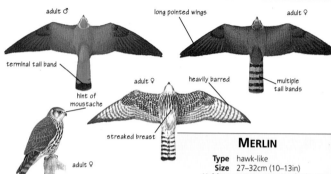

adult ♂

long pointed wings

adult ♀

terminal tail band

adult ♀

hint of moustache

heavily barred

multiple tail bands

streaked breast

adult ♀

Small, dark, fast-flying falcon of hills and moors; haunts coastlines and adjacent marshes in winter. Male smaller; blue-grey above with dark terminal band on tail. Female brown with multiple-barred buff and brown tail. Both sexes heavily streaked below and heavily barred across underwing. Flies low and fast in pursuit of smaller birds. *Status:* resident in hilly districts of north and west, but nowhere common. Winter visitor elsewhere, mostly to coasts.
Similar Species: Hobby (p.79), a summer visitor, is also dark but with prominent white sides to neck and clear-cut, dark moustache; wings are longer, narrower and more angular.

MERLIN

Type	hawk-like
Size	27–32cm (10–13in)
Habitat	moors, estuaries, freshwater marshes
Behaviour	perches openly, takes off and lands on vegetation or ground
Flocking	solitary
Flight	soars, glides, aerial dive; strong and powerful; direct
Voice	chattering *kee-kee-kee*

IDENTIFICATION

Adult ♂

Crown	blue-grey
Upperparts	blue-grey
Rump	blue-grey
Tail	blue, dark terminal band
Throat	buff
Breast	buff, heavy blackish streaks
Belly	buff, heavy blackish streaks
Bill	yellow; hooked
Legs	yellow; short

Ad. ♀ and juv.

brown above, heavily barred and streaked below

BREEDING

Nest	hollow on ground
Eggs	5–6; buff, heavily spotted reddish
Incubation	28–32 days, mainly ♀
Young	helpless; downy
Fledging	25–30 days
Broods	1; Apr–May
Food	small birds
Population	600–800 pairs

J	F	M	A	M	J	J	A	S	O	N	D
3	3	3	3	3	3	3	3	3	3	3	3

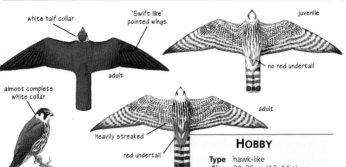

white half collar

'Swift-like' pointed wings

juvenile

no red undertail

adult

almost complete white collar

adult

heavily streaked

red undertail

adult

S ummer visitor to heaths and downland; often hunts over water or marshland for insects and small birds. Resembles Common Kestrel but wings longer and narrower, almost Swift-like; tail slightly shorter. Upperparts slate-grey; prominent black moustache and almost complete white 'neck ring'. Neck ring is most prominent field mark. Underparts heavily streaked and barred; undertail coverts rust-red. Juvenile dark brown above; lacks rusty undertail coverts. *Status:* summer visitor to central and southern England.
Similar Species: Merlin (p.78) and Common Kestrel (p.77) both have broad wings and lack white 'neck ring'.

HOBBY

Type	hawk-like
Size	30–36cm (12–14in)
Habitat	heaths, fields and hedges
Behaviour	perches openly, takes off and lands on vegetation
Flocking	1 or 2
Flight	soars, glides, aerial dive; strong and powerful; direct
Voice	*kew-kew* repeated; also high-pitched *ki-ki-ki*

IDENTIFICATION

Adult

Crown	black
Upperparts	slate-grey, white 'neck ring' and black moustache
Rump	grey
Tail	grey, undertail coverts rust-red; medium length, square
Throat	white
Breast	buff, heavily streaked
Belly	buff, heavily streaked
Bill	yellow; hooked
Legs	yellow; short
Juvenile	dark brown above; lacks red undertail

BREEDING

Nest	nest of other species in tree
Eggs	2–3; yellowish, speckled reddish
Incubation	28 days, mainly ♀
Young	helpless; downy
Fledging	28–32 days
Broods	1; May–June
Food	insects, small birds
Population	150–450 pairs

J	F	M	A	M	J	J	A	S	O	N	D
0	0	0	0	0	0	0	0	0	1	0	0

Peregrine Falcon *Falco peregrinus*

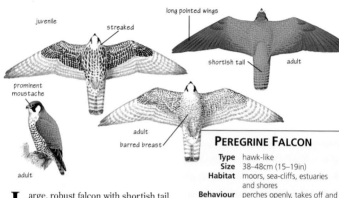

juvenile

streaked

long pointed wings

shortish tail

adult

prominent moustache

adult

barred breast

adult

Large, robust falcon with shortish tail and long, angular wings. Flies with deep sweeps of long, pointed wings producing impression of immense speed and power. Upperparts slate-grey with paler rump and delicately barred tail. White face and sides of neck with bold black moustaches. Underparts and underwing finely barred. Juvenile brown above with heavily streaked body. Haunts cliffs, both coastal and inland; in winter also frequents estuaries where rests on ground or small hummock.

Status: resident in hilly and coastal districts mainly north and west; elsewhere scarce winter visitor.

Similar Species: no other large falcons.

PEREGRINE FALCON

Type	hawk-like
Size	38–48cm (15–19in)
Habitat	moors, sea-cliffs, estuaries and shores
Behaviour	perches openly, takes off and lands on ground
Flocking	solitary
Flight	soars, glides, aerial stoop; strong and powerful; direct
Voice	loud *kek-kek-kek*; repeated *wee-chew*

IDENTIFICATION

Adult

Crown	slate-grey
Upperparts	slate-grey, white face and sides of neck; prominent black moustache
Rump	grey
Tail	grey; shortish and square
Throat	white
Breast	white, barred black
Belly	white, barred black
Bill	yellow; hooked
Legs	yellow; short
Juvenile	brown above; heavily streaked

BREEDING

Nest	bare scrape on cliff
Eggs	3–4; buff, speckled red
Incubation	28–29 days, mainly ♀
Young	helpless; downy
Fledging	35–42 days
Broods	1; Apr–June
Food	birds
Population	1000+ pairs

J	F	M	A	M	J	J	A	S	O	N	D
3	3	3	3	3	3	3	3	3	3	3	3

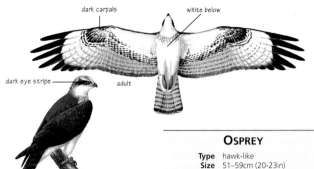

dark carpals — white below

dark eye stripe — adult

adult

Large, pale raptor, sometimes mistaken for large gull. Upperparts dark brown and grey; underparts white with black carpal patches, wingtips and wingbar. Flies gull-like on bowed wings. Head and nape white with prominent black eye stripe. Small head and long neck apparent at all times. Catches fish in spectacular feet-first dive; often after hovering high overhead. Found in lakes in forested areas in summer; reservoirs and other large waters at other times. Hunts in sea abroad. *Status:* recolonized in 1955 after lengthy absence. Scarce summer visitor to Scotland; elsewhere increasing passage migrant. *Similar Species:* none.

OSPREY

Type	hawk-like
Size	51–59cm (20-23in)
Habitat	freshwater, sea, estuaries, forests and woods
Behaviour	perches openly; dives from air; takes off and lands on vegetation, ground, or water
Flocking	solitary
Flight	hovers, soars, glides, aerial dive; strong and powerful; direct
Voice	whistling *chew-chew*

IDENTIFICATION

Adult

Crown	white
Upperparts	brown and grey
Rump	brown
Tail	brown; medium length, square
Throat	white
Breast	white, faint brown band
Belly	white
Bill	black; hooked
Legs	grey; medium length

BREEDING

Nest	mass of sticks in tree
Eggs	3; creamy, blotched reddish
Incubation	35–38 days ♂ ♀
Young	helpless, downy
Fledging	51–59 days
Broods	1; Mar–June
Food	fish
Population	70+ pairs

J	F	M	A	M	J	J	A	S	O	N	D
0	0	0	3	3	3	3	3	3	3	0	0

Common Quail *Coturnix coturnix*

adult ♂

prominent head pattern

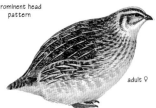

adult ♀

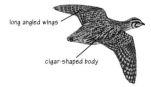

long angled wings

cigar-shaped body

Small, fast-flying, migratory gamebird; more often heard than seen. Ventriloquial call makes bird's location difficult to assess. Good views of bird on ground exceptional. Usually seen when flushed (deliberately or accidentally); flies when almost trodden on. Combination of stocky body and long, pointed wings is unique. Upperparts brown, streaked and barred; underparts warm buffy orange. Pattern of bold creamy eyebrow and dark facial streaks more pronounced in male than female.

Status: scarce and declining summer visitor.

Similar Species: none.

J	F	M	A	M	J	J	A	S	O	N	D
0	0	0	2	2	2	2	1	1	1	0	0

COMMON QUAIL

Type	partridge-like
Size	17–18.5cm (6–7in)
Habitat	moors, heaths, fields, hedges
Behaviour	walks, runs, takes off and lands on ground
Flocking	solitary
Flight	glides; strong and powerful; direct
Voice	distinctive *whic-we-whic*, repeated; often rendered 'wet-me-lips'

IDENTIFICATION

Adult

Crown	black and white
Upperparts	brown and black; pale streaks
Rump	brown
Tail	brown; short and rounded
Throat	white; ♂ black central stripe
Breast	buffy orange
Belly	white
Bill	black; short and stubby
Legs	grey; short

BREEDING

Nest	hollow on ground
Eggs	7–12; creamy, spotted brown
Incubation	16–21 days ♀
Young	active; downy
Fledging	19 days
Broods	1 sometimes 2; May–June
Food	seeds, insects
Population	less than 100 pairs

red comb

rich, dark chestnut

rufous brown

adult ♂

adult ♀

The grouse of grouse-moor fame; widespread resident of hilly, heather-clad regions. Sub-species of Willow Grouse, which is widespread in northern hemisphere. Most numerous in northern Britain where moorland is managed to suit its needs. Both sexes dark reddish brown, heavily spotted and barred black. Male considerably darker than female, with bold red comb above eye. Generally seen when flushed from heather; flies away strongly before gliding back to cover on bowed wings. In early morning, often seen along moorland roads collecting grit. Colour and dumpy, rotund shape identify. *Status:* largely confined to moorland of north and west. *Similar Species:* Ptarmigan (p.84) is much scarcer and less widespread.

J	F	M	A	M	J	J	A	S	O	N	D
4	4	4	4	4	4	4	4	4	4	4	4

RED GROUSE

Type	partridge-like
Size	33–39cm (13–19in)
Habitat	moors
Behaviour	walks, takes off and lands on ground
Flocking	1–15
Flight	glides; strong and powerful; direct
Voice	characteristic *go-back, go-back, go-back, back-back-back*

IDENTIFICATION

Adult ♂	
Crown	red-brown, barred black
Upperparts	red-brown, barred black
Rump	red-brown, barred black
Tail	red-brown, barred black
Throat	red-brown, barred black
Breast	red-brown, barred black
Belly	red-brown, barred black
Bill	grey; short and stubby
Legs	white; short
Adult ♀	paler, reduced red comb

BREEDING

Nest	hollow on ground
Eggs	6–11; yellowish, blotched dark brown
Incubation	20–26 days
Young	active; downy
Fledging	12–13 days
Broods	1; May–June
Food	heather
Population	less than 500,000 pairs

Ptarmigan *Lagopus mutus*

red comb

dark lores

greyish-brown

adult ♀ winter

white wing

white belly

adult ♂ winter

adult ♂ summer

Close relative of Red Grouse that lives at higher altitudes but is similarly resident and unknown away from breeding grounds. Mottled greys and browns camouflage against scant vegetation and broken rocks of high mountain tops. In winter, whole plumage white; in summer, only wingtips white. Even intermediate white and grey patchy birds difficult to see. Male has prominent red comb in summer; black mark between bill and eye in winter.
Status: scarce resident of mountain tops of Scottish Highlands.
Similar Species: in summer, Red Grouse (p.83) but Ptarmigan paler, in shades of grey-brown rather than russet.

PTARMIGAN

Type	partridge-like
Size	33–36cm (13–14in)
Habitat	moors
Behaviour	walks, perches openly, takes off and lands on ground
Flocking	1–15
Flight	glides; strong and powerful; direct
Voice	cackling *aar-aar-ka-ka-ka*

IDENTIFICATION

Ad. ♂ summer	
Crown	grey-brown
Upperparts	grey-brown, bared black
Rump	grey-brown
Tail	black; short and rounded
Throat	grey-brown
Breast	grey-brown, barred black
Belly	white
Bill	black; short and stubby
Legs	white; short
Ad. ♀ summer	
	mottled brown and buff; underparts less white than ♂
Ad. winter	all white; ♂ dark lores

BREEDING

Nest	bare hollow on ground
Eggs	5–10; white, blotched dark brown
Incubation	24–26 days ♀
Young	active; downy
Fledging	10 days
Broods	1; May–June
Food	shoots, berries
Population	less than 10,000 pairs

J	F	M	A	M	J	J	A	S	O	N	D
2	2	2	2	2	2	2	2	2	2	2	2

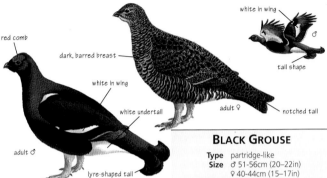

red comb

dark, barred breast

white in wing

white in wing

white undertail

adult ♂

lyre-shaped tail

white in wing

♂

tail shape

adult ♀

notched tail

Large grouse of woodland margins and birch scrub, best seen at communal lekking grounds in early morning or evening. Generally gregarious, forming small flocks and family groups. Sexes quite distinct. Male (Blackcock) predominantly black, with longish lyre-shaped tail, erected in display to show bold white undertail. Large red comb above eye, bold white wingbar in flight. Female (Greyhen) heavily barred brown and black above, black and buff below. Longish tail shows distinct notch in flight. *Status:* resident of moorlands. *Similar Species:* Capercaillie (p.86) is larger, has white bill and tail is a different shape.

J	F	M	A	M	J	J	A	S	O	N	D
3	3	3	3	3	3	3	3	3	3	3	3

BLACK GROUSE

Type	partridge-like
Size	♂ 51-56cm (20–22in)
	♀ 40-44cm (15–17in)
Habitat	moors, fields and hedgerows, forests
Behaviour	walks, takes off and lands on ground
Flocking	1-15
Flight	glides; strong and powerful; direct
Voice	*roo-koo* repeated at lek; a sneezed *chew-oosh*

IDENTIFICATION

Adult ♂	
Crown	black
Upperparts	black, white wingbar
Rump	black
Tail	black, undertail white; long and forked
Throat	black
Breast	black
Belly	black and white
Bill	black; short and stubby
Legs	black; short
Adult ♀	mottled; notched tail
Juvenile	like small, dull ♀

BREEDING

Nest	hollow on ground
Eggs	6–10; buffy, spotted brown
Incubation	23–26 days ♀
Young	active; downy
Fledging	4 weeks
Broods	1; May–June
Food	shoots, berries
Population	10,000–50,000 pairs

85

Capercaillie *Tetrao urogallus*

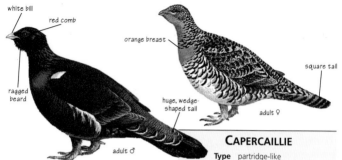

white bill
red comb
orange breast
square tail
ragged beard
huge, wedge-shaped tail
adult ♀
adult ♂

Largest of the grouse; huge male reminiscent of Turkey. Native birds shot out of existence in eighteenth century but successfully re-introduced in nineteenth. Male black with brown back and wings; long tail spread and raised to form fan in display. Large head with ragged 'beard'; red wattle above eye; fearsome white bill. Highly aggressive, will even attack human intruders. Female smaller and camouflaged in barred shades of brown with distinctive orange breast. Confined to conifer forests.
Status: resident in Scottish Highland forests; unknown elsewhere.
Similar Species: smaller Black Grouse (p.85) has lyre-shaped tail in male; female lacks orange breast.

CAPERCAILLIE

Type	partridge-like
Size	♂ 82–90cm (32–35in)
	♀ 58–64cm (22–25in)
Habitat	forests and woods
Behaviour	walks, perches openly, takes off and lands on vegetation and ground
Flocking	1–10
Flight	glides; strong and powerful; direct
Voice	crowing *ko-ko-kok*; series of clicks ending in pop

IDENTIFICATION

Adult ♂

Crown	black
Upperparts	brown
Rump	black
Tail	black; long and rounded
Throat	black
Breast	black
Belly	black; spotted white
Bill	white; short and stubby
Legs	grey; medium length
Adult ♀	smaller; buff and brown with orange breast

BREEDING

Nest	lined depression on ground
Eggs	5–8; buff, blotched reddish
Incubation	26–29 days ♀
Young	active; downy
Fledging	2–3 weeks
Broods	1; Apr–June
Food	shoots, berries, conifer needles
Population	1000–10,000 pairs

J	F	M	A	M	J	J	A	S	O	N	D
2	2	2	2	2	2	2	2	2	2	2	2

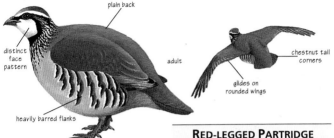

plain back

distinct face pattern

adult

chestnut tail corners

glides on rounded wings

heavily barred flanks

R otund, stocky bird successfully introduced from the Continent. Distinctive facial pattern consists of black eye stripe extending across ear coverts and neck to join broad, speckled breast band and enclose creamy chin and throat. Blue flanks barred black and chestnut. Gregarious, found in small flocks in open fields; also in overgrown areas with scattered vegetation. Flies low over ground and on bowed wings. In recent years, closely related Chukar introduced; hybrids may be found in some areas.

Status: resident mainly in south and east Britain; absent Ireland.

Similar Species: Grey Partridge (p.88) is similar shape but Red-legged is more boldly marked. Chukar has 'clean-cut' (not spotted) black breast band and fewer, broader bars on flanks.

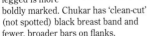

J	F	M	A	M	J	J	A	S	O	N	D
5	5	5	5	5	5	5	5	5	5	5	5

RED-LEGGED PARTRIDGE

Type	partridge-like
Size	33–36cm (13–14in)
Habitat	heaths, fields
Behaviour	walks, runs, perches openly, takes off and lands on ground
Flocking	1–15
Flight	glides; strong and powerful; direct
Voice	loud chuk-chuk-chukar-chukar

IDENTIFICATION

Adult

Crown	buff
Upperparts	buff
Rump	buff
Tail	buff; short and rounded
Throat	black and white
Breast	grey
Belly	orange
Bill	red; short and stubby
Legs	red; medium length

BREEDING

Nest	hollow on ground
Eggs	10–16; yellowish, spotted reddish
Incubation	23–25 days; often 2 nests, one incubated ♂, one incubated ♀
Young	active; downy
Fledging	10+ days
Broods	1 or 2; Apr–May
Food	seeds, leaves, insects
Population	100,000–200,000 pairs

Grey Partridge *Perdix perdix*

streaked back

chestnut tall corners

grey breast

♂

chestnut horseshoe

Stocky gamebird of open fields that prefers to run when threatened. When pressed, flies low over ground on bowed wings. Generally gregarious, occurring in small flocks (coveys). Pale, washed-out coloration makes it appear buffy at any distance. A closer approach reveals pale orange face, grey breast, brown bars on flanks and bold chestnut horseshoe on belly – reduced to chestnut smudge in female.
Status: declining resident of agricultural land throughout Britain and Ireland.
Similar Species: Red-legged Partridge (p.87).

GREY PARTRIDGE

Type	partridge-like
Size	29–32cm (11–13in)
Habitat	heaths, fields
Behaviour	walks, runs, takes off and lands on ground
Flocking	1–15
Flight	glides; strong and powerful; direct
Voice	decelerating *krikrikri-kri-krikri*; also rusty hinge sound, *kirr-ik*

IDENTIFICATION

Adult	
Crown	buff
Upperparts	brown and black, streaked
Rump	buff
Tail	buff; short and rounded
Throat	orange
Breast	grey
Belly	buff; ♂ chestnut horseshoe, ♀ chestnut smudge
Bill	grey; short and stubby
Legs	grey; medium length

BREEDING

Nest	hollow on ground
Eggs	9–20; buff
Incubation	23–25 days ♀
Young	active; downy
Fledging	16 days
Broods	1; Apr–May
Food	seeds, leaves, insects
Population	less than 500,000 pairs

J	F	M	A	M	J	J	A	S	O	N	D
5	5	5	5	5	5	5	5	5	5	5	5

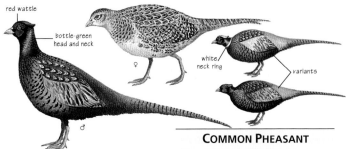

red wattle

bottle-green
head and neck

♀

white
neck ring

variants

♂

COMMON PHEASANT

Type	partridge-like
Size	♂ 75–90cm (30–35in)
	♀ 52–64cm (20–25in)
Habitat	heaths, forests and fields
Behaviour	walks, runs, takes off and lands on vegetation or ground
Flocking	1–15
Flight	glides; strong and powerful; direct
Voice	far carrying *kok...kok-kok*

IDENTIFICATION

Adult ♂	
Crown	green
Upperparts	brown, spotted black; lower back grey
Rump	russet
Tail	brown, barred black; long and pointed
Throat	green
Breast	brown, spotted black
Belly	brown, spotted black
Bill	buff; short and stubby
Legs	grey; medium length
Adult ♀	mottled buff and brown; long, pointed tail

BREEDING

Nest	hollow on ground
Eggs	7–15; plain olive-brown
Incubation	23–27 days ♀
Young	active; downy
Fledging	12–14 days
Broods	1; Apr–June
Food	shoots, seeds, berries
Population	8,000,000 individuals

Widespread, ground-dwelling
gamebird of woods, hedgerows
and fields. Plumage of male highly
variable due to introduction of sub-
species from different parts of natural
range. Female buffy; heavily speckled
black above and on flanks. Generally
found in small groups. When disturbed,
often runs or flies to cover; takes off
powerfully and then glides on bowed
wings, often quite low. Seldom makes
prolonged flights. Among vegetation,
often crouches and
is difficult to find.
Status: widespread
resident (except
north-western
Scotland); locally
abundant when
reared.
Similar Species:
none.

J	F	M	A	M	J	J	A	S	O	N	D
6	6	6	6	6	6	6	6	6	6	6	6

Water Rail *Rallus aquaticus*

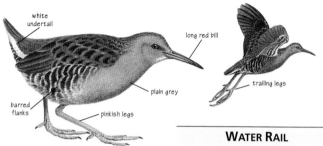

white undertail
long red bill
trailing legs
plain grey
barred flanks
pinkish legs

Highly secretive, marsh-dwelling bird, similar to Moorhen but with long, red, bill. More frequently heard than seen; calls sound more like a squealing pig than a bird. Laterally compressed for easy passage through dense vegetation, especially reeds. In winter, may emerge on open ground, though seldom far from water and cover. Upperparts dark brown, heavily streaked black; sides of head, throat and breast metallic grey. Flanks and belly barred black and white. Long legs and toes and short, rounded wings. Short, cocked tail frequently flicked showing white undertail coverts. *Status:* widespread resident but not common; Continental birds are winter visitors.
Similar Species: only rail with long bill.

WATER RAIL

Type	rail-like
Size	27–29cm (10–11in)
Habitat	freshwater marshes
Behaviour	wades, takes off and lands on water or ground
Flocking	1–2
Flight	laboured; legs trailing
Voice	repeated *kip-kip-kip*; variety of shrill squeals and harsh grunts

IDENTIFICATION

Adult	
Crown	brown and black
Upperparts	brown, streaked black
Rump	brown and black
Tail	brown and black, undertail white; short and pointed
Throat	grey
Breast	grey
Belly	black and white, barred
Bill	red; very long and thin
Legs	pinkish or greenish; long
BREEDING	
Nest	cup of reeds hidden above water
Eggs	6–10; creamy, spotted reddish
Incubation	19-20 days, mainly ♀
Young	active; downy
Fledging	7–8 weeks
Broods	2; Apr–June
Food	amphibians, vegetation, invertebrates
Population	2000–4000 pairs

J	F	M	A	M	J	J	A	S	O	N	D
3	3	3	3	3	3	3	3	3	3	3	3

chestnut wings

barred flanks and undertail

adult

trailing legs

pinkish legs

S ecretive summer visitor to hay and cereal fields. More often heard than seen, uttering harsh, rasping call; in some areas walks openly and even perches to call. When flushed, bold, chestnut wings and trailing legs diagnostic. Upperparts have black feather-centres edged with buffy brown, producing 'scalloped' effect. In summer, male has pale grey face and upper breast; less grey in winter. Underparts buff, barred chestnut, including undertail coverts; latter often obvious as bird walks away. *Status:* summer visitor April– September. Once widespread, now decidedly scarce; still relatively numerous in Ireland and Hebrides. *Similar Species:* short-billed rails, especially rare Little and Baillon's Crake.

CORN CRAKE

Type	rail-like
Size	25–28cm (10–11 in)
Habitat	fields and hedgerows
Behaviour	walks, takes off and lands on ground
Flocking	solitary
Flight	laboured; legs trailing
Voice	grating *crek-crek*, repeated

IDENTIFICATION

Ad. ♂ summer

Crown	black and brown
Upperparts	black, brown feather margins; wings chestnut
Rump	buff and black
Tail	buff and black, undertail buff, barred chestnut; short and pointed
Throat	white
Breast	grey
Belly	buff, barred chestnut
Bill	yellow; short and pointed
Legs	pink; long

Ad. ♂ winter

	less grey on breast (like ♀ and juvenile)

BREEDING

Nest	platform hidden on ground
Eggs	8–12; greenish, blotched brown
Incubation	15–18 days ♀
Young	active; downy
Fledging	5 weeks
Broods	1; May–June
Food	invertebrates, plants
Population	less than 100 pairs

J	F	M	A	M	J	J	A	S	O	N	D
0	0	0	1	3	3	2	2	2	1	0	0

Moorhen *Gallinula chloropus*

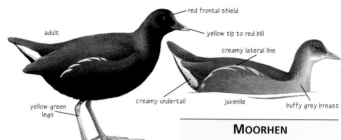

red frontal shield

yellow tip to red bill

adult

creamy lateral line

creamy undertail

yellow-green legs

juvenile

buffy grey breast

Common bird of ponds, rivers, canals and marshes; most often seen walking waterside banks with jerking, chicken-like movements of head. On land, long legs and toes obvious, as is white, cocked tail. In adult, white lateral line separates dark grey underparts from dark brown wings. Juvenile brown with whitish chin and foreneck; lateral line creamy; bill and legs dullish green. Swims well but flies laboriously with legs trailing after lengthy pattering take-off. Dives rarely. Seldom found in flocks.

Status: widespread resident except for higher hills; winter visitors arrive from September onwards.

Similar Species: Common Coot (p. 93) is all black with white frontal shield and often forms large winter flocks.

MOORHEN

Type	rail-like
Size	31–35cm (12–14in)
Habitat	freshwater, fields and hedges
Behaviour	swims, wades, walks, takes off and lands on water or ground
Flocking	1–15
Flight	laboured; legs trailing
Voice	loud *currick*; high-pitched *kik-kik-kik-kik*

IDENTIFICATION

Adult	
Crown	dark grey
Upperparts	dark brown, white lateral line
Rump	brown
Tail	brown, undertail black and white; short and pointed
Throat	dark grey
Breast	dark grey
Belly	dark grey
Bill	red, tip yellow; short and pointed
Legs	yellow-green; long
Juvenile	brown, whitish throat and foreneck; lateral line creamy

BREEDING

Nest	cup near ground
Eggs	5–11; buff, spotted
Incubation	19-22 days ♂ ♀
Young	active; downy
Fledging	6–7 weeks
Broods	2–3; Mar–Aug
Food	aquatic insects, molluscs, seeds, plants
Population	300,000 pairs

J	F	M	A	M	J	J	A	S	O	N	D
6	6	6	6	6	6	6	6	6	6	6	6

white frontal shield and bill

adult

juvenile

grey-green legs

whitish foreparts

Bulky, sooty black waterbird distinguished by white bill and frontal shield. Juvenile brownish with whitish face and foreneck; lacks frontal shield. Swims buoyantly and frequently dives for food; also up-ends in shallow water. Walks well and often feeds on splashy grassland, though always adjacent to open water. Forms large winter flocks tightly packed together. Evades danger by running over water surface rather than flying. Once airborne, flies strongly on broad, rounded wings with long legs trailing behind. *Status:* widespread resident; winter visitors arrive from the Continent October–April. *Similar Species:* Moorhen (p.92) has red bill and white undertail.

COMMON COOT

Type	duck-like
Size	36–40cm (14–16in)
Habitat	open freshwater, estuaries
Behaviour	swims, dives, wades, walks, takes off and lands on water
Flocking	1–1000
Flight	laboured; legs trailing
Voice	explosive *kook* or *teuk*

IDENTIFICATION

Adult

Crown	black; white frontal shield
Upperparts	black
Rump	black
Tail	black; short and pointed
Throat	black
Breast	black
Belly	black
Bill	white; short and pointed
Legs	grey-green; medium length
Juvenile	brownish with whitish foreparts; lacks frontal shield

BREEDING

Nest	bulky cup among aquatic vegetation or adjacent bush
Eggs	6–9; buff, spotted black
Incubation	21–24 days ♂♀
Young	active; downy
Fledging	6–8 weeks
Broods	2; mid Mar–June
Food	mostly plants but omnivorous
Population	10,000–100,000 pairs

J	F	M	A	M	J	J	A	S	O	N	D
6	6	6	6	6	6	6	6	6	6	6	6

Oystercatcher *Haematopus ostralegus*

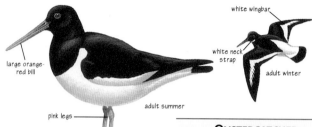

large orange-red bill

white wingbar

white neck strap

adult winter

pink legs

adult summer

L large, striking black and white bird with long, thick, orange-red bill and long, pink legs. Eyes red with bright orange-red eye ring. In winter, adult has brownish wash over black upperparts and white half collar. Juvenile as adult winter but browner above with only rudimentary half collar. Typically a bird of rocky and sandy shores; often gathers in large flocks on favoured estuaries. Highly vocal with loud piping calls; flies strongly, often low along shoreline. Frequently feeds on wet grasslands and freshwater marshes near sea; also along banks of shingle rivers.
Status: widespread coastal resident; winter visitors arrive August–April. Some British breeders migrate to France and Spain.
Similar Species: none.

J	F	M	A	M	J	J	A	S	O	N	D
6	6	6	6	6	6	6	6	6	6	6	6

OYSTERCATCHER

Type	wader-like
Size	41–45cm (16–18in)
Habitat	marshes, estuaries and shores, fields
Behaviour	wades, walks, perches openly, takes off and lands on water or ground
Flocking	1–several thousand
Flight	strong and powerful; direct
Voice	loud, penetrating *kleep;* also *kleep-a-kleep*

IDENTIFICATION

Ad.summer
Crown	black
Upperparts	black
Rump	white 'V'
Tail	white, black band; medium length, square
Throat	black
Breast	black, forming breast band
Belly	white
Bill	orange; long and thick
Legs	pink; long
Ad.winter	white chin bar
Juvenile	browner upperparts than Ad.winter; legs grey

BREEDING

Nest	scrape
Eggs	3; buff, blotched black
Incubation	24–27 days ♂♀
Young	active; downy
Fledging	34–37 days
Broods	1; mid Apr–June
Food	molluscs, worms
Population	c30,000 pairs; c300,000 winter

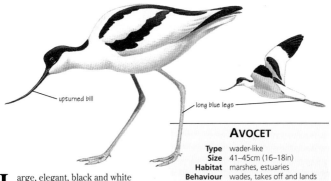

upturned bill

long blue legs

Large, elegant, black and white wader with long legs and distinctly upcurved bill. At rest, black areas form a white-filled oval pattern on wings. Scarce, seen mostly on coasts and marshes, mainly in south and east England. Feeds head-down with regular side-to-side scything movements of head and bill. Generally occurs in small groups; sometimes in much larger winter flocks. Often rather noisy.

Status: regular breeding colonies in East Anglia and elsewhere on east coast of England. Winters in Tamar Estuary, Devon. Elsewhere scarce passage migrant along south and east coasts in spring and autumn.

Similar Species: Oystercatcher (p.94) has straight orange-red bill.

J	F	M	A	M	J	J	A	S	O	N	D
1	1	2	2	3	3	2	2	2	2	1	1

AVOCET

Type	wader-like
Size	41–45cm (16–18in)
Habitat	marshes, estuaries
Behaviour	wades, takes off and lands on water or ground
Flocking	1–100
Flight	strong and powerful; direct; legs trailing
Voice	loud *kloo-eet*

IDENTIFICATION

Adult

Crown	black
Upperparts	black and white stripes
Rump	white
Tail	white; medium length, square
Throat	white
Breast	white
Belly	white
Bill	black; long, thin and upturned
Legs	blue-grey; very long
Juvenile	dark brown where adult black

BREEDING

Nest	bare scrape on ground, often on low island
Eggs	4; buff, spotted and blotched black
Incubation	22–24 days ♂ ♀
Young	active; downy
Fledging	6 weeks
Broods	1; Apr–May
Food	insects, crustaceans
Population	450 pairs

95

Stone-curlew *Burhinus oedicnemus*

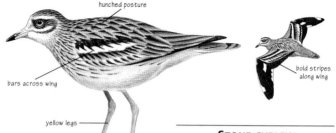

hunched posture

bars across wing

yellow legs

bold stripes along wing

Large, plover-like summer visitor to stony or other sparsely vegetated ground, mainly in south-eastern England. Most active at dawn and dusk. When disturbed, prefers to run rather than fly. Buffy brown streaked with black above and on breast; wings have bold horizontal white bar with black border. Complex faced pattern of brown and white stripes. Long, yellow legs and penetrating yellow eye. Difficult to pick out at any distance due to cryptic camouflage. In flight, shows bold pattern of black and white on long, pointed wings.
Status: scarce summer visitor March–October; winters southern Europe and Africa.
Similar Species: none.

STONE-CURLEW

Type	wader-like
Size	38–43cm (15–17in)
Habitat	heaths, fields
Behaviour	walks, runs, takes off and lands on ground
Flocking	1–2
Flight	strong and powerful; direct
Voice	rippling *cooree*, similar to tin whistle

IDENTIFICATION

Adult	
Crown	buff
Upperparts	buff, streaked black; black and white bars across wings
Rump	buff
Tail	buff, black tip; medium length, rounded
Throat	white
Breast	buff, streaked brown
Belly	white
Bill	yellow with black tip; short and pointed
Legs	yellow; long
Juvenile	paler with less marked wingbars

BREEDING

Nest	bare scrape
Eggs	2; creamy, speckled and blotched brown
Incubation	25–27 days ♂ ♀
Young	active; downy
Fledging	6 weeks
Broods	1 occasionally 2; Apr–May
Food	insects, worms
Population	140–150 pairs

J	F	M	A	M	J	J	A	S	O	N	D
0	0	1	2	2	2	2	2	1	1	0	0

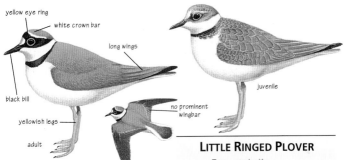

yellow eye ring

white crown bar

long wings

black bill

yellowish legs

adult

juvenile

no prominent wingbar

LITTLE RINGED PLOVER

S carce summer visitor to inland freshwaters (especially gravel pits) of southern and central England. Smaller, slimmer version of Ringed Plover with similar round-headed appearance, short bill and typical 'run-stop' plover behaviour. Adult has white forehead with black band across crown bordered by narrow white line; yellow eye ring. In flight, lacks wingbar; shows white outer tail feathers. Juvenile similar but with darker brown (not black) head markings; breast band often incomplete.
Status: scarce summer visitor and passage migrant March–October.
Similar Species: Ringed Plover (p.98) has orange-yellow, not black, bill and shows wingbar in flight.

Type	wader-like
Size	14–16cm (5–6in)
Habitat	freshwater
Behaviour	wades, runs, takes off and lands on ground
Flocking	1–2
Flight	strong and powerful; direct
Voice	short, down-slurred *piu*
IDENTIFICATION	
Adult	
Crown	white, black and brown
Upperparts	brown
Rump	brown
Tail	black and white; short and square
Throat	white
Breast	white with black band
Belly	white
Bill	black; short and pointed
Legs	dull pink or yellow; medium length
Juvenile	brownish above; head and breast bands brownish, incomplete
BREEDING	
Nest	bare scrape on ground
Eggs	4; buffish, spotted and streaked brown
Incubation	24–26 days ♂ ♀
Young	active; downy
Fledging	21–24 days
Broods	1 or 2; Mar–June
Food	insects, molluscs
Population	400–500 pairs

J	F	M	A	M	J	J	A	S	O	N	D
0	0	0	3	3	3	2	3	3	2	0	0

Ringed Plover *Charadrius hiaticula*

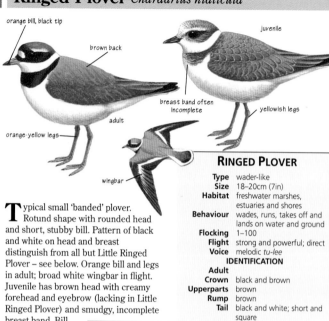

orange bill, black tip

brown back

juvenile

breast band often incomplete

yellowish legs

adult

orange-yellow legs

wingbar

Typical small 'banded' plover. Rotund shape with rounded head and short, stubby bill. Pattern of black and white on head and breast distinguish from all but Little Ringed Plover – see below. Orange bill and legs in adult; broad white wingbar in flight. Juvenile has brown head with creamy forehead and eyebrow (lacking in Little Ringed Plover) and smudgy, incomplete breast band. Bill black; legs yellowish.

Status: resident breeder, passage migrant and winter visitor to coasts and estuaries. Also occurs and breeds inland but never commonly.

Similar Species: Little Ringed Plover (p.97).

RINGED PLOVER

Type	wader-like
Size	18–20cm (7in)
Habitat	freshwater marshes, estuaries and shores
Behaviour	wades, runs, takes off and lands on water and ground
Flocking	1–100
Flight	strong and powerful; direct
Voice	melodic *tu-lee*

IDENTIFICATION

Adult	
Crown	black and brown
Upperparts	brown
Rump	brown
Tail	black and white; short and square
Throat	white
Breast	white with black band
Belly	white
Bill	orange; short and pointed
Legs	orange-yellow; medium length
Juvenile	incomplete breast band; bill black; legs yellowish

BREEDING

Nest	bare scrape on ground
Eggs	4; buff, spotted brown
Incubation	23–26 days ♂♀
Young	active; downy
Fledging	25 days
Broods	2 sometimes 3; May–July
Food	invertebrates
Population	9,000 pairs; 350,000 winter; more on passage

J	F	M	A	M	J	J	A	S	O	N	D
3	3	4	4	4	4	4	4	5	5	4	4

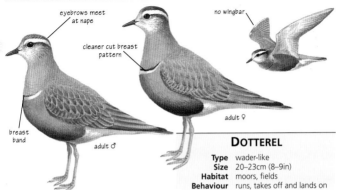

eyebrows meet at nape

cleaner cut breast pattern

no wingbar

adult ♀

breast band

adult ♂

Small, rotund plover; easily overlooked on stony mountain-top habitat where well camouflaged among lichens and mosses. Summer adults have distinctive grey breast and chestnut underparts separated by white band. Prominent white eyebrows meet on nape. In winter and juvenile plumages, becomes greyish; marked only by white eyebrow and indistinct breast band. Plain wings and no distinctive tail pattern in flight. Runs and stops in typical plover manner.
Status: rare summer visitor; breeds on a few Scottish mountain-tops. Scarce passage migrant in East Anglia in May.
Similar Species: none.

J	F	M	A	M	J	J	A	S	O	N	D
0	0	0	1	2	2	2	2	1	1	0	0

DOTTEREL

Type	wader-like
Size	20–23cm (8–9in)
Habitat	moors, fields
Behaviour	runs, takes off and lands on ground
Flocking	1–15
Flight	strong and powerful; direct
Voice	quiet *peep-peep* in flight; *titi-ri-titi-ri* repeated

IDENTIFICATION

Ad.summer	
Crown	black
Upperparts	grey; wings brown and black
Rump	buff and brown
Tail	buff and brown; short and rounded
Throat	white
Breast	grey, white band
Belly	chestnut
Bill	black; short and thin
Legs	yellow; medium length
Ad.winter & juvenile	grey above and below, good white eyebrow, indistinct breast band

BREEDING

Nest	hollow on ground
Eggs	3; buffy, spotted blackish brown
Incubation	21–26 days ♀
Young	active; downy
Fledging	4 weeks
Broods	1; May–une
Food	insects
Population	60–100 pairs; very scarce migrant

European Golden Plover *Pluvialis apricaria*

adult northern summer

more black on face

narrow wingbar

adult winter

little streaking on buffy breast

adult winter

black belly

adult southern summer

Medium-sized plover with typically rotund body, round head, short bill and long legs. Upperparts spangled black and gold. In winter, underparts whitish with buffy breast markings. In summer, southern sub-species has black belly extending to central breast stripe and grey face. Northern sub-species has more black on belly and breast with black face. In flight, shows faint wingbar and plain barred tail pattern. Found among hills in summer and on marshes and grassland in winter. *Status:* widespread and numerous winter visitor. *Similar Species:* similarly shaped Grey Plover (p.101) is spangled grey and black above; shows black 'arm pits' in flight.

EUROPEAN GOLDEN PLOVER

Type	wader-like
Size	27–29cm (10–11in)
Habitat	moors, heaths, fields, marshes
Behaviour	walks, runs, takes off and lands on ground
Flocking	1–1000
Flight	strong and powerful; direct
Voice	whistled *tlui*
IDENTIFICATION	
Ad.summer	
Crown	black and gold
Upperparts	spangled black and gold
Rump	black and gold
Tail	black and gold; short and square
Throat	black
Breast	black, white margins
Belly	black, white margins
Bill	black; short and thin
Legs	grey; long
Ad.winter	lacks black face and underparts; buffy breast markings
BREEDING	
Nest	scrape on ground
Eggs	4; buff, blotched brown
Incubation	27–28 days, mainly ♀
Young	active; downy
Fledging	4 weeks
Broods	1; Apr–June
Food	worms, insects
Population	30,000 pairs; 700,000 winter

J	F	M	A	M	J	J	A	S	O	N	D
3	3	3	3	3	3	3	3	3	3	3	3

black and pale grey

little streaking on white breast

winter

black face and belly

adult summer

winter

black 'arm pits'

Similar to European Golden Plover, but larger and confined to coasts, estuaries and adjacent marshes. Upperparts spangled grey and black. In winter, underparts white with grey speckling on breast. In summer, belly, breast and face black, with white margins on sides of breast and head. In flight, shows wingbar, white rump and black axillaries (arm pits). Legs longer than European Golden Plover and extend just beyond tip of tail in flight. Found in large flocks on favoured estuaries and shorelines.
Status: common winter visitor and passage migrant to all coasts.
Similar Species: European Golden Plover (p.100).

GREY PLOVER

Type	wader-like
Size	28–31cm (11–12in)
Habitat	estuaries, shores
Behaviour	wades, walks, takes off and lands on water or ground
Flocking	1–1000
Flight	strong and powerful; direct
Voice	plaintive whistled *tlee-oo-ee*

IDENTIFICATION

Ad.summer	
Crown	grey and black
Upperparts	spangled grey and black
Rump	white
Tail	black and white; short and square
Throat	black
Breast	black, white margins
Belly	black
Bill	black; short and thin
Legs	black; long
Ad.winter	grey above, white below

BREEDING

Nest	hollow on ground
Eggs	4; buff, spotted
Incubation	23 days ♂ ♀
Young	active; downy
Fledging	?
Broods	1; June–July
Food	invertebrates, worms
Population	20,000 winter

J	F	M	A	M	J	J	A	S	O	N	D
3	3	3	3	3	1	1	2	3	3	3	3

Lapwing *Vanellus vanellus*

wispy crest

adult winter

black breast

adult summer

rounded wings

white rump
black tail
band

Common throughout Britain and Ireland. Looks black and white at any distance; distinctive crest. Close approach reveals upperparts have glossy green and purple sheen. Head white with intricate pattern of black markings; throat black, widening into black breast band. In winter, throat and upper breast become white. Gregarious outside breeding season.
Status: widespread and numerous breeding bird; huge winter influx from the Continent.
Similar Species: none.

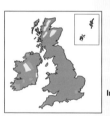

LAPWING

Type	wader-like
Size	29–32cm (11–12in)
Habitat	freshwater marshes, moors, estuaries, fields
Behaviour	wades, walks, takes off and lands on ground
Flocking	1–1000
Flight	laboured; direct; aerial dive
Voice	plaintive *pee-wit*
IDENTIFICATION	
Adult	
Crown	black and white; wispy crest
Upperparts	green-black
Rump	white
Tail	black and white, undertail pale brown; short and square
Throat	black and white
Breast	black
Belly	white
Bill	black; short and thin
Legs	dark red; long
BREEDING	
Nest	hollow on ground
Eggs	4; buff, blotched black
Incubation	24–29 days, mainly ♀
Young	active; downy
Fledging	33 days
Broods	1; Mar–Apr
Food	invertebrates
Population	200,000 pairs; 1,000,000+ winter

J	F	M	A	M	J	J	A	S	O	N	D
6	6	6	6	6	6	6	6	6	6	6	6

short straight bill

eyebrow

chestnut underparts

adult summer

wingbar

grey rump

adult winter

Medium-sized, stocky shorebird similar to Dunlin, but considerably larger, with shorter bill and legs. Highly gregarious at all seasons with majority concentrated at relatively few favoured estuaries. In winter, grey above with pale feather margins; underparts white with faint speckling on breast and flanks; well marked eye stripe and eyebrow. In summer face and underparts chestnut. In flight, shows faint wingbar and distinctive grey rump.
Status: abundant, though localized winter visitor.
Similar Species: winter Dunlin (p.109) but Knot much larger with proportionately shorter bill.

KNOT

Type	wader-like
Size	24–27cm (9–10in)
Habitat	estuaries and shores
Behaviour	wades, takes off and lands on water or ground
Flocking	1–20,000
Flight	strong and powerful; direct
Voice	low *knut*

IDENTIFICATION

Ad.winter

Crown	grey
Upperparts	grey
Rump	grey
Tail	grey; short and square
Throat	white
Breast	grey
Belly	white
Bill	black; straight and thin
Legs	dark green; medium length

Ad.summer

face and underparts chestnut-red; mantle spangled black and chestnut

BREEDING

Nest	lined hollow
Eggs	4; pale green, spotted brown
Incubation	20–25 days ♂ ♀ ?
Young	active; downy
Fledging	20 days?
Broods	1; June
Food	molluscs, crustaceans, worms
Population	200,000–400,000 winter

J	F	M	A	M	J	J	A	S	O	N	D
4	4	4	4	3	2	2	3	4	4	4	4

Sanderling *Calidris alba*

short bill

pale grey
upperparts

heavily streaked
breast

adult summer

black at bend
of wing

adult winter

bold wingbar

Palest of the shorebirds with light grey upperparts and white below; prominent black mark at bend of wing. Gregarious, forms small flocks that characteristically feed in fast, running motion up and down beaches with movement of waves. In summer, head, breast and back spangled black and chestnut for brief period. Summer birds away from shoreline, may provoke thoughts of other, rarer, species.
Status: widespread winter visitor and numerous passage migrant; confined to coasts and sometimes adjacent marshes.
Similar Species: no other wader runs up and down beach with the waves or is so pale in winter plumage.

SANDERLING

Type	wader-like
Size	19–22cm (7–8½in)
Habitat	shores
Behaviour	wades, runs, takes off and land on water or ground
Flocking	1–100
Flight	strong and powerful; direct
Voice	*quit-quit*, repeated
IDENTIFICATION	
Ad.winter	
Crown	grey
Upperparts	grey; black at bend of wing
Rump	black and white
Tail	black and white; short and square
Throat	white
Breast	white
Belly	white
Bill	black; short and straight
Legs	black; medium length
Ad.summer	
	head, back and breast spangled black and chestnut
BREEDING	
Nest	neat hollow on ground
Eggs	4; greenish, spotted brown
Incubation	23–24 days ♂♀
Young	active; downy
Fledging	23-24 days
Broods	1; June–July
Food	molluscs, crustaceans
Population	12,000 winter; 30,000 May

J	F	M	A	M	J	J	A	S	O	N	D
3	3	3	3	3	1	0	2	2	3	3	3

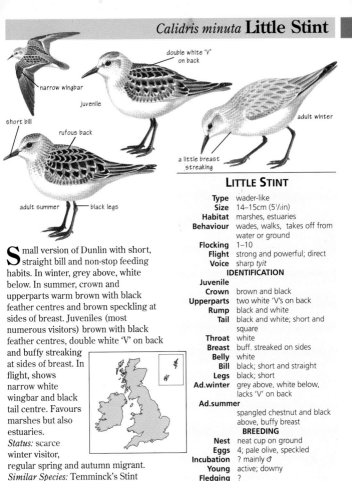

double white 'V' on back

narrow wingbar

juvenile

short bill

rufous back

adult winter

a little breast streaking

adult summer — black legs

S mall version of Dunlin with short, straight bill and non-stop feeding habits. In winter, grey above, white below. In summer, crown and upperparts warm brown with black feather centres and brown speckling at sides of breast. Juveniles (most numerous visitors) brown with black feather centres, double white 'V' on back and buffy streaking at sides of breast. In flight, shows narrow white wingbar and black tail centre. Favours marshes but also estuaries.
Status: scarce winter visitor, regular spring and autumn migrant.
Similar Species: Temminck's Stint (p.106).

LITTLE STINT

Type	wader-like
Size	14–15cm (5½in)
Habitat	marshes, estuaries
Behaviour	wades, walks, takes off from water or ground
Flocking	1–10
Flight	strong and powerful; direct
Voice	sharp *tyit*

IDENTIFICATION

Juvenile	
Crown	brown and black
Upperparts	two white 'V's on back
Rump	black and white
Tail	black and white; short and square
Throat	white
Breast	buff. streaked on sides
Belly	white
Bill	black; short and straight
Legs	black; short
Ad.winter	grey above, white below, lacks 'V' on back
Ad.summer	spangled chestnut and black above, buffy breast

BREEDING

Nest	neat cup on ground
Eggs	4; pale olive, speckled
Incubation	? mainly ♂
Young	active; downy
Fledging	?
Broods	1; June–July
Food	molluscs, crustaceans
Population	less than 30 winter; 200+ September

J	F	M	A	M	J	J	A	S	O	N	D
1	1	1	1	1	1	1	1	2	3	1	1

Temminck's Stint *Calidris temminckii*

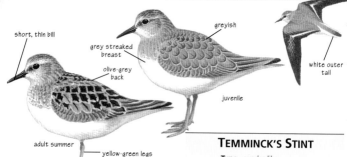

short, thin bill

grey streaked breast

olive-grey back

greyish

white outer tail

juvenile

adult summer

yellow-green legs

Marginally smaller than Little Stint and much more grey and uniformly marked. Winter adult and juvenile grey above, with slightly paler feather margins. White below with grey breast. In summer, upperparts olive-grey with black streaks. Shortish legs and extended body shape, together with picking feeding action, recall Common Sandpiper rather than Dunlin or Little Stint. Prefers fresh marshes with emergent vegetation.
Status: scarce, but regular double passage migrant. Breeds regularly in small numbers in Scotland.
Similar Species: Little Stint (p.105). Temminck's is more uniform and less 'contrasting' in all plumages.

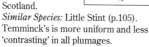

TEMMINCK'S STINT

Type	wader-like
Size	13–15cm (5–5½in)
Habitat	freshwater marshes
Behaviour	wades, walks, takes off from water or ground
Flocking	1 or 2
Flight	strong and powerful; direct; flitting
Voice	high-pitched *trrrr-trrrr*

IDENTIFICATION

Ad.winter and juvenile

Crown	grey
Upperparts	grey
Rump	black and white
Tail	black and white; short and square
Throat	white
Breast	grey
Belly	white
Bill	black; short, straight and thin
Legs	yellow green; medium length

Ad.summer

upperparts olive-grey, speckled black; breast grey

BREEDING

Nest	hollow on ground
Eggs	4; pale olive, speckled brownish
Incubation	21–22 days, mainly ♂
Young	active; downy
Fledging	15–18 days
Broods	1; June
Food	insects
Population	rare breeder; scarce migrant

J	F	M	A	M	J	J	A	S	O	N	D
0	0	0	1	1	1	1	0	1	1	1	0	0

long neck, rounded head

decurved bill

adult winter

juvenile

longish legs

adult summer

juvenile

square white rump

buffy unstreaked breast

Double passage migrant, mostly in autumn. Shape distinctive; long legs, long neck, decurved bill. White rump diagnostic. Adults constitute first wave of autumn birds (July–August); most show some chestnut feathers on breast. Later autumn wave (Aug–Sept) mainly juveniles; grey above with buffy feather margins giving scaled appearance. Buff wash over unstreaked breast. Some late adult migrants (Sept–Oct) are grey above and unstreaked white below. In spring, chestnut head and body contrast with grey wings.
Status: regular in autumn, mostly Aug-Sept. Scarce spring.
Similar Species: Dunlin (p.109) is smaller, shorter-necked and less elegant.

CURLEW SANDPIPER

Type	wader-like
Size	18–20cm (7–8in)
Habitat	freshwater marshes, estuaries and shores
Behaviour	wades, walks, takes off and lands on ground
Flocking	1–15
Flight	strong and powerful; direct
Voice	*churrip*

IDENTIFICATION

Juvenile	
Crown	grey
Upperparts	grey and buff
Rump	white
Tail	white, grey tip; short and square
Throat	white
Breast	buff-white
Belly	white
Bill	black, long and decurved
Legs	black; long
Ad.winter	grey above, white below
Ad.summer	chestnut head and underparts; grey wings

BREEDING

Nest	hollow on ground
Eggs	3–4; olive, blotched brown
Incubation	?; ♂♀
Young	active; downy
Fledging	?
Broods	1; June-July
Food	insects, molluscs, crustaceans
Population	variable autumn; a few in spring

J	F	M	A	M	J	J	A	S	O	N	D
0	0	0	1	1	1	1	3	3	0	0	0

Purple Sandpiper *Calidris maritima*

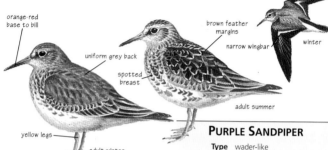

orange-red base to bill

uniform grey back

spotted breast

yellow legs

adult winter

brown feather margins

narrow wingbar

winter

adult summer

T he most maritime of all shorebirds, seldom found away from rocky shorelines. Stockily-built, short-legged wader with bill about same length as head; base of bill orange-red. Few distinguishing features apart from shape and general dark coloration. In winter, head and breast dark grey with white eye ring and throat. Upperparts black with dark grey feather margins. Belly white with dark spots. In summer, back and wings dark with broad, brown edges to feathers. Head, neck, breast and belly heavily streaked. Feeds busily among rocks and seaweed, often with Turnstones.
Status: winter visitor to rocky coasts.
Similar Species: no waders are as dark.

PURPLE SANDPIPER

Type	wader-like
Size	20–22cm (7½–8½in)
Habitat	coasts
Behaviour	walks, wades, perches openly, takes off and lands on water or ground
Flocking	1–20
Flight	strong and powerful; direct
Voice	mostly silent, occasional *weet-weet*

IDENTIFICATION

Ad.winter	
Crown	dark grey
Upperparts	black and grey
Rump	black and white
Tail	black and white; short and rounded
Throat	white
Breast	dark grey
Belly	white, dark spots
Bill	black, orange base; straight
Legs	yellow; short
Ad.summer	
	black and buff above; heavily streaked breast

BREEDING

Nest	leaf-lined hollow
Eggs	4; pale greenish, blotched brown
Incubation	21–22 days, mainly ♂
Young	active; downy
Fledging	3–4 weeks
Broods	1; June–July
Food	molluscs, crustaceans
Population	25,000 winter

J	F	M	A	M	J	J	A	S	O	N	D
3	3	3	2	1	0	0	0	0	2	3	3

buff feather margins

winter

white wingbar

white tail patches

juvenile

adult winter

longish bill slight decurve

streaked breast

black belly

adult summer

M ost widespread and abundant small wader, found in enormous flocks on estuaries and shorelines. Dumpy little bird that feeds busily and generally adopts a hunched-up attitude. In winter, upperparts grey with paler feather margins; underparts white with grey streaks on breast. In summer, chestnut and black on crown and back; breast streaked, black belly patch. Juvenile brown above with narrow buff margins. *Status:* widespread moorland breeder. Passage migrant and winter visitor to all coasts and floods.
Similar Species: the standard wader.

DUNLIN

Type	wader-like
Size	16–19cm (6–8in)
Habitat	marshes, estuaries and shores, moors
Behaviour	walks, wades, takes off from water and ground
Flocking	1–10,000
Flight	strong and powerful; direct
Voice	rasped *schreep*

IDENTIFICATION

Ad.winter

Crown	grey
Upperparts	grey
Rump	black and white
Tail	black and white; short and square
Throat	white
Breast	white, streaked grey
Belly	white
Bill	black; long and thin, decurved tip
Legs	black; medium length

Ad.summer

brown above; black belly

Juvenile	brown above, buff breast

BREEDING

Nest	hollow on ground
Eggs	4; greenish, blotched brown
Incubation	21–22 days ♂ ♀
Young	active; downy
Fledging	25 days
Broods	1; May–June
Food	molluscs, crustaceans
Population	4000–8000 pairs; 650,000 winter

J	F	M	A	M	J	J	A	S	O	N	D
5	5	4	4	4	3	3	4	4	5	5	5

109

Ruff *Philomachus pugnax*

varlants

small head, long neck

broad buff margins to feathers create 'scaly' effect

juvenile

buffy breast

adult ♂ summer

adult ♂ winter

white oval patches

orange-red legs — adult ♀

Rare breeder but relatively common double passage migrant and increasing winter visitor. Male (Ruff) much larger than female (Reeve). Male in summer, even on passage, boasts elaborate multi-coloured plumes on head and neck and has wattled, bare red face. Females, juveniles and males at other times have long necks, small heads, fine, medium-length, pointed bills and longish red, pink, yellow or green legs. Back always scalloped with buff margins.
Status: scarce breeder; regular double passage migrant; scarce winter visitor.
Similar Species: Common Redshank (p.119) also has reddish legs but shape quite different.

J	F	M	A	M	J	J	A	S	O	N	D
2	2	2	2	2	1	1	3	3	2	2	2

RUFF

Type	wader-like
Size	♂ 27–31cm (10–12in)
	♀ 22–25cm (8–9in)
Habitat	freshwater marshes, flooded grassland
Behaviour	wades, walks, takes off from water or ground
Flocking	1–100
Flight	strong and powerful; direct
Voice	*chuk-uck*
IDENTIFICATION	
Ad. ♂ winter and ♀	
Crown	buff
Upperparts	buff and brown, 'scalloped'
Rump	black and white
Tail	black and white; short
Throat	white
Breast	buff, speckled
Belly	white
Bill	black; straight and thin
Legs	pinkish red or yellowish; long
Ad. ♂ summer	
	elaborate head plumes
Juvenile	uniformly buff below
BREEDING	
Nest	hollow on ground
Eggs	4; olive, blotched brown
Incubation	20–21 days ♀
Young	active; downy
Fledging	?
Broods	1; Apr–May
Food	insects, invertebrates
Population	20+ Reeves; 1400 winter

adult

striped crown

medium bill

adult

wedge-shaped tail, no white

adult

S maller, shorter-billed version of Common Snipe but much less common and more elusive, keeping itself well hidden in cover. Frequents freshwater marshes and flooded ground. Usually seen only when flushed; flies when in danger of being trodden on. Silent take-off and brief, low, straight flight with no towering or zig-zagging. No white on tail margins.
Status: passage migrant and winter visitor from September–April.
Similar Species: Common Snipe (p.112) is larger, with longer bill, zig-zag flight and harsh flight note.

JACK SNIPE

Type	wader-like
Size	18–20cm (7–8in)
Habitat	freshwater and marshes, fields and hedges
Behaviour	wades, walks, runs, takes off and lands on water or ground
Flocking	1–2
Flight	strong and powerful; direct
Voice	usually silent

IDENTIFICATION
Adult

Crown	white with black stripe
Upperparts	brown and black, streaked
Rump	brown and black
Tail	brown and black; short and rounded
Throat	white
Breast	buff and brown, streaked
Belly	white
Bill	brown; straight and thin
Legs	green; medium length

BREEDING

Nest	lines cup on ground
Eggs	4; green, blotched brown
Incubating	17–24 days ♀
Young	active; downy
Fledging	?
Broods	1; June–July
Food	molluscs, worms, insects
Population	winter ?

J	F	M	A	M	J	J	A	S	O	N	D
2	2	2	2	1	0	0	0	1	2	2	2

111

Common Snipe *Gallinago gallinago*

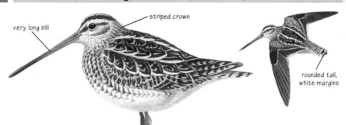

very long bill

striped crown

rounded tail, white margins

Heavily streaked, well camouflaged wader with long, straight bill. Mottled brown and black above with bold, buff stripes on back forming 'V'. Buff crown stripe and eyebrow plus dark eye stripe and dark margins to ear coverts produce distinctive striped pattern. Found mostly on freshwater marshes and flooded fields; generally gregarious. Tends to keep to cover but also feeds quite openly when not alarmed. If disturbed, flies off with pronounced zig-zagging, often towering into the air. Distinctive harsh flight note; also produces bleating sound in aerial diving display. *Status:* widespread resident and abundant winter visitor. *Similar Species:* Jack Snipe (p.111) smaller with low, straight flight.

COMMON SNIPE

Type	wader-like
Size	25–27cm (9½–10½in)
Habitat	freshwater marshes, moors, fields
Behaviour	wades, walks, runs, takes off from water and ground
Flocking	1–100
Flight	strong and powerful
Voice	harsh *scarp*, aerial 'drumming'

IDENTIFICATION

Adult	
Crown	dark brown with buff stripe
Upperparts	brown and black, streaked
Rump	brown and black
Tail	brown and black, edged white; short and rounded
Throat	white
Breast	buff and brown, streaked
Belly	white
Bill	brown; very long, thin and straight
Legs	green; long

BREEDING

Nest	lined hollow on ground
Eggs	4; pale green, blotched brown
Incubation	18–20 days ♀
Young	active; downy
Fledging	19-20 days
Broods	1,2?; Apr–May
Food	worms, insects
Population	80,000–110,000 pairs; many hundreds of thousands winter

J	F	M	A	M	J	J	A	S	O	N	D
4	4	4	4	4	4	4	4	4	4	4	4

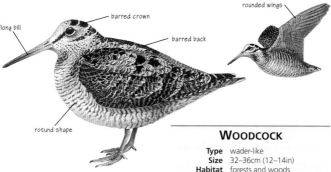

long bill — barred crown — barred back — rounded wings — rotund shape

Bulky, Snipe-like wader of moist, open woodland. Well camouflaged by brown and buff bars creating a 'dead leaves' effect. Hardly ever seen on ground but occasional bird may be flushed from nest. In flight, bulky shape, long, down-pointed bill and broad, rounded wings diagnostic. Mainly nocturnal. Territorial display flight (roding) at dawn and dusk.
Status: resident virtually throughout Britain and Ireland; some immigration from the Continent in winter.
Similar Species: Common Snipe (p.112) has longer bill, is smaller and slimmer and lives in different habitat.

WOODCOCK

Type	wader-like
Size	32–36cm (12–14in)
Habitat	forests and woods
Behaviour	walks, takes off or lands on ground
Flocking	solitary
Flight	strong and powerful; direct
Voice	shrill *tssick* flight note when roding

IDENTIFICATION

Adult	
Crown	buff, transverse black bars
Upperparts	dark brown and buff, bars and stripes
Rump	brown and black
Tail	brown and black; short and rounded
Throat	buff
Breast	buff and brown, barred
Belly	buff and brown, barred
Bill	buff, very long and thin
Legs	pink; short and stout

BREEDING

Nest	leaf-lined hollow on ground
Eggs	4; buff, blotched brown
Incubation	20–23 days ♀
Young	active; downy
Fledging	5–6 weeks
Broods	2; Mar–May
Food	worms, insects
Population	10,000–50,000 pairs

J	F	M	A	M	J	J	A	S	O	N	D
2	2	2	2	3	3	2	2	2	2	2	2

Black-tailed Godwit *Limosa limosa*

long straight bill

uniform greyish
upperparts

bold black and
white wings

adult winter

black tail
bar

legs extend
in flight

chestnut
breast

adult winter

chestnut ends at
breast, white belly

adult summer

Large, long-legged, long-billed wader of freshwater marshes, flooded fields and estuaries. In summer, adult has chestnut head, neck and breast with white chin and white eyebrow. Back spangled black and chestnut; wings grey. Belly white, barred black and brown. In winter, grey back and wings with no prominent streaking. Breast pale grey; belly white. Juvenile brown and buff; upperparts 'scalloped'. In flight, shows black band at tip of white tail and broad white wingbar. *Status:* scarce breeder; double passage migrant and winter visitor.
Similar Species: Bar-tailed Godwit (p.115) is smaller, has shorter legs and shorter, upturned bill; lacks wingbar.

BLACK-TAILED GODWIT

Type	wader-like
Size	38–43cm (14½–16½in)
Habitat	marshes, estuaries, field
Behaviour	wades, walks, takes off and lands on water or ground
Flocking	1–200
Flight	strong and powerful; direct
Voice	loud *reeka-reeka-reeka*

IDENTIFICATION

Ad.winter	
Crown	grey
Upperparts	grey
Rump	white
Tail	white with black band; short and square
Throat	white
Breast	pale grey
Belly	white
Bill	dark with pink base; very long, straight and thin
Legs	black; very long
Ad.summer	chestnut foreparts, barred white belly
Juvenile	upperparts dark brown and buff, scalloped; breast buff

BREEDING

Nest	lined hollow on ground
Eggs	4; green, blotched brown
Incubation	22–24 days ♂♀
Young	active; downy
Fledging	4 weeks
Broods	1; Apr–June
Food	worms, molluscs, insects
Population	60–70 pairs; 12,000–15,000 winter

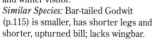

J	F	M	A	M	J	J	A	S	O	N	D
2	2	2	2	2	2	2	4	4	2	2	2

long bill, slightly upturned

adult winter

streaked back

no wingbar

adult winter

chestnut on whole of underparts

adult summer

L arge, long-legged, long-billed wader of estuaries and shorelines; occasionally roosts in coastal freshwater marshes. In summer, males have chestnut underparts, extending to undertail. Back spangled black and chestnut; wings grey. Summer females paler than males. In winter, upperparts buffy grey, heavily streaked black; underparts white. Juvenile streaked buff and black. In flight, appears uniformly greyish with white 'V' extending upwards from rump; feet barely extend beyond tail. *Status:* passage migrant and winter visitor.

Similar Species: larger Black-tailed Godwit (p.114) shows black and white in flight.

J	F	M	A	M	J	J	A	S	O	N	D
5	5	5	4	2	0	0	3	3	5	5	5

BAR-TAILED GODWIT

Type	wader-like
Size	36–40cm (14–16in)
Habitat	estuaries and shores
Behaviour	wades, walks, takes off from water and ground
Flocking	1–1000
Flight	strong and powerful; direct
Voice	*kirrick-kirrick*
IDENTIFICATION	
Ad.winter	
Crown	buff and brown
Upperparts	buffy grey, streaked black
Rump	white
Tail	barred black; short and square
Throat	white
Breast	buff
Belly	white
Bill	dark with pink base; very long and thin, upturned
Legs	black; long
Ad.summer	chestnut head and all underparts
Juvenile	heavily streaked and mottled black and buff above; breast buff with clear streaking
BREEDING	
Nest	lined hollow on ground
Eggs	4; olive, blotched brown
Incubation	20–21 days ♂♀
Young	active; downy
Fledging	?
Broods	1; May–June
Food	molluscs, worms
Population	58,000 winter

Whimbrel *Numenius phaeopus*

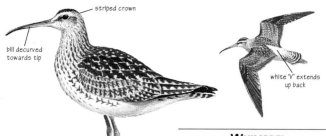

striped crown

bill decurved towards tip

white 'V' extends up back

S maller version of Eurasian Curlew that breeds in small numbers in northern Scotland but is otherwise double passage migrant. Central crown stripe, pale bordered black; pale eyebrow. Bill decurved towards tip. Upperparts greyish brown with dark centres and pale edges to feathers. Neck and breast buff with dark streaking. In flight, shows white 'V' up back; feet just protrude beyond tail. Distinctive call. *Status:* scarce breeder in Scotland; regular double passage migrant April–June, July–October. *Similar Species:* Eurasian Curlew (p.117) lacks crown stripe and has longer, more decurved bill. Beware young Eurasian Curlews with short bills.

WHIMBREL

Type	wader-like
Size	39–43cm (15–17in)
Habitat	freshwater marshes, estuaries, moors
Behaviour	wades, walks, takes off from water and ground
Flocking	1–15
Flight	strong and powerful; direct
Voice	rapidly whistled *whi-whi-whi-whi-whi-whi-whi*

IDENTIFICATION

Adult	
Crown	pale central stripe, bordered black
Upperparts	greyish brown, dark feather centres
Rump	white
Tail	black and white; short and square
Throat	buff and brown
Breast	buff, brown streaks
Belly	white
Bill	black; long and decurved near tip
Legs	grey; long

BREEDING

Nest	hollow on ground
Eggs	4; olive-green, blotched brown
Incubation	24–28 days ♂♀
Young	active; downy
Fledging	5–6 weeks
Broods	1; May–June
Food	molluscs, crabs
Population	less than 200 pairs

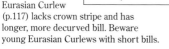

J	F	M	A	M	J	J	A	S	O	N	D
0	0	0	3	3	2	2	3	3	1	0	0

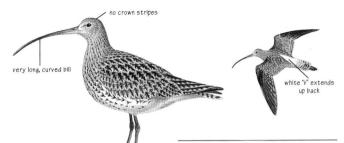

no crown stripes

very long, curved bill

white 'V' extends up back

Large shorebird with long legs and very long, decurved bill. Upperparts brown with buffy feather margins; underparts heavily streaked brown on neck and breast. In flight, shows uniform wings and white 'V' extending up rump. Generally gregarious, forming large flocks on estuaries, marshes and adjacent fields. *Status:* widespread breeding bird, mainly in northern and western hill districts; also on lowland heaths and marshes. Numerous winter visitor and passage migrant. *Similar Species:* Whimbrel (p.116) has striped crown, marked eyebrow and shorter bill with downward curve nearer the tip.

EURASIAN CURLEW

Type	wader-like
Size	51–61cm (20–24in)
Habitat	freshwater marshes, estuaries and shores, moors and heaths, fields
Behaviour	wades, walks, takes off and lands on water or ground
Flocking	1–1000
Flight	strong and powerful; direct
Voice	drawn out *coor-lee*; bubbling call summer

IDENTIFICATION

Adult	
Crown	buff and brown
Upperparts	buff and brown
Rump	white
Tail	buff and brown; short and square
Throat	buff and brown; streaked
Breast	buff and brown; streaked
Belly	white
Bill	black; very long and decurved
Legs	dark green; long

BREEDING

Nest	lined hollow on ground
Eggs	4; olive, blotched brown
Incubation	26-30 days, mainly ♀
Young	active; downy
Fledging	5–6 weeks
Broods	1; Apr–June
Food	worms, molluscs, crabs
Population	40,000–70,000 pairs; 200,000 winter

J	F	M	A	M	J	J	A	S	O	N	D
5	5	5	5	5	4	4	5	5	5	5	5

Spotted Redshank *Tringa erythropus*

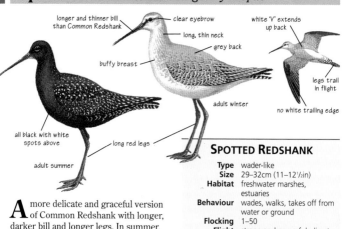

longer and thinner bill than Common Redshank

clear eyebrow

long, thin neck

grey back

buffy breast

white 'V' extends up back

legs trail in flight

adult winter

no white trailing edge

all black with white spots above

long red legs

adult summer

A more delicate and graceful version of Common Redshank with longer, darker bill and longer legs. In summer, adult is completely black above and below with white spangling on wings and back. In winter, upperparts grey; wing feathers spotted black with white margins. In late spring and early autumn, adults often show traces of black in plumage. Juveniles resemble Common Redshank more closely but brown upperparts finely spotted black and white. In flight white rump extends up back in a 'V'; no wingbar. Feet trail beyond tip of tail.
Status: regular double passage migrant.
Similar Species: Common Redshank (p.119) is less elegant.

SPOTTED REDSHANK

Type	wader-like
Size	29–32cm (11–12½in)
Habitat	freshwater marshes, estuaries
Behaviour	wades, walks, takes off from water or ground
Flocking	1–50
Flight	strong and powerful; direct
Voice	loud *choo-it*
IDENTIFICATION	
Ad.winter	
Crown	grey
Upperparts	grey; wing feathers white margins, spotted black
Rump	white
Tail	black and white; short and square
Throat	white
Breast	grey
Belly	white
Bill	red; long and thin
Legs	red; long
Ad.summer	uniformly black with white speckling on upperparts
Juvenile	upperparts brown, spotted black and white
BREEDING	
Nest	hollow on ground
Eggs	4; olive, blotched blackish
Incubation	?; ♂
Young	active; downy
Fledging	?
Broods	1; May–June
Food	molluscs, crustaceans
Population	80–200 winter; 700 Sept.

J	F	M	A	M	J	J	A	S	O	N	D
2	2	2	2	3	2	2	4	3	2	2	2

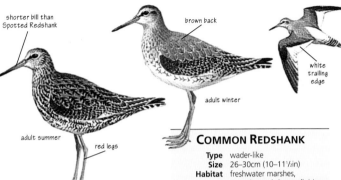

shorter bill than
Spotted Redshank

brown back

white
trailing
edge

adult winter

adult summer

red legs

Common and widespread wader of
coasts, estuaries, inland marshes
and wetlands. In winter, large flocks
found on favoured estuaries; also occurs
along rocky and muddy shores.
Upperparts brown, paler and more
uniform in winter. Underparts white with
heavy streaking, particularly in summer.
Legs and base of bill bright red. In flight
shows broad
white trailing
edge to wing.
Status: breeds
over large areas,
particularly in north
and west Britain
and Ireland.
Abundant passage
migrant and winter
visitor, mainly to coasts and estuaries.
Similar Species: Spotted Redshank
(p.118) and Ruff (p.110).

COMMON REDSHANK

Type	wader-like
Size	26–30cm (10–11½in)
Habitat	freshwater marshes, estuaries and shores, fields
Behaviour	wades, walks, takes off from water and ground
Flocking	1–1000
Flight	strong and powerful; direct
Voice	melodic *tyew-yew-yew*; and repeated *twek*

IDENTIFICATION

Adult	
Crown	brown
Upperparts	brown
Rump	white
Tail	black and white; short and square
Throat	white, heavy brown streaking
Breast	white, heavy brown streaking
Belly	white
Bill	dark brown, base red; long and thin
Legs	red; long

BREEDING

Nest	lined hollow on ground
Eggs	4; buff, blotched blackish
Incubation	23–24 days ♂♀
Young	active; downy
Fledging	30 days
Broods	1; Apr–June
Food	worms, molluscs
Population	40,000–50,000 pairs; 95,000 winter

J	F	M	A	M	J	J	A	S	O	N	D
5	5	5	5	4	4	4	5	5	5	5	5

Greenshank *Tringa nebularia*

grey, uptilted bill

grey and black back

grey back

white extends in 'V' up back

adult winter

legs trail in flight

no white on wing

adult summer

green legs

Long-legged, long-billed, greyish wader of marshes and estuaries. Upperparts grey, marked with streaks of black in summer. Underparts mainly white, speckled grey in summer. Long green legs and long, grey, slightly upturned bill. Always appears graceful and elegant. In flight, wings uniformly dark grey with white rump extending in 'V' up back; feet extend beyond tip of tail.
Status: scarce breeder in Scottish Highlands and Islands and western Ireland. Double passage migrant, most numerous in autumn; scarce winter visitor to south-west England and Wales and coast of Ireland.
Similar Species: none.

GREENSHANK

Type	wader-like
Size	29–32cm (11–12½in)
Habitat	freshwater marshes, moors, estuaries
Behaviour	wades, walks, takes off and lands on water and ground
Flocking	1–15
Flight	strong and powerful; direct
Voice	loud *tu-tu-tu*
IDENTIFICATION	
Ad.winter	
Crown	grey
Upperparts	grey
Rump	white
Tail	grey; short and square
Throat	white
Breast	grey
Belly	white
Bill	grey; long and thin
Legs	green; long
Ad.summer	black streaks on upperparts; underparts speckled grey
BREEDING	
Nest	hollow on ground
Eggs	4; buff, blotched brown
Incubation	24–25 days, mainly ♀
Young	active; downy
Fledging	4 weeks
Broods	1; May–June
Population	800–900 pairs; 1000–1500 winter; 2000 September

J	F	M	A	M	J	J	A	S	O	N	D
1	2	1	3	3	2	2	3	3	2	1	1

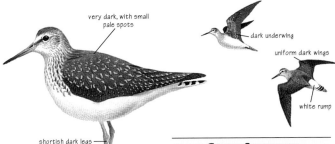

very dark, with small pale spots

dark underwing

uniform dark wings

white rump

shortish dark legs

Medium-sized wader; dark brown above and white below but always appears black and white at any distance. Speckled on breast; short white eyebrow. In flight, shows uniformly dark wings and back, white rump and barred tail. Generally solitary or in small groups on freshwater marshes, particularly along dykes and ditches. Bobs head and tail.

Status: double passage migrant but never numerous. Has bred in Scotland.

Similar Species: Wood Sandpiper (p.122) is paler brown above and has longer, paler legs and shorter, thicker bill.

GREEN SANDPIPER

Type	wader-like
Size	22–24cm (8½–9in)
Habitat	freshwater marshes
Behaviour	wades, walks, takes off from water and ground
Flocking	1–10
Flight	strong and powerful; direct
Voice	rising *tluit-weet-wit* of alarm

IDENTIFICATION

Adult

Crown	black and brown
Upperparts	dark brown
Rump	white
Tail	black and white, barred; short and square
Throat	white
Breast	white, brown streaks
Belly	white
Bill	black; straight and thin
Legs	dark green; medium length

BREEDING

Nest	disused bird's nest in tree
Eggs	4; olive, spotted reddish brown
Incubation	20–23 days, mainly ♀
Young	active; downy
Fledging	4 weeks
Broods	1; Apr–June
Food	molluscs, crustaceans, insects
Population	very rare breeder; several hundred passage; 500–1000 winter

J	F	M	A	M	J	J	A	S	O	N	D
1	1	1	2	2	1	1	2	3	1	1	1

Wood Sandpiper *Tringa glareola*

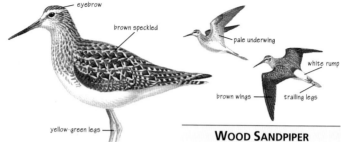

- eyebrow
- brown speckled
- pale underwing
- white rump
- brown wings
- trailing legs
- yellow-green legs

S imilar to Green Sandpiper but always browner above with heavily speckled plumage and more pronounced eyebrow. Slimmer build and longer, pale legs produce a more elegant impression. Generally occurs singly or in small groups on freshwater marshes, often where vegetation emerges above the water. In flight, shows white rump, barred tail and uniform wing, but never appears black and white like Green Sandpiper.

Status: regular double passage migrant, most numerous in autumn. Rare breeder in Scotland.

Similar Species:
Green Sandpiper (p.121). Speckled upperparts may produce similar pattern to small female Ruff (p.110).

WOOD SANDPIPER

Type	wader-like
Size	19–21cm (7–8in)
Habitat	freshwater marshes
Behaviour	wades, walks, takes off and lands on water or ground
Flocking	1–15
Flight	strong and powerful; direct
Voice	flat *chi-chi-chi*

IDENTIFICATION

Adult	
Crown	brown
Upperparts	brown, speckled buff and white
Rump	white
Tail	black and white; short and square
Throat	white
Breast	buff, faint streaks
Belly	white
Bill	black; straight and thin
Legs	yellow-green; long

BREEDING

Nest	hollow on ground
Eggs	4; pale green, blotched brown
Incubation	22–23 days mainly ♀
Young	active; downy
Fledging	?
Broods	1; May–June
Food	molluscs, crustaceans, insects
Population	less than 5 pairs; passage 1000 or more?

J	F	M	A	M	J	J	A	S	O	N	D
0	0	0	2	2	1	1	3	3	1	0	0

122

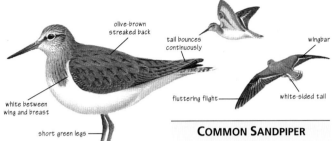

olive-brown streaked back

tail bounces continuously

wingbar

white between wing and breast

fluttering flight

white-sided tail

short green legs

Distinctive sandpiper with brown upperparts and white below. Brown streaking at side of breast forms clear line above bend of wing; distinctive white wedge between the two. Clear-cut eyestripe and eyebrow. Short green legs accentuate long body; folded wings do not reach tip of tail. Continuous wagging motion when feeding and at rest. Flickering, shallow wing beats produce characteristic flight, usually low over water; usually solitary.
Status: breeding summer visitor to hill districts of north and west. Common double passage migrant elsewhere.
Similar species: Wood Sandpiper (p.122) and Green Sandpiper (p.121) also 'bob'.

COMMON SANDPIPER

Type	wader-like
Size	18–21cm (7–8in)
Habitat	freshwater marshes, estuaries
Behaviour	wades, walks, takes off and lands on water or ground
Flocking	1–2
Flight	direct; flitting
Voice	whistled *sweeswee-swoo*

IDENTIFICATION

Adult	
Crown	brown
Upperparts	olive-brown
Rump	buff
Tail	buff; short and square
Throat	white
Breast	white, streaked buff on sides
Belly	white
Bill	black; straight and thin
Legs	green; short
BREEDING	
Nest	hollow on ground
Eggs	4; buff, speckled brown
Incubation	20–23 days ♂ ♀
Young	active; downy
Fledging	13–21 days
Food	molluscs, crustaceans, insects
Population	50,000 pairs; 100 winter

J	F	M	A	M	J	J	A	S	O	N	D
0	0	0	3	3	3	4	4	4	2	0	0

Turnstone *Arenaria interpres*

remnant face pattern

greyish

complex head and face pattern

rich chestnut

adult winter

legs orange

adult summer

complex pattern of bars and stripes

Stocky, short-legged, stubby-billed wader of coastal pools and beaches, especially rocky shores. Generally gregarious. Characteristic habit of turning stones in search of food; also picks and probes at surface. In summer, upperparts rich chestnut marked with black and buff. Head and neck white with intricate black markings extending to broad black breast band. Remaining underparts white. In winter, same overall pattern but in shades of grey. In flight, wingbar and wing patch combine with white rump and double tail bands to produce unmistakable pattern.

Status: common double passage migrant and winter visitor.

Similar Species: none.

TURNSTONE

Type	wader-like
Size	22–24cm (8–9in)
Habitat	estuaries and shores
Behaviour	wades, walks, perches openly, takes off from water and ground
Flocking	1–300
Flight	strong and powerful; direct
Voice	distinctive rattling *tukatuk*

IDENTIFICATION

Ad.winter	
Crown	grey and black
Upperparts	grey and black
Rump	white
Tail	white, two black bands; short and square
Throat	white
Breast	grey
Belly	white
Bill	black; short and thin
Legs	orange; short
Ad.summer	rich chestnut above with bold black and white face pattern

BREEDING

Nest	scrape on ground
Eggs	4; greenish, blotched brown
Incubation	22–23 days ♂♀
Young	active; downy
Fledging	?
Broods	1; May–July
Food	invertebrates
Population	50,000 winter

J	F	M	A	M	J	J	A	S	O	N	D
4	4	4	2	3	3	1	2	2	4	4	4

Phalaropus lobatus **Red-necked Phalarope**

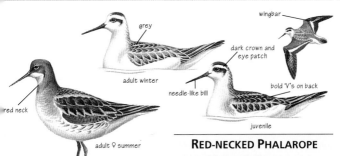

grey

adult winter

wingbar

dark crown and
eye patch

needle-like bill

bold 'V's on back

juvenile

red neck

adult ♀ summer

Delicate little wader that spends
most of its time swimming. In
summer, breeds on a few marshy pools
in north of Scotland and western
Ireland; winters at sea. In breeding
season, female has grey crown, nape,
lower breast and back; the latter is
marked by two buffy 'V's. Chin white,
neck and upper breast orange-red. Male
duller. In winter, grey above and white
below; small dark
comma extends
behind eye.
Juvenile slate grey
with buffy feather
markings, two buff
'V's on back.
Status: passage
migrant (usually
storm-driven)
mostly in autumn.
Similar Species: Grey Phalarope (p.126)
has thicker bill.

RED-NECKED PHALAROPE

Type	wader-like
Size	17–19cm (6½–7in)
Habitat	freshwater marshes, sea
Behaviour	swims, wades, takes off from water and ground
Flocking	1–15
Flight	strong and powerful; direct
Voice	quiet *tyit*

IDENTIFICATION

Ad. ♀ summer	
Crown	grey
Upperparts	grey and buff; wings black
Rump	black and white
Tail	black and white; short and square
Throat	white chin, red neck
Breast	orange-red
Belly	white
Bill	black; straight and fine
Legs	black; medium length
Ad. ♂ summer	
	as ♀ but paler
Ad.winter	grey above with eye mark
Juvenile	dark brown on crown and back; dark eye mark

BREEDING

Nest	neat cup in marsh
Eggs	4; pale green, blotched
Incubation	18–20 days ♂
Young	active; downy
Fledging	18–22 days
Broods	1; June–July
Food	insects, crustaceans
Population	16–20 pairs; variable autumn migration

J	F	M	A	M	J	J	A	S	O	N	D
0	0	0	0	2	2	2	1	2	2	0	0

Grey Phalarope *Phalaropus fulicarius*

bill thicker and shorter than Red-necked

grey

adult winter

dark crown and eye patch

wingbar

juvenile

bold 'V's on back

red

adult ♀ summer

Similar to Red-necked Phalarope but slightly larger and decidedly more bulky, with stouter and proportionately shorter bill. In breeding plumage, rust-red on neck and underparts. Back is black with double buffy 'V' and broad buffy margins to wings. Crown, forehead and chin black, face white. Bill has yellow base. Winter and juvenile birds similar to Red-necked and best separated by stocky shape and thicker bill.
Status: autumn passage migrant in variable number, mostly storm-driven.
Similar Species:
Red-necked
Phalarope (p.125), see above.

GREY PHALAROPE

Type	wader-like
Size	19–21cm (7–8in)
Habitat	freshwater, sea, estuaries
Behaviour	swims, wades, takes off from water and ground
Flocking	1–2
Flight	strong and powerful; direct
Voice	high-pitched *twit*
IDENTIFICATION	
Ad.winter	
Crown	grey
Upperparts	grey
Rump	black and white
Tail	black and white; short and square
Throat	white
Breast	white
Belly	white
Bill	black, yellow base; straight and thin
Legs	yellow; medium length
Ad.summer	chestnut red underparts; white face
Juvenile	dark brown on crown and back; dark eye mark
BREEDING	
Nest	hollow in marsh
Eggs	4; pale green, blotched brown
Incubation	19 days ♂
Young	active; downy
Fledging	16–21 days
Broods	1: June–July
Food	insects, molluscs, crustaceans
Population	variable, autumn migrant

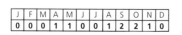

J	F	M	A	M	J	J	A	S	O	N	D
0	0	0	1	1	0	0	1	2	2	1	0

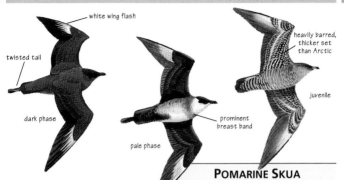

white wing flash

twisted tail

dark phase

heavily barred, thicker set than Arctic

juvenile

prominent breast band

pale phase

L ike Arctic Skua, occurs in two phases – light and dark. Both phases show white wing flashes, but pale phase has smudgy breast band (more prominent than pale Arctic). Spring adults easily separated from Arctic by broad, twisted, central feathers extending well beyond rest of tail. In autumn and juveniles, structure more important than plumage details; Pomarine always heavier and more bulky than Arctic. Juvenile heavily barred above and below. Generally seen offshore during extended sea-watches in spring and autumn. *Status:* regular but scarce passage migrant in first half of May and August–October.
Similar Species: Arctic Skua (p.128).

POMARINE SKUA

Type	gull-like
Size	43–53cm (16–21in)
Habitat	open sea; and shores
Behaviour	swims, takes off and lands on water
Flocking	1–10
Flight	strong and powerful; direct
Voice	silent at sea

IDENTIFICATION

Ad.pale	
Crown	black
Upperparts	brown
Rump	brown
Tail	brown; rounded; central feathers long and twisted
Throat	yellow
Breast	buff; smudgy breast band
Belly	white
Bill	buff; short and thin
Legs	brown; medium length
Ad.dark	uniformly brown; white wing flashes
Juvenile	heavily barred

BREEDING

Nest	hollow on ground
Eggs	2; buff, spotted brown
Incubation	27–28 days ♂ ♀
Young	semi-helpless; downy
Fledging	5–6 weeks
Broods	1; June–July
Food	fish
Population	scarce passage migrant

J	F	M	A	M	J	J	A	S	O	N	D
0	0	0	1	2	1	0	1	1	1	1	0

Arctic Skua *Stercorarius parasiticus*

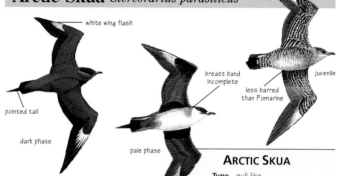

white wing flash

pointed tail

dark phase

pale phase

breast band incomplete

less barred than Pomarine

juvenile

Most commonly seen of the four skua species and the 'base' from which others must be differentiated. Fast, highly agile, dashing flight reminiscent of Peregrine. Pursues other seabirds. Occurs in two phases – light and dark – both of which show white wing flashes. Pale phase has dark cap and upperparts; underparts pale with indistinct dark breast band. Dark phase uniformly brown. Spring adults have two central tail feathers extended; absent in juveniles and (usually) autumn adults.
Status: summer visitor to far north; regular passage migrant to all coasts.
Similar Species: lighter and more agile than Pomarine Skua (p.127).

ARCTIC SKUA

Type	gull-like
Size	38–48cm (14½–18½in)
Habitat	sea, moors, estuaries
Behaviour	swims, perches openly, takes off from water and ground
Flocking	1–15
Flight	strong and powerful; direct; glides, aerial dive
Voice	high *kee-ow*; silent at sea

IDENTIFICATION

Ad.pale	
Crown	black
Upperparts	brown
Rump	brown
Tail	black; long central feathers
Throat	yellow
Breast	white; indistinct band
Belly	white
Bill	black; short and thin
Legs	brown; medium length
Ad.dark	uniformly brown; white wing flashes, as pale phase
Juvenile	heavily barred; lacks long central tail feathers

BREEDING

Nest	unlined hollow on ground
Eggs	2; greenish, blotched brown
Incubation	24–28 days ♂♀
Young	semi-helpless; downy
Fledging	30 days
Broods	1; May–June
Food	fish
Population	1000 pairs; regular passage migrant, mostly autumn.

J	F	M	A	M	J	J	A	S	O	N	D
0	0	0	2	3	3	3	3	3	3	1	0	0

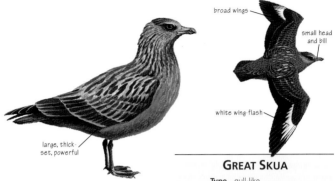

broad wings

small head and bill

white wing-flash

large, thick-set, powerful

Largest of the skuas with uniformly dark brownish plumage and bold white wing flashes. Wings much broader than other skuas and flight less agile. Smaller head and bill than large gulls and easier, dashing flight, especially in pursuit of other seabirds.
Status: scarce breeder in far north of Britain; passage migrant to all other coasts.
Similar Species: often said to resemble large immature gull but not really confusable once known.

GREAT SKUA

Type	gull-like
Size	56–61cm (22–24in)
Habitat	sea, estuaries, moors
Behaviour	swims, perches openly, takes off and lands on water or ground
Flocking	1–2
Flight	strong and powerful; direct; glides, aerial dive
Voice	harsh *uk-uk-uk*; nasal *skeerr*
IDENTIFICATION	
Adult	
Crown	brown and black
Upperparts	dark brown, streaked buff
Rump	dark brown, streaked buff
Tail	dark brown and buff; medium length, rounded
Throat	buff and brown, streaked
Breast	buff and brown; streaked
Belly	buff and brown, streaked
Bill	black; stout
Legs	brown; medium length
BREEDING	
Nest	unlined hollow on ground
Eggs	2; olive, spotted brown
Incubation	28–30 days ♂♀
Young	semi-helpless; downy
Fledging	6–7 weeks
Broods	1; May–June
Food	fish, eggs, birds
Population	3800 pairs; scarce passage migrant

J	F	M	A	M	J	J	A	S	O	N	D
0	0	1	3	3	3	3	3	2	0	0	0

Mediterranean Gull *Larus melanocephalus*

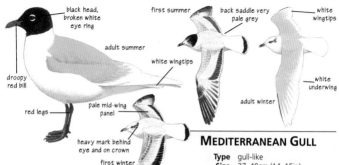

black head, broken white eye ring

adult summer

droopy red bill

red legs

pale mid-wing panel

heavy mark behind eye and on crown

first winter

pale inner primaries

first summer

back saddle very pale grey

white wingtips

white wingtips

adult winter

white underwing

adult winter

Very pale gull with heavy, droopy, red bill and red legs. Adult in summer has black, not brown, head with prominent broken white eye ring. Back and wings pale grey, with white primaries and white underwing. In winter, black head replaced by dark smudge behind eye and streaked hind crown.

Status: rare breeder; scarce passage migrant and winter visitor.

Similar Species: adult Black-headed Gull (p.133). Juvenile more like Common Gull (p.131), but with paler central wing panel. First winter similar, but Common Gull has pale grey (not white) 'saddle' on back.

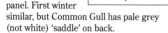

MEDITERRANEAN GULL

Type	gull-like
Size	37–40cm (14–15in)
Habitat	freshwater marshes, sea, estuaries and shores
Behaviour	swims, wades, walks, perches openly, takes off from water and ground
Flocking	1–3
Flight	soars, glides; strong and powerful; direct
Voice	plaintive *kee-ow*
IDENTIFICATION	
Ad.winter	
Crown	white, streaked hind crown
Upperparts	grey
Rump	white
Tail	white; medium length, square
Throat	white
Breast	white
Belly	white
Bill	red; short and thin
Legs	red; medium length
Ad.summer	black hood, white eye ring
Juvenile	brown across wings, pale central wing patch
BREEDING	
Nest	lined hollow near water
Eggs	3; creamy, spotted black
Incubation	23–25 days ♂♀
Young	partly-active; downy
Fledging	35–40 days
Broods	1; May–June
Food	invertebrates, fish
Population	15–23 pairs; 100–150 winter

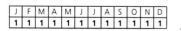

J	F	M	A	M	J	J	A	S	O	N	D
1	1	1	1	1	1	1	1	1	1	1	1

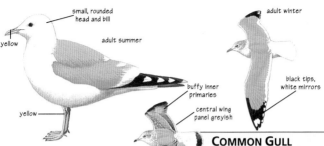

small, rounded head and bill

yellow

adult summer

yellow

adult winter

buffy inner primaries

black tips, white mirrors

central wing panel greyish

first winter

Abundant inland and along coasts in winter, but virtually confined to north and north-west in summer. Grey upperparts with black wingtips and white 'mirrors' create similar pattern to Herring Gull (p.134), but head and bill significantly smaller, giving more gentle look. Thin, yellow bill lacks red spot. Juvenile and first winter birds show dark trailing edge to secondaries and pale mid-wing panel.

Status: breeds inland in north and west Britain and Ireland; abundant winter visitor.

Similar Species: Kittiwake (p.137) has similar benign look; first winter Mediterranean Gull (p.130) separated from first winter Common Gull with care.

COMMON GULL

Type	gull-like
Size	38–43cm (14–16¹⁄₂in)
Habitat	towns, freshwater marshes, moors, sea, estuaries, fields
Behaviour	swims, wades, walks, perches openly, takes off from water and ground
Flocking	1–1000
Flight	soars, glides; strong and powerful; direct
Voice	high *kee-aa*

IDENTIFICATION

Adult	
Crown	white
Upperparts	grey; black wingtips with white 'mirrors'
Rump	white
Tail	white; medium length, square
Throat	white
Breast	white
Belly	white
Bill	yellow; short and thin
Legs	yellow-green; medium length
Juvenile	brown wings, grey 'saddle'

BREEDING

Nest	lined hollow on ground
Eggs	3; blotched brown
Incubation	22–27 days ♂♀
Young	partly-active; downy
Fledging	4 weeks
Broods	1; May
Food	worms, insects, molluscs
Population	50,000 pairs; 700,000 winter

J	F	M	A	M	J	J	A	S	O	N	D
5	5	5	5	5	5	5	5	5	5	5	5

131

Little Gull *Larus minutus*

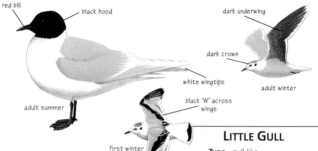

red bill

black hood

dark underwing

dark crown

white wingtips

adult winter

adult summer

white wingtips

black 'W' across wings

first winter

S mall, dainty, tern-like gull, most often seen feeding in flight, picking insects from surface of water like a marsh tern. Adult has uniformly pale grey wings lacking black tips; underwing dark grey. In summer, head black, tiny bill red. In winter, hood replaced by dark hind crown and spot behind eye. Juvenile and first winter birds have inverted black 'W' across upperwings in flight – like Kittiwake (p.137) of same age; Kittiwake is larger. *Status:* has bred. Regular passage migrant and scarce winter visitor; may gather in good numbers at a few particularly favoured spots. *Similar Species:* smaller size precludes confusion.

LITTLE GULL

Type	gull-like
Size	27–29cm (10–11in)
Habitat	freshwater marshes, sea, estuaries and shores
Behaviour	swims, wades, walks, perches openly, takes off from water or ground
Flocking	1–100
Flight	soars, glides, flitting; strong and powerful
Voice	*ka-ee* and low *ka-ka-ka*

IDENTIFICATION

Ad.winter	
Crown	white, dark hind crown
Upperparts	grey
Rump	white
Tail	white; medium length, square
Throat	white
Breast	white
Belly	white
Bill	black; short and thin
Legs	black; short
Ad.summer	black hood, red bill
Juvenile	'W' across upperwing

BREEDING

Nest	reeds and rushes
Eggs	3; pale green, blotched black
Incubation	20–21 days ♂ ♀
Young	partly-active; downy
Fledging	21–24 days
Broods	1; May–June
Food	invertebrates, fish, insects
Population	double-passage migrant; scarce winter visitor

J	F	M	A	M	J	J	A	S	O	N	D
2	2	2	2	2	2	2	2	3	3	3	2	2

Larus ridibundus **Black-headed Gull**

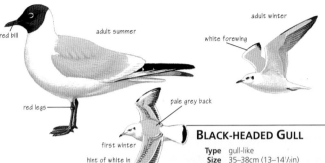

red bill

adult summer

adult winter

white forewing

red legs

pale grey back

first winter

hint of white in forewing

Most common and widespread gull, equally at home inland and along shorelines. In all plumages distinguished by white outer primaries creating a white forewing. Outer underwing dark. Adult in summer has chocolate hood, red bill and red legs. In winter, hood reduced to spot behind eye. First winter birds have pale grey backs with brown markings across wings. Gregarious, forming huge nocturnal roosts. *Status:* widespread and numerous colonial breeder; abundant winter visitor. *Similar Species:* Mediterranean Gull (p.130) and Little Gull (p.132).

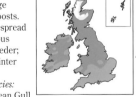

BLACK-HEADED GULL

Type	gull-like
Size	35–38cm (13–14¹/₂in)
Habitat	towns, marshes, moors, sea, shoreline, fields
Behaviour	swims, wades, walks, perches openly, takes off from water or ground
Flocking	1–40,000
Flight	soars, glides; strong and powerful; direct
Voice	repeated *kuk-kuk*, angry *kee-ar*

IDENTIFICATION

Ad.winter	
Crown	white
Upperparts	grey
Rump	white
Tail	white; medium length
Throat	white
Breast	white
Belly	white
Bill	red; short and thin
Legs	red; medium length
Ad.summer	chocolate hood
Juvenile	brown on head and back

BREEDING

Nest	scrape or cup of vegetation
Eggs	3; buffy, spotted black
Incubation	21–27 days ♂♀
Young	partly active; downy
Fledging	5–6 weeks
Broods	1; Apr–May
Food	invertebrates, seeds
Population	150,000–300,000 pairs; 3,000,000 winter

J	F	M	A	M	J	J	A	S	O	N	D
6	6	6	6	6	6	6	6	6	6	6	6

Herring Gull *Larus argentatus*

adult summer

first winter

pale grey (saddle) back

yellow bill, red spot

pink legs

black tips, white mirrors

dark trailing edge

pale inner primaries

second winter

streaked head

adult winter

Most common and familiar of the larger gulls. Grey back; grey wings with black tips and white 'mirrors'. Large yellow bill with red spot; flesh coloured legs. In winter, head variably streaked black. Immatures must be separated with care from Lesser Black-backed Gulls of same age. Juvenile Herring Gulls have wider pale margins to upperparts and pale inner primaries that break up hind wing pattern. First summer birds have creamy upperparts. Second winter birds have pale grey 'saddles'. *Status:* widespread resident and winter visitor; breeds along most coasts. *Similar Species:* immature Lesser Black-backed Gull (p.135) as above.

HERRING GULL

Type	gull-like
Size	53–59cm (20–23in)
Habitat	towns, freshwater marshes, sea-cliffs, shores
Behaviour	swims, wades, walks
Flocking	1–10,000
Flight	soars, glides; strong and powerful; direct
Voice	loud ringing *kyow-kyow*

IDENTIFICATION

Adult	
Crown	white
Upperparts	grey; black wingtips with white 'mirrors'
Rump	white
Tail	white; medium length, square
Throat	white
Breast	white
Belly	white
Bill	yellow, red spot; straight and thick
Legs	pink; medium length
Juvenile	speckled brown above

BREEDING

Nest	cup of vegetation on cliff, dunes, marsh, building
Eggs	2–3; pale green, blotched brown
Incubation	25–33 days, mainly ♀
Young	partly-active; downy
Fledging	6 weeks
Broods	1; Apr–May
Food	virtually anything
Population	over 300,000 pairs

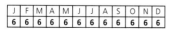

J	F	M	A	M	J	J	A	S	O	N	D
6	6	6	6	6	6	6	6	6	6	6	6

134

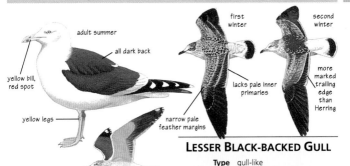

first winter

second winter

adult summer

all dark back

yellow bill, red spot

yellow legs

lacks pale inner primaries

more marked trailing edge than Herring

narrow pale feather margins

adult winter

L arge, dark-backed gull with yellow legs and yellow bill with red spot. Scandinavian sub-species, *L.f. fuscus*, nearly as black on back as Great Black-backed, but considerably smaller. Younger birds separated from Herring Gulls of similar age by narrower, paler margins to upperparts and bolder spots on underparts.

Status: widespread breeder mostly around coasts; passage migrant and increasing winter visitor.

Similar Species: adult Herring Gull (p.134) has lighter grey back and pink, not yellow, legs. Adult Great Black-backed Gull (p.136) is much larger, almost black on back and has pale pink legs.

LESSER BLACK-BACKED GULL

Type	gull-like
Size	51–56cm (20–22in)
Habitat	marshes, moors, sea, estuaries, shores, fields
Behaviour	swims, wades, walks, perches openly, takes off from water and ground
Flocking	1–1000
Flight	soars, glides; strong and powerful; direct
Voice	*kyow-kyow, kee-aa*

IDENTIFICATION

Adult

Crown	white
Upperparts	slate-grey; black wingtips with white 'mirrors'
Rump	white
Tail	white; medium length, square
Throat	white
Breast	white
Belly	white
Bill	yellow with red spot; straight and thick
Legs	yellow; medium length
Juvenile	speckled brown above

BREEDING

Nest	lines hollow on flat ground
Eggs	3; olive, blotched blackish
Incubation	25–29 days ♂♀
Young	partly-active; downy
Fledging	35-40 days
Broods	1; Apr–June
Food	virtually anything
Population	50,000 pairs; 70,000 winter

J	F	M	A	M	J	J	A	S	O	N	D
4	4	5	5	5	5	5	5	5	5	4	4

Great Black-backed Gull *Larus marinus*

first winter
dark trailing edge

thick yellow bill, red spot

massive head and bill

black back

adult summer

flesh legs

adult

back as black as wingtips

Massive gull that stands larger than Herring and Lesser Black-backed Gulls in all plumages. Sheer size of bird picks it out from any mixed gull flock. Adult has black back and wings, huge head and large, deep bill. Immatures have almost white margins to dark brown feathers of upperparts and are much more contrasted than Herring and Lesser Black-backed Gulls of similar age. Mainly marine, but penetrates inland in winter, mostly to rubbish tips and reservoirs. *Status:* breeds along most western coasts; winter visitor elsewhere. *Similar Species:* adult Lesser Black-backed Gull (p.135) is smaller with less massive head and bill.

J	F	M	A	M	J	J	A	S	O	N	D
5	5	5	5	5	5	5	5	5	5	5	5

GREAT BLACK-BACKED GULL

Type	gull-like
Size	63–39cm (24½–27in)
Habitat	sea, estuaries, marshes
Behaviour	swims, wades, walks, perches openly, takes off from water or ground
Flocking	1–100s
Flight	soars, glides; strong and powerful; direct
Voice	harsh *owk*, also *uk-uk-uk*

IDENTIFICATION

Adult

Crown	white
Upperparts	black; black wingtips with white 'mirrors'
Rump	white
Tail	white; medium length, square
Throat	white
Breast	white
Belly	white
Bill	yellow with red spot; large and thick
Legs	pink; medium length
Juvenile	dark trailing edge to wing

BREEDING

Nest	large mass of sticks and seaweed on ground
Eggs	2–3; olive, speckled brown
Incubation	26–30 days ♂ ♀
Young	partly-active; downy
Fledging	7–8 weeks
Broods	1; Apr–May
Food	seabirds, offal, rubbish
Population	25,000 pairs

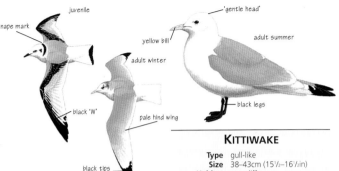

juvenile

nape mark

yellow bill

'gentle head'

adult summer

adult winter

black 'W'

pale hind wing

black legs

black tips
no mirrors

Totally maritime gull about same size as Common Gull and superficially similar. Both species have small head, short yellow bill and benign expression. Kittiwake has shorter legs and longer, narrower wings; black wingtips lack white 'mirrors'. Immatures show black inverted 'W' across upperwings in flight (like much smaller Little Gull p.132) and black neck bar. Spends most of time at sea flying lightly and buoyantly; breeds on cliffs, forming large colonies.
Status: breeds on most cliff-bound shores, especially numerous in north and west.
Similar Species: Common Gull (p.131) as above.

KITTIWAKE

Type	gull-like
Size	38–43cm (15½–16½in)
Habitat	sea, cliffs
Behaviour	swims, perches openly, takes off and lands on water or ground
Flocking	1–1000s
Flight	soars, glides; strong and powerful; direct
Voice	repeated *kitti-week*

IDENTIFICATION

Adult	
Crown	white
Upperparts	grey; black wingtips
Rump	white
Tail	white; medium length, square
Throat	white
Breast	white
Belly	white
Bill	yellow; short and thin
Legs	black; short
Juvenile	black 'W' across wings, black tail band, black bill

BREEDING

Nest	neat cup of seaweed on tiny cliff edge
Eggs	2; creamy, speckled brown
Incubation	25–30 days ♂♀
Young	partly-active; downy
Fledging	43 days
Broods	1; May–June
Food	fish
Population	c500,000 pairs

J	F	M	A	M	J	J	A	S	O	N	D
4	4	4	4	4	4	4	4	4	4	4	4

Sandwich Tern *Sterna sandvicensis*

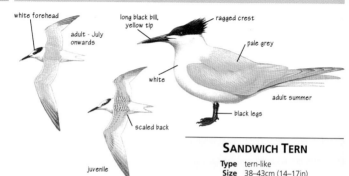

white forehead

adult - July onwards

long black bill, yellow tip

ragged crest

pale grey

white

adult summer

black legs

scaled back

juvenile

Largest of the terns with typical buoyant flight on long, narrow wings. Sandwich is much paler than other terns and has black legs and long, black bill with yellow tip. Black cap forms ragged crest on hind crown. Confined to coastlines where dives into sea for food. Forms dense colonies. *Status:* summer visitor like other terns. Breeds very locally along all coasts. Passage migrant away from colonies. *Similar Species:* no terns are as large, as white or have black bills.

SANDWICH TERN

Type	tern-like
Size	38–43cm (14–17in)
Habitat	sea, estuaries and adjacent marshes
Behaviour	swims, dives from air, perches openly, takes off from water or ground
Flocking	1–1000s
Flight	hovers, aerial dive; strong and powerful; direct
Voice	loud *ker-rik*

IDENTIFICATION

Ad.summer	
Crown	black, with ragged crest
Upperparts	whitish grey
Rump	white
Tail	white; long and forked
Throat	white
Breast	white
Belly	white
Bill	black with yellow tip; straight and thin
Legs	black; short
Ad.winter & juvenile	white forehead and crown; black hind crown; juvenile barred 'saddle'

BREEDING

Nest	bare scrape; highly colonial
Eggs	2; buffy, speckled brown
Incubation	20–24 days ♂♀
Young	partly-active; downy
Fledging	35 days
Broods	1; Apr–May
Food	fish
Population	c12,000 pairs

J	F	M	A	M	J	J	A	S	O	N	D
0	0	2	4	4	4	4	4	3	2	0	0

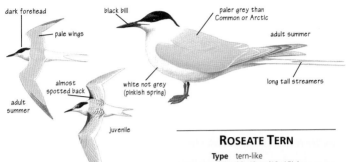

dark forehead

black bill

paler grey than
Common or Arctic

pale wings

adult summer

almost
spotted back

white not grey
(pinkish spring)

long tail streamers

adult
summer

juvenile

Rarest of the breeding terns with a
few isolated colonies, mostly on
islands, holding bulk of population.
Elsewhere decidedly rare or overlooked.
A small tern somewhere between
Common and Little Tern in size but with
long tail streamers boosting measured
length. Best picked out from more
abundant Common and Arctic Terns by
paler colour – almost white above and
below. Identification
confirmed by black
bill and tail
streamers (may
become broken). In
spring has pink
flush on breast.
Status: rare
summer visitor and
passage migrant;
arrives later than other terns.
Similar Species: Common Tern (p.140)
and Arctic Tern (p.141).

ROSEATE TERN

Type	tern-like
Size	32–40cm (12–15in)
Habitat	sea, estuaries and adjacent marshes
Behaviour	swims, dives from air, perches openly, takes off and lands on water or ground
Flocking	1–100
Flight	hovers; strong and powerful; direct
Voice	*kee-a, pee-pee-pee,* similar to Common Tern

IDENTIFICATION

Ad.summer	
Crown	black
Upperparts	whitish grey
Rump	white
Tail	white; long and forked
Throat	white
Breast	white, pink flush in spring
Belly	white
Bill	black; short and thin
Legs	red; short
Ad.winter & juvenile	white forehead; juvenile scaled upperparts

BREEDING

Nest	unlined hollow
Eggs	1–2; creamy, speckled brown
Incubation	21–26 days ♂♀
Young	partly-active; downy
Fledging	27–30 days
Broods	1; June
Food	fish
Population	100–500 pairs

J	F	M	A	M	J	J	A	S	O	N	D
0	0	0	1	2	2	2	2	1	0	0	0

Common Tern *Sterna hirundo*

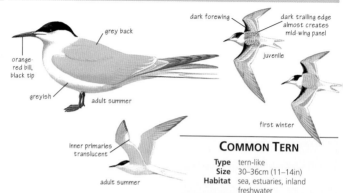

adult summer

juvenile

first winter

inner primaries translucent

adult summer

dark forewing
dark trailing edge almost creates mid-wing panel
grey back
orange-red bill, black tip
greyish

Common and widespread summer visitor. Essentially pale grey above and white below but underparts have pale greyish wash. Black cap; red legs. Bill usually red with black tip but sometimes pure red or almost black. (Beware separating Common Terns from Arctic or Roseate Terns by bill colour alone.) Deeply forked tail; light and buoyant flight. Dives for food; also picks food from surface of water. Autumn adults and juveniles have black leading edge to wing that forms bar when folded.
Status: breeds along most coasts in concentrated colonies, also inland in smaller numbers.
Similar Species: Arctic Tern (p.141) and Roseate Tern (p.139).

COMMON TERN

Type	tern-like
Size	30–36cm (11–14in)
Habitat	sea, estuaries, inland freshwater
Behaviour	swims, dives from air, perches openly, takes off and lands on water or ground
Flocking	1–1000
Flight	hovers, aerial dive; strong and powerful; direct
Voice	harsh *key-arr, kirri-kirri*

IDENTIFICATION

Ad.summer	
Crown	black
Upperparts	pale grey
Rump	white
Tail	white; long and forked
Throat	white
Breast	white
Belly	white
Bill	red with black tip; short and thin
Legs	red; short
Ad.winter & juvenile	white forehead; juvenile barred brownish on upperparts

BREEDING

Nest	unlined hollow
Eggs	2–3; creamy, blotched black
Incubation	20–23 days, mainly ♀
Young	partly-active; downy
Fledging	28 days
Broods	1,2?; May–June
Food	fish
Population	15,000–20,000 pairs

J	F	M	A	M	J	J	A	S	O	N	D
0	0	0	3	4	4	4	4	4	2	0	0

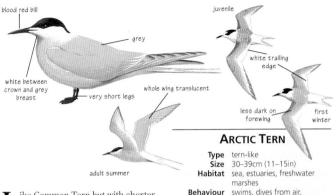

blood red bill

grey

juvenile

white trailing edge

white between crown and grey breast

very short legs

whole wing translucent

less dark on forewing

first winter

adult summer

L ike Common Tern but with shorter, darker red bill (without black tip), longer tail and fully translucent wing when seen from below. Common Tern has translucent patch only on inner primaries. Generally greyer below with white cheeks standing out pure white. More confined to coast than Common Tern. Juveniles have less black on leading edge of wing than Common Tern and prominent white trailing edge to secondaries.
Status: summer visitor mainly to northern coasts; passage migrant in south
Similar Species: Common Tern (p.140) as above.

ARCTIC TERN

Type	tern-like
Size	30–39cm (11–15in)
Habitat	sea, estuaries, freshwater marshes
Behaviour	swims, dives from air, perches openly, takes off and lands on water and ground
Flocking	1–1000
Flight	hovers, aerial dive; strong and powerful; direct
Voice	*key-rrr*, similar to Common Tern but briefer

IDENTIFICATION

Ad.summer

Crown	black
Upperparts	grey
Rump	white
Tail	white; long and forked
Throat	white
Breast	whitish grey
Belly	whitish grey
Bill	red; short and thin
Legs	red; short
Ad. winter & juvenile	white forehead

BREEDING

Nest	bare scrape
Eggs	2; buffy, blotched brown
Incubation	20–22 days ♂♀
Young	partly-active; downy
Fledging	20–22 days
Broods	1; May–June
Food	fish
Population	c40,000 pairs

J	F	M	A	M	J	J	A	S	O	N	D
0	0	0	3	4	4	4	4	4	2	0	0

141

Little Tern *Sterna albifrons*

very narrow wings

adult

white forehead

yellow bill, black tip

juvenile

Tiny, fast flying tern. Long, narrow wings, almost Swift-like in shape, flicker in fast wing beats. Essentially marine, feeding close inshore, diving for small fish; breeds along shingle beaches. Legs and bill yellow, the latter with black tip. Black cap always incomplete; forehead white
Status: declining due to disturbance of breeding grounds; summer visitor to coasts.
Similar Species: small size separates from most other terns.

LITTLE TERN

Type	tern-like
Size	23–26cm (9–10in)
Habitat	sea, estuaries and adjacent freshwater
Behaviour	swims, dives from air, perches openly, takes off from water and ground
Flocking	1–50
Flight	hovers, aerial dive; strong and powerful; direct
Voice	various chatterings; high-pitched, sharp *kitik*

IDENTIFICATION

Ad.summer	
Crown	black with white forehead
Upperparts	grey; black wingtips
Rump	white
Tail	white; forked
Throat	white
Breast	white
Belly	white
Bill	yellow, black tip
Legs	yellow; short
Ad.winter	more white on crown;
& juvenile	juvenile sandy buff above, 'saddle' barred

BREEDING

Nest	bare scrape near sea
Eggs	2–3; olive, blotched brown
Incubation	19–22 days ♂♀
Young	partly-active; downy
Fledging	15–17 days
Broods	1; May–June
Food	fish
Population	c1800 pairs

J	F	M	A	M	J	J	A	S	O	N	D
0	0	0	3	3	3	3	3	2	1	0	0

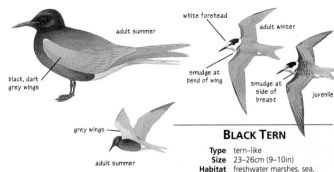

adult summer

white forehead

adult winter

black, dark grey wings

smudge at bend of wing

smudge at side of breast

juvenile

grey wings

adult summer

BLACK TERN

Type	tern–like
Size	23–26cm (9–10in)
Habitat	freshwater marshes, sea, estuaries
Behaviour	swims, dives from air, perches openly, takes off from water and ground
Flocking	1–15
Flight	hovers, flitting; undulating
Voice	high-pitched *kik*

IDENTIFICATION

Ad.summer	
Crown	black
Upperparts	black; dark grey wings
Rump	dark grey
Tail	grey; medium length, notched
Throat	black
Breast	black
Belly	black
Legs	red-brown; short
Ad.winter & juvenile	grey above, white below, white forehead, dark smudge at sides of breast

BREEDING

Nest	mound of vegetation in marshy lagoon
Eggs	3; buffy, spotted brown
Incubation	14–17 days, mainly ♀
Young	partly-active; downy
Fledging	4 weeks
Broods	1; May
Food	insects
Population	very rare breeder; several 100s spring and autumn

Summer adult all black with dark grey wings. Juvenile and winter adult grey above and white below, with black cap, white forehead and black smudge at sides of breast. Tail notched rather than forked. Black Terns feed by taking insects from surface of water in flight. Flight easy but erratic as they twist and swoop over the water.
Status: regular double passage migrant through southern and eastern England; more numerous in autumn than spring. Has bred on occasion.
Similar Species: other terns and Little Gull (p.132) feed in similar way, but Black Terns always smaller and darker.

J	F	M	A	M	J	J	A	S	O	N	D
0	0	0	2	2	1	1	2	3	1	1	0

143

Common Guillemot *Uria aalge*

sharply pointed bill

narrow white eye ring and line

adult 'bridled' form

adult winter

white face

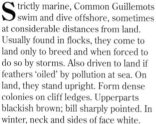

adult summer

Strictly marine, Common Guillemots swim and dive offshore, sometimes at considerable distances from land. Usually found in flocks, they come to land only to breed and when forced to do so by storms. Also driven to land if feathers 'oiled' by pollution at sea. On land, they stand upright. Form dense colonies on cliff ledges. Upperparts blackish brown; bill sharply pointed. In winter, neck and sides of face white. Some Common Guillemots have white eye ring and white line extending across ear coverts – known as bridled form. *Status:* breeds mainly in north and west; widespread offshore at other times. *Similar Species:* Razorbill (p.145) and Puffin (p.146).

COMMON GUILLEMOT

Type	auk-like
Size	40–44cm (15–17in)
Habitat	sea and cliffs
Behaviour	swims, dives from surface, perches openly, takes off and lands on water and ground
Flocking	1-1000s
Flight	laboured; direct
Voice	various growling and moaning notes

IDENTIFICATION

Ad.summer	
Crown	blackish brown
Upperparts	blackish brown
Rump	blackish brown
Tail	blackish brown; short and rounded
Throat	blackish brown
Breast	white
Belly	white
Bill	black; short and thin; pointed
Legs	black; short
Ad.winter	white throat and sides of face

BREEDING

Nest	bare cliff ledge
Eggs	1; highly variable, blotched black
Incubation	28-25 days ♂ ♀
Young	helpless; downy
Fledging	18–25 days
Broods	1; May–June
Food	fish, crustaceans, molluscs
Population	1,000,000 pairs

J	F	M	A	M	J	J	A	S	O	N	D
2	2	3	4	4	4	4	3	2	2	2	2

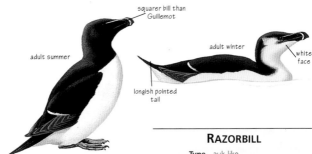

squarer bill than
Guillemot

adult winter

adult summer

white
face

longish pointed
tail

Similar to Common Guillemot; often forms mixed flocks. Generally blacker above. Bill shape much deeper than Common Guillemot, with distinctive vertical white line. In flight at sea, pointed tail particularly useful feature; gives bird elongated silhouette. Like Common Guillemot, black neck lost in winter. Nests in rock crevices rather than on open cliff ledges.

Status: breeds in north and west, often on same cliffs as Common Guillemot.

Similar Species: Common Guillemot (p.144) and Puffin (p.146).

RAZORBILL

Type	auk-like
Size	39–43cm (15–16½in)
Habitat	sea and cliffs
Behaviour	swims, dives from surface, perches openly, takes off and lands on water and ground
Flocking	1–100
Flight	laboured
Voice	growls and grunts

IDENTIFICATION

Ad.summer	
Crown	black
Upperparts	black
Rump	black
Tail	black; short and pointed
Throat	black
Breast	white
Belly	white
Bill	black, vertical white line; short and thin
Legs	black; short
Ad.winter	throat and sides of face white

BREEDING

Nest	crevice or hole in cliff
Eggs	1; variable, blotched brown
Incubation	25–35 days ♂ ♀
Young	helpless; downy
Fledging	14–24 days
Broods	1; May–June
Food	fish, crustaceans, molluscs
Population	c144,000 pairs

J	F	M	A	M	J	J	A	S	O	N	D
2	2	2	3	3	3	3	2	2	2	2	2

Puffin *Fratercula arctica*

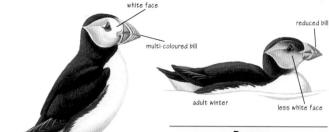

white face

multi-coloured bill

adult summer

reduced bill

adult winter

less white face

Small, comical seabird; forms colonies on offshore islands and sea stacks in north and west. Upperparts black; underparts white; face white. Outstanding feature is large parrot-like bill vertically striped in yellow and red. Size of bill reduced (horny plates at base shed) and colours paler in winter and juvenile plumages. At sea, short, rapidly whirring wings and white face are best features. Nests in burrows, but off-duty birds form groups that loaf around cliff-tops.
Status: locally abundant resident, especially in north and west; some winter wandering.
Similar Species: Common Guillemot (p.144) and Razorbill (p.145).

PUFFIN

Type	auk-like
Size	29–31cm (11–12in)
Habitat	sea and cliffs
Behaviour	swims, dives from surface, walks, perches openly, takes off and lands on water or ground
Flocking	1–1000
Flight	laboured; direct
Voice	deep *arr-arr*

IDENTIFICATION

Ad.summer	
Crown	black and white
Upperparts	black
Rump	black
Tail	black; short and square
Throat	black
Breast	white
Belly	white
Bill	blue-grey, red and yellow, striped; short and stubby
Legs	red; short
Ad.winter	bill smaller with paler colours
Juvenile	bill smaller and all dark

BREEDING

Nest	burrow
Eggs	1; white
Incubation	40–43 days ♀ only
Young	helpless; downy
Fledging	47–51 days
Broods	1; May
Food	fish, crustaceans, molluscs
Population	c500,000 pairs

J	F	M	A	M	J	J	A	S	O	N	D
1	1	3	3	3	3	3	3	1	1	1	1

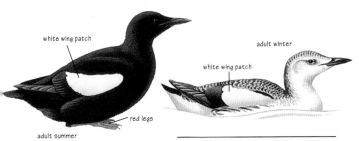

white wing patch

adult winter

white wing patch

red legs

adult summer

S carce seabird most often seen on
water below nesting cliffs. In
summer, plumage all black with bold
white oval patch on wings. Feet and
inside of mouth bright red. In winter,
mottled greyish all over, with darker
wings still marked by whitish ovals.
Status: scarce resident around northern
and western cliffs; virtually unknown
further south.
Similar Species: none

BLACK GUILLEMOT

Type	auk-like
Size	33–35cm (12½–13½in)
Habitat	sea and cliffs
Behaviour	swims, dives from surface, perches openly, takes off and lands on water or ground
Flocking	1–15
Flight	laboured; direct
Voice	whistling cries

IDENTIFICATION

Ad.summer	
Crown	black
Upperparts	black with white patches on wings
Rump	black
Tail	black; short and square
Throat	black
Breast	black
Belly	black
Bill	black; short and thin
Legs	red; short
Ad.winter	white below, grey above; black wings retain white oval patches

BREEDING

Nest	hole among boulders
Eggs	2; white, spotted blackish
Incubation	21–25 days ♂ ♀
Young	helpless; downy
Fledging	34–40 days
Broods	1; May–June
Food	fish, crustaceans, molluscs
Population	16,000–25,000 pairs

J	F	M	A	M	J	J	A	S	O	N	D
1	1	2	2	2	2	2	2	2	2	1	1

147

Rock Dove *Columba livia*

pale grey

wingbars

wingbars

white rump

Genuine Rock Doves are now confined to cliffs in extreme north and west. Elsewhere, they have interbred over the centuries with feral pigeons – domesticated Rock Doves escaped from captivity. Pigeons occur in wide variety of plumages, but genuine wild bird is pale grey with patch of iridescent purple and green at sides of neck. Folded wing shows two black bars. Rump white; tail broadly tipped black. Some feral pigeons show close resemblance to this plumage.
Status: highly localized resident in extreme north and west; feral birds widespread and numerous in cities and along cliffs.
Similar Species:
Stock Dove (p.149) lacks white rump.

ROCK DOVE

Type	pigeon-like
Size	31–35cm (12–13in)
Habitat	sea cliffs, towns
Behaviour	walks, perches openly, takes off and lands on ground
Flocking	1–100
Flight	glides; strong and powerful; direct
Voice	familiar *oo-roo-coo* repeated
IDENTIFICATION	
Adult	
Crown	grey
Upperparts	grey
Rump	white
Tail	grey, black tip; medium length, square
Throat	grey
Breast	grey
Belly	grey
Bill	black and white; short and thin
Legs	pink; short
BREEDING	
Nest	crevices and ledges in cliffs and buildings
Eggs	2; white
Incubation	17–19 days ♂ ♀
Young	helpless; downy
Fledging	30–35 days
Broods	2 or 3; Mar–Sept
Food	seeds, grain
Population	c100,000 pairs

J	F	M	A	M	J	J	A	S	O	N	D
3	3	3	3	3	3	3	3	3	3	3	3

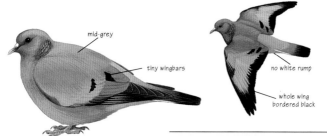

mid-grey

tiny wingbars

no white rump

whole wing bordered black

STOCK DOVE

Type	pigeon-like
Size	31–35cm (12–13in)
Habitat	forests and woods, fields and hedges, gardens, heaths
Behaviour	walks, perches openly, takes off and lands on vegetation and ground
Flocking	1–100
Flight	strong and powerful; direct
Voice	*coo-roo-oo*, repeated monotonously

IDENTIFICATION

Adult	
Crown	grey
Upperparts	grey
Rump	grey
Tail	grey, broad black tip; medium length, square
Throat	grey
Breast	pink
Belly	grey
Bill	red; short and thin
Legs	red; short

BREEDING

Nest	hole in tree or cliff
Eggs	2; white
Incubation	16–18 days ♂ ♀
Young	helpless; downy
Fledging	27–28 days
Broods	2–3; Mar–une
Food	crops, seeds, grain
Population	50,000–60,000 pairs

Grey above and paler grey below, with pale pink breast and less marked double wingbar than Rock Dove. In flight, shows grey wings with broad black borders – quite characteristic once seen. Tail broadly tipped black. Though found in similar areas toWood Pigeon, can be distinguished by lack of white on neck and wing.
Status: widespread resident.
Similar Species: Rock Dove (p.148) and Wood Pigeon (p.150) as above.

J	F	M	A	M	J	J	A	S	O	N	D
4	4	4	4	4	4	4	4	4	4	4	4

Wood Pigeon *Columba palumbus*

white neck slash

white bars across wing

white wing edge

Largest of the pigeons; marked by white neck flash and broad white bar across open wings. Grey above, pinkish below. In flight, outer wing is black; tail grey with black terminal band. Familiar bird throughout the country, including city-centres.
Status: abundant and widespread resident; abundant winter visitor.
Similar Species: Stock Dove (p.149).

WOOD PIGEON

Type	pigeon-like
Size	39–43cm (15–16½in)
Habitat	forests and woods, fields and hedges, towns, gardens, heaths
Behaviour	walks, perches openly, takes off and lands on vegetation or ground
Flocking	1–1000
Flight	strong and powerful; direct
Voice	coo-coo-coo-cu-coo, repeated endlessly

IDENTIFICATION

Adult	
Crown	grey
Upperparts	grey
Rump	grey
Tail	grey with black band; medium length, square
Throat	grey
Breast	pink
Belly	grey
Bill	red; short and thin
Legs	red; short
Juvenile	lacks white neck patch

BREEDING

Nest	twig platform in tree
Eggs	2; white
Incubation	17 days ♂ ♀
Young	helpless; downy
Fledging	29–35 days
Broods	3; Apr–June
Food	crops, seeds, grain
Population	4,800,000 individuals

J	F	M	A	M	J	J	A	S	O	N	D
6	6	6	6	6	6	6	6	6	6	6	6

black neck slash

buffy

pale, white-edged tail

broad white undertail

First nested in Norfolk in 1955 and has since spread throughout the country. Pale buffy above, pinkish below; neat black line (collar) on sides of neck. In flight, undertail has black base and broad white tip. Haunts gardens with conifers as well as grain stores, where may form substantial flocks.
Status: widespread resident, reaches high densities in south-east; continued immigration probable.
Similar Species:
Turtle Dove (p.152) is rust-brown on back.

COLLARED DOVE

Type	pigeon-like
Size	29–32cm (11–12in)
Habitat	towns and gardens, fields and hedges
Behaviour	walks, perches openly, takes off and lands on vegetation or ground
Flocking	1–50
Flight	glides; strong and powerful; direct
Voice	*coo-cooo-coo* repeated at length; plaintive *weer*

IDENTIFICATION

Adult

Crown	buff
Upperparts	buff
Rump	buff
Tail	buff with white corners, undertail black with broad white tip; medium length, rounded
Throat	buff
Breast	buff
Belly	buff
Bill	brown; short and thin
Legs	red; short

BREEDING

Nest	platform of twigs in tree
Eggs	2; white
Incubation	14 days ♂♀
Young	helpless; downy
Fledging	18 days
Broods	2–5; Mar–Sept
Food	seeds, grain
Population	50,000+

J	F	M	A	M	J	J	A	S	O	N	D
5	5	5	5	5	5	5	5	5	5	5	5

Turtle Dove *Streptopelia turtur*

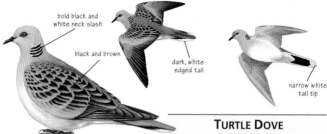

bold black and white neck slash

black and brown

dark, white-edged tail

narrow white tail tip

Small, fast-flying dove; purring call is characteristic sound of summer. Grey-brown on head and back; pinkish below. Wing coverts black; each feather broadly edged rust, creating turtle-shell appearance. Shows rufous back and wing coverts in flight. Black tail edged white; smudged black and white neck slash. Forms flocks in autumn.
Status: summer visitor to south and east England.
Similar Species:
Collared Dove (p.151) is similar size, but plain buff above.

TURTLE DOVE

Type	pigeon-like
Size	26–29cm (10–11in)
Habitat	forests and woods, fields and hedges, gardens
Behaviour	walks, perches openly, takes off and lands on vegetation or ground
Flocking	1–50
Flight	strong and powerful; direct
Voice	purring *roor-rr*
IDENTIFICATION	
Adult	
Crown	grey
Upperparts	brown and black, 'scalloped'
Rump	brown
Tail	black edged white; medium length, rounded
Throat	pink
Breast	pink
Belly	white
Bill	black; short and thin
Legs	red; short
BREEDING	
Nest	platform of twigs in tree
Eggs	2; white
Incubation	13–14 days ♂♀
Young	helpless; downy
Fledging	19–21 days
Broods	2; May–June
Food	seeds
Population	c125,000 pairs

J	F	M	A	M	J	J	A	S	O	N	D
0	0	0	3	5	5	5	5	4	2	1	0

long tail

adult

long narrow wings

adult ♀

hepatic phase

juvenile

small head and bill

adult

juvenile

long narrow wings

grey head and neck

barred below

adult

COMMON CUCKOO

Type	pigeon-like/hawk-like
Size	32–34cm (12–13in)
Habitat	gardens, marshes, moors and heaths, woods, fields and hedges
Behaviour	hops, perches openly, takes off and lands on vegetation or ground
Flocking	1–2
Flight	direct
Voice	*cuc-coo* repeated

IDENTIFICATION

Adult

Crown	grey
Upperparts	grey
Rump	grey
Tail	grey; long and rounded
Throat	grey
Breast	grey
Belly	black and white, barred
Bill	black; short and thin
Legs	yellow; short
Juvenile	mottled and barred brown, black, buff and white
Hepatic ♀	chestnut and white, heavily barred

BREEDING

Nest	parasitic
Eggs	8–12; highly variable
Incubation	12½ days; by host
Young	helpless; naked
Fledging	20–23 days
Broods	not applicable
Food	insects
Population	17,000–35,000 pairs

Harbinger of spring and Britain's most familiar bird call. Usually seen in flight when long pointed wings, long tail and small head are reminiscent of a hawk. When perched, often on overhead wire, appears ungainly and off-balance; seems to have difficulty folding wings. Upperparts and breast grey; underparts barred black and white. Juvenile darker; heavily barred above and below. Hepatic female is rare colour phase; chestnut above and white below.
Status: widespread summer visitor.
Similar Species: beware female Sparrowhawk (p.74).

J	F	M	A	M	J	J	A	S	O	N	D
0	0	1	3	4	4	4	3	3	2	0	0

153

Barn Owl *Tyto alba*

bold facial disc

white breast

pale rounded wings

rare dark breasted form

flat white face

The ghost-like, white owl of country folklore. Most often seen quartering fields at dusk when white underparts identify. Upperparts pale orange-buff with darkish spots. Flat-faced appearance with dark ring around facial disc. The dark-breasted form is a rare immigrant from central Europe.
Status: widespread resident but nowhere common; declining in numbers.
Similar Species: all other owls are brown and buff, except rare Snowy Owl, which is white, mottled black.

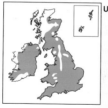

BARN OWL

Type	owl-like
Size	33–36cm (12½–14in)
Habitat	heaths, woods, fields and hedges
Behaviour	perches openly, takes off and lands on vegetation or ground
Flocking	solitary
Flight	hovers, glides
Voice	variety shrill shrieks, hisses and snoring notes

IDENTIFICATION

Adult	
Crown	buffy orange
Upperparts	buffy orange, dark spots
Rump	buffy orange
Tail	buffy orange; short and square
Throat	white
Breast	white
Belly	white
Bill	grey; hooked
Legs	white; medium length

BREEDING

Nest	hole in tree or building
Eggs	4–7; white
Incubation	32-34 days ♀
Young	helpless; naked
Fledging	60 days
Broods	1–2; Mar–May
Food	small mammals, birds
Population	5000-10,000 pairs

J	F	M	A	M	J	J	A	S	O	N	D
3	3	3	3	3	3	3	3	3	3	3	3

fierce expression, bold eyebrows

yellow eyes

round wings, bounding flight

resting posture

alert posture

S mall brown and buff owl; most often seen perched openly during daylight. When disturbed, flies away with distinctive bouncing flight, like a woodpecker. Staring yellow eyes and prominent facial disc with bold 'eyebrows' create fierce expression. *Status:* introduced resident of England and Wales. *Similar Species:* only tiny owl.

LITTLE OWL

Type	owl-like
Size	21–23cm (8–9in)
Habitat	towns and gardens, heaths, woods, fields and hedges
Behaviour	perches openly, takes off and lands on vegetation or ground
Flocking	solitary
Flight	glides; undulating
Voice	plaintive *keeoo*

IDENTIFICATION

Adult	
Crown	brown and buff, spotted
Upperparts	brown and buff, spotted
Rump	brown and buff, spotted
Tail	brown and buff; short and square
Throat	brown and buff, streaked
Breast	brown and buff, streaked
Belly	white, streaked brown
Bill	grey; hooked
Legs	white, medium length

BREEDING

Nest	hole in tree or building
Eggs	3–5; white
Incubation	28–29 days ♀
Young	helpless; downy
Fledging	4–5 weeks
Broods	1,2?; Apr–May
Food	insects, small mammals, small birds
Population	7000–14,000 pairs

J	F	M	A	M	J	J	A	S	O	N	D
3	3	3	3	3	3	3	3	3	3	3	3

Short-eared Owl *Asio flammeus*

rounded head, yellow eyes

dark carpals

gliding, hovering harrier-like flight on long, rounded wings

Diurnal owl, associated with marshes and moorland; the owl most frequently seen hunting during daylight. Flat head and long, rounded wings with dark carpal patches above. Pale, almost white, below with dark wingtips and carpal patches. Quarters territory like a harrier – weaves, hovers and glides with wings held in shallow 'V'.

Status: resident mainly in north and along east coast of Britain; passage migrant and winter visitor elsewhere.

Similar Species: only regular diurnal owl of moors and marshes.

SHORT-EARED OWL

Type	owl-like
Size	36–39cm (14–15in)
Habitat	freshwater marshes, moors, estuaries
Behaviour	perches openly, takes off and lands on ground
Flocking	1–2
Flight	hovers, glides; laboured
Voice	high-pitched *kee-aw*; deep *boo-boo-boo*

IDENTIFICATION
Adult

Crown	buff
Upperparts	brown and buff, barred
Rump	brown and buff, barred
Tail	brown and buff; short and square
Throat	brown and buff, streaked
Breast	brown and buff, streaked
Belly	pale buff
Bill	black; hooked
Legs	white; medium length

BREEDING

Nest	hollow on ground
Eggs	4–8; white
Incubation	24-28 days ♀
Young	helpless; downy
Fledging	22–27 days
Broods	1 (sometimes 2); Apr–June
Food	small mammals
Population	1000+ pairs

J	F	M	A	M	J	J	A	S	O	N	D
3	3	3	3	3	3	3	3	3	3	3	3

ear tufts

orange eyes

dark carpals

Medium-sized owl with striking orange eyes, prominent facial disc and conspicuous ear tufts. Upperparts mottled buff and brown; underparts buffy, streaked brown. Scarce and secretive owl, lacking obviously distinctive voice. Mainly found in old conifers; sometimes forms communal roosts in winter.
Status: widespread, but patchy, throughout Britain and Ireland. Continental immigrants in winter.
Similar Species: Tawny Owl (p.158) also occurs in woodlands.

LONG-EARED OWL

Type	owl-like
Size	34–37cm (13–14in)
Habitat	forests and woods, heaths
Behaviour	takes off and lands on vegetation or ground
Flocking	solitary
Flight	glides; laboured; direct
Voice	low *oo-oo-oo*, juvenile a rusty-hinge contact squeak

IDENTIFICATION

Adult	
Crown	buff and brown, mottled
Upperparts	buff and brown, mottled
Rump	buff and brown, mottled
Tail	buff and brown; short and square
Throat	buff, streaked brown
Breast	buff, streaked brown
Bill	black; hooked
Legs	buff; medium length
BREEDING	
Nest	old nest of different species in tree
Eggs	4–5; white
Incubation	25–30 days ♀
Young	helpless; downy
Fledging	23–24 days
Broods	1 (rarely 2); Feb–May
Food	small mammals
Population	3000–10,000 pairs; 10,000–35,000 winter

J	F	M	A	M	J	J	A	S	O	N	D
2	2	2	2	2	2	2	2	2	2	2	2

Tawny Owl *Strix aluco*

dark eyes

large rounded head

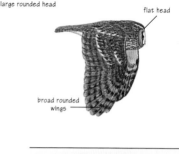

flat head

broad rounded wings

The brown owl of the countryside and source of the most familiar owl hoots and shrieks. Although widespread (except Ireland), surprisingly seldom seen. Upperparts brown, mottled buff; underparts buffy, broadly streaked brown. Well-marked facial disc set off by large, dark eyes. In flight, wings long and rounded.

Status: widespread and numerous resident throughout Britain; absent Ireland.

Similar Species: can be confused with much scarcer Long-eared Owl (p.157) but calls completely different.

TAWNY OWL

Type	owl-like
Size	36–40cm (14–15½in)
Habitat	towns and gardens, heaths, forests and woods, fields and hedges
Behaviour	perches openly, takes off and lands on vegetation
Flocking	solitary
Voice	hooted *hoo-hoo-hoo-oo-oo-oo*; harsh *ke-wick*

IDENTIFICATION

Adult	
Crown	brown, mottled buff
Upperparts	brown, mottled buff
Rump	brown, mottled buff
Tail	buff and brown; short and square
Throat	buff, streaked brown
Breast	buff, streaked brown
Belly	buff
Bill	grey; hooked
Legs	white; medium length

BREEDING

Nest	hole in tree or building
Eggs	2–4; white
Incubation	28–30 days ♀
Young	helpless; downy
Fledging	32–37 days
Broods	1; Mar–May
Food	small mammals, small birds
Population	50,000–100,000 pairs

J	F	M	A	M	J	J	A	S	O	N	D
4	4	4	4	4	4	4	4	4	4	4	4

tiny bill

♀

long tail

♂

long wings

white wing and
tail patches

EUROPEAN NIGHTJAR

Type	hawk-like/owl-like
Size	25–28cm (9½–11in)
Habitat	heaths, forests and woods
Behaviour	takes off and lands on vegetation or ground
Flocking	solitary
Flight	glides; flitting
Voice	distinctive churring
IDENTIFICATION	
Adult ♂	
Crown	grey
Upperparts	brown, spotted
Rump	brown
Tail	brown, white patches; long and square
Throat	buff and brown, barred
Breast	buff and brown, barred
Belly	buff and brown, barred
Bill	black; short and thin
Legs	buff; short
Adult ♀	lacks white wing and tail patches
BREEDING	
Nest	bare hollow
Eggs	2; white, spotted light brown
Incubation	18 days ♂♀
Young	partly-active; downy
Fledging	16–18 days
Broods	2; May–July
Food	insects
Population	3000–6000 pairs

M edium-sized nocturnal bird with long wings and tail. Heavily mottled and barred in browns, buffs and greys, creating excellent camouflage when bird nests on ground on open heaths. Male has conspicuous white patches on wing and tail, lacking in female. Best located by distinctive churring call (similar to that made by vibrating tongue in mouth), which continues for long periods. Claps wings in display. *Status:* widespread but scarce and declining summer visitor. *Similar Species:* none.

J	F	M	A	M	J	J	A	S	O	N	D
0	0	0	1	2	2	2	2	1	1	0	0

Common Swift *Apus apus*

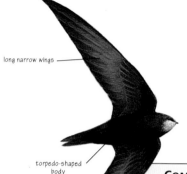

long narrow wings

torpedo-shaped body

S uperficially similar to
Barn Swallow and martins
but easily distinguished by
longer and narrower
sickle-shaped wings and all-black
coloration. Most aerial of birds, coming
to land (buildings and caves) only to lay
and incubate eggs and feed young.
Flickers wings and
forms 'screaming'
parties over
colonies on
summer evenings.
Status: common
summer visitor.
Similar Species:
Barn Swallow
and martins
(pp. 169-171).

COMMON SWIFT

Type	swallow-like
Size	16–17cm (6in)
Habitat	towns, freshwater, moors, heaths, fields and hedges
Behaviour	totally aerial, takes off and lands on buildings
Flocking	1–1000
Flight	glides; strong and powerful; flitting
Voice	high-pitched scream

IDENTIFICATION

Adult	
Crown	black
Upperparts	black
Rump	black
Tail	black; short and forked
Throat	grey
Breast	black
Belly	black
Bill	black; short and thin
Legs	black; short

BREEDING

Nest	leaves and debris inside building
Eggs	3; white
Incubation	14–20 days ♂♀
Young	helpless; naked
Fledging	5–8 weeks
Broods	1; May–June
Food	insects
Population	c100,000 pairs

J	F	M	A	M	J	J	A	S	O	N	D
0	0	0	2	5	6	6	5	2	0	0	0

Alcedo atthis **Common Kingfisher**

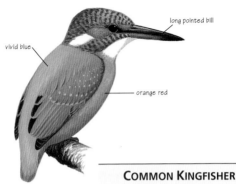

long pointed bill

vivid blue

orange red

E xotic, jewel-like bird, most often
seen as a flash of bright blue as it
dashes upstream. Confined to small
streams, though may move to larger
rivers and even coastal marshes during
hard weather. Upperparts blue-green
with vividly blue rump; underparts
bright orange-red. Catches fishes by
diving head-first into water.
Status: declining resident, becoming
decidedly scarce.
Similar Species:
none.

COMMON KINGFISHER

Type	unique
Size	15–16cm (5½–6in)
Habitat	inland freshwater
Behaviour	dives from air, perches openly, takes off and lands in vegetation
Flocking	solitary
Flight	direct; aerial dive
Voice	metallic *chee*, or *chee-kee*, often rapidly repeated

IDENTIFICATION

Adult	
Crown	blue-green, barred black
Upperparts	blue-green; wings barred black
Rump	bright blue
Tail	blue-green; short and square
Throat	white
Breast	orange-red
Belly	orange-red
Bill	black; straight and thin
Legs	red; short
BREEDING	
Nest	hole in bank
Eggs	6–7; white
Incubation	19–21 days ♂♀
Young	helpless; naked
Fledging	23–27 days
Broods	2; Apr–June
Food	fish
Population	5000–9000 pairs

J	F	M	A	M	J	J	A	S	O	N	D
3	3	3	3	3	3	3	3	3	3	3	3

Wryneck *Jynx torquilla*

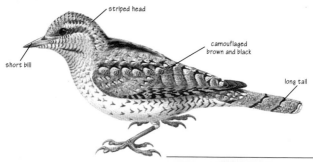

striped head

camouflaged
brown and black

short bill

long tail

Highly elusive, well-camouflaged, relative of the woodpeckers; spends most of its time on the ground or perched inconspicuously in bushes. Does not behave like a woodpecker, although voice similar to Lesser Spotted. Upperparts brown, variously mottled, streaked and barred with black, buff and grey. Short bill, striped head pattern and long tail produce unusual appearance. Name comes from habit of twisting neck right round when startled or handled. *Status:* formerly bred southern England; now may be colonizing Scotland. Regular but scarce passage migrant – especially in autumn on south and east coasts. *Similar Species:* none.

J	F	M	A	M	J	J	A	S	O	N	D
0	0	1	1	1	1	1	1	1	2	2	0	0

WRYNECK

Type	woodpecker-like
Size	15–16cm (5½–6in)
Habitat	gardens, heaths, woods, fields
Behaviour	perches openly, hops, takes off from vegetation or ground
Flocking	solitary
Flight	direct
Voice	far-carrying *kyee-kyee-kyee*, repeated

IDENTIFICATION

Adult	
Crown	buff and brown
Upperparts	brown with black, buff and grey markings
Rump	buff and brown
Tail	grey, barred black; long, square
Throat	buff
Breast	barred buff and brown
Belly	barred buff and brown
Bill	black; short and thin
Legs	brown; short
BREEDING	
Nest	hole in tree or wall
Eggs	7–10; white
Incubation	12–14 days, mainly ♀
Fledging	19–21 days
Broods	1, occasionally 2; May–June
Food	insects
Population	0–10 pairs; passage migrant

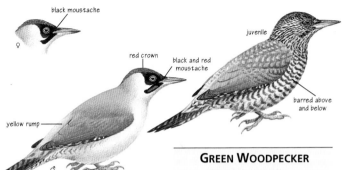

black moustache ♀

juvenile

red crown

black and red
moustache

barred above
and below

yellow rump

♂

arge green and yellow woodpecker which spends much time on ground, feeding. Bright red crown; moustachial stripe red, bordered black in male, pure black in female. Upperparts green, rump yellow, tail dark brown and pointed. Underparts white with faint greenish wash; undertail barred brown. Dagger-like silver-grey bill; grey legs. Typical undulating flight. Unlike other woodpeckers, rarely drums. *Status:* widespread resident of woods and heaths in most of Britain except northern Scotland; absent Ireland. *Similar Species:* only large green woodpecker to occur in Britain.

GREEN WOODPECKER

Type	woodpecker-like
Size	30–33cm (11½–13in)
Habitat	gardens, woods, heaths, fields
Behaviour	climbs, hops, take off from vegetation or ground
Flocking	1–2
Flight	laboured; undulating
Voice	loud, laughing *keu-keu-keu*

IDENTIFICATION

Adult	
Crown	red
Upperparts	green
Rump	yellow
Tail	dark brown, barred below; short and pointed
Throat	grey
Breast	grey
Belly	white with greenish wash
Bill	silver-grey; short and thin
Legs	grey; short
Juvenile	face and underparts heavily barred black; less conspicuous moustaches

BREEDING

Nest	bare tree hold
Eggs	5–7; white
Incubation	18–19 days ♂♀
Young	helpless; naked
Fledging	18–21 days
Broods	1; Apr–May
Food	insects
Population	15,000–30,000 pairs

J	F	M	A	M	J	J	A	S	O	N	D
3	3	3	3	3	3	3	3	3	3	3	3

Great Spotted Woodpecker
Dendrocopus major

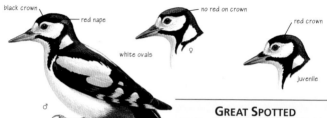

black crown · red nape · white ovals · no red on crown · ♀ · red crown · juvenile · ♂

Most common and widespread of the three British woodpeckers. Upperparts black broken by white cheeks, neck patch, and two bold white ovals on back. Underparts buffy white; red undertail coverts. Adult male has red patch on hind crown (lacking in female). Juvenile has red crown. Largely confined to woodland; climbs trees easily. Both sexes frequently drum on dead wood producing loud, far-carrying hollow sound. Deeply undulating flight. *Status:* widespread resident; absent Ireland.
Similar Species: much smaller and more elusive Lesser Spotted Woodpecker (p.165) lacks red undertail and white ovals on back.

GREAT SPOTTED WOODPECKER

Type	woodpecker-like
Size	22–24cm (8–9in)
Habitat	woods, gardens, hedges
Behaviour	climbs, takes off and lands on vegetation
Flocking	1–2
Flight	laboured; undulating
Voice	loud *tchack*; also far-carrying, hollow drumming

IDENTIFICATION

Adult ♂	
Crown	black; red patch on nape
Upperparts	black and white; bold white ovals on back
Rump	black
Tail	black, undertail red; short and rounded
Throat	white
Breast	buffy white
Belly	buffy white; red on lower belly
Bill	grey; short and thin
Legs	grey; short
Adult ♀	lacks red on nape
Juvenile	red crown

BREEDING

Nest	tree hole
Eggs	4–7; white
Incubation	16 days, mainly ♀
Young	helpless; naked
Fledging	18–21 days
Broods	1; May–June
Food	insects
Population	60,000–80,000 pairs

J	F	M	A	M	J	J	A	S	O	N	D
4	4	4	4	4	4	4	4	4	4	4	4

Lesser Spotted Woodpecker
Dendrocopus minor

red crown

ladder back

♂

buffy crown

♀

Tiny, sparrow-sized, black and white woodpecker; spends most of its time among the woodland canopy where easily overlooked. Agile climber, often on thin twigs near tops of trees. Male has red crown, female buffy white. Upperparts black, boldly barred white across back; white cheeks. Underparts buffy white. Both sexes drum on dead branches producing faster, higher-pitched sound than Great Spotted. Frequently calls early in breeding season. Needs dead and decaying trees for nesting.
Status: resident breeder.
Similar Species:
Great Spotted Woodpecker (p.164) is larger and has white shoulder patches and red undertail.

LESSER SPOTTED WOODPECKER

Type	woodpecker-like
Size	14–15cm (5½–6in)
Habitat	heaths, woods, hedgerows, parks
Behaviour	climbs, takes off and lands on vegetation
Flocking	solitary
Flight	undulating
Voice	high-pitched *kee-kee-kee-kee*, repeated; similar to Wryneck

IDENTIFICATION

Adult ♂	
Crown	red
Upperparts	black, barred white
Rump	black
Tail	black; short and rounded
Throat	white
Breast	buffy white
Belly	buffy white
Bill	grey; short and thin
Legs	grey; short
Adult ♀	lacks red crown

BREEDING

Nest	tree hole
Eggs	4–6; white
Incubation	14 days ♂ ♀
Young	helpless, naked
Fledging	21 days
Broods	1; May–June
Food	insects
Population	5000–10,000 pairs

J	F	M	A	M	J	J	A	S	O	N	D
2	2	2	2	2	2	2	2	2	2	2	2

Wood Lark *Lullula arborea*

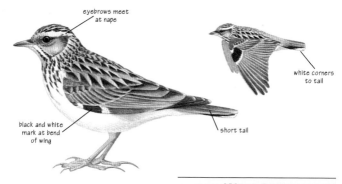

eyebrows meet at nape

white corners to tail

black and white mark at bend of wing

short tail

Small, stockily-built lark; scarce inhabitant of heaths and open woodlands. Favours areas of short grass with scattered trees and shrubs, on which it frequently lands. Similar to Sky Lark but tail obviously shorter and only hint of crest; prominent pale eyebrows meet at nape. Small black and white patch at bend of wing. Upperparts streaked brown and buff; underparts white with brown and buff streaked on breast. Distinctive song uttered from tree-top or in flight; melodic and liquid series of repeated phrases.

Status: fast-declining resident of southern England.

Similar Species: Sky Lark (p.167)

WOOD LARK

Type	lark-like
Size	14.5–16cm (5½–6in)
Habitat	heaths, woodlands
Behaviour	walks, takes off and lands on vegetation or ground
Flocking	1–2
Flight	**h**overs; undulating
Voice	fluty *too-loo-eet*

IDENTIFICATION

Adult	
Crown	buff and brown
Upperparts	buff and brown, streaked
Rump	buff and brown
Tail	buff and brown, tipped white; short and notched
Throat	white
Breast	white, streaked buff
Belly	white
Bill	brown; short and thin
Legs	pink; medium length

BREEDING

Nest	cup on ground
Eggs	3–4; buffy, spotted brown
Incubation	12–16 days ♀
Young	helpless; downy
Fledging	15–17 days?
Broods	2; Mar–May
Food	seeds, insects
Population	60–360 pairs

J	F	M	A	M	J	J	A	S	O	N	D
1	1	1	2	2	2	2	1	1	1	1	1

Alauda arvensis **Sky Lark**

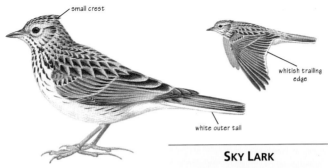

small crest

whitish trailing edge

white outer tail

Heavily-streaked, ground dwelling bird of wide variety of habitats; widespread at all seasons. Most often seen in towering song flight during spring and early summer. Thickish bill and bulky shape distinguish from pipits; noticeable crest and long, white-edged tail separate from Wood Lark. Gregarious outside breeding season. *Status:* breeds throughout Britain and Ireland, but declining in numbers; also double passage migrant and winter visitor. *Similar Species:* Wood Lark (p.166).

SKY LARK

Type	lark-like
Size	17–18cm (6½–7in)
Habitat	moors, heaths, fields, marshes
Behaviour	walks, takes off and lands on ground
Flocking	1–100
Flight	hovers; undulating
Voice	liquid *chirrup*, also fine warbling song in towering flight

IDENTIFICATION

Adult

Crown	buff and brown; small crest
Upperparts	buff and brown; heavily-streaked
Rump	buff and brown
Tail	buff and brown, white-edged; long and notched
Throat	white'
Breast	buff; streaked brown
Belly	white
Bill	brown; short and thickish
Legs	pinkish; medium length

BREEDING

Nest	cup on ground
Eggs	3–4; greyish, blotched brown
Incubation	11 days ♀
Young	helpless; downy
Fledging	20 days
Broods	2–3; Apr–June
Food	seeds, insects
Population	2,000,000–3,000,000 pairs

J	F	M	A	M	J	J	A	S	O	N	D
5	5	5	5	5	5	5	5	5	5	5	5

Shore Lark *Eremophila alpestris*

bold face pattern

white outer tail

winter

♂ summer

Scarce autumn and winter visitor to east coast of Britain. Usually confined to shorelines, saltings and shingle with sparse growth of vegetation. Difficult to locate until it flies. Buffy brown above and white below. Shows white outer tail feathers; distinctive black and yellow face pattern and two tiny black 'horns' on top of head. Face pattern subdued in winter but still unmistakable. Usually occurs in small flocks, often in same areas occupied by Snow Buntings. *Status:* scarce in autumn, even scarcer in winter. Has bred in Scotland. *Similar Species:* none.

SHORE LARK

Type	lark-like
Size	16–17cm (6–6½in)
Habitat	estuaries and shores
Behaviour	walks, takes off and lands on ground
Flocking	1–15
Flight	undulating
Voice	shrill *tseep* or *tseep-seep*, similar to wagtail or pipit

IDENTIFICATION
Adult

Crown	buff; black 'horns'
Upperparts	buff and brown
Rump	buff
Tail	buff and brown, white outer feathers; medium length, notched
Throat	yellow
Breast	black crescent
Belly	white
Bill	black; short and thin
Legs	black; short
Juvenile	darker above, spotted buff-white; lacks black and yellow face pattern

BREEDING

Nest	cup on ground
Eggs	4; greenish, speckled brown
Incubation	10–14 days ♀
Young	helpless; downy
Fledging	?
Broods	2; May–June
Food	seeds, insects
Population	less than 300 winter

J	F	M	A	M	J	J	A	S	O	N	D
2	2	1	0	0	0	0	0	0	0	2	2

completely brown
upperparts

breast band

S mallest of the swallow-like birds, with shallow, forked tail and sharply angled wings. Erratic flight with less frequent glides than similar species. Upperparts sandy brown; underparts white. Distinctive brown breast band. Always gregarious, forming highly vocal, twittering flocks; frequently gathers to feed over water. Nests in colonies in sand-banks and cliffs. In winter and on passage roosts among dense reeds, often in company with Barn Swallows.
Status: widespread summer visitor, except to northern and western isles. Sharp decline in mid-1980s associated with drought in Africa.
Similar Species:
Barn Swallow (p.170) and House Martin (p.171) have blackish upperparts.

SAND MARTIN

Type	swallow-like
Size	11–12cm (4¹/₂–5in)
Habitat	inland freshwater, sea cliffs
Behaviour	aerial, takes off and lands on ground
Flocking	1–100s
Flight	flitting
Voice	continuous twittering, harsh *chirrup*

IDENTIFICATION

Adult	
Crown	sandy brown
Upperparts	sandy brown
Rump	sandy brown
Tail	sandy brown; short and notched
Throat	white
Breast	sandy brown band
Belly	white
Bill	black; short and thin
Legs	black; short

BREEDING

Nest	hole in sand-band; colonial
Eggs	4–5; white
Incubation	1–12 days ♂♀
Young	helpless; downy
Fledging	19 days
Broods	2; May–June
Food	insects
Population	less than 250,000 pairs

J	F	M	A	M	J	J	A	S	O	N	D
0	0	2	4	4	4	4	4	4	3	3	0	0

169

Barn Swallow *Hirundo rustica*

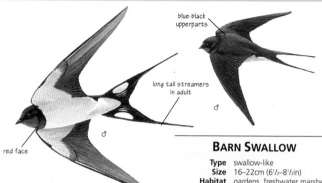

blue-black
upperparts

long tail streamers
in adult

♂

red face

♂

S ummer visitor to farms and gardens;
most frequently nests inside barns,
sheds, garages and other outbuildings.
Fast, highly acrobatic flight in search of
flying insects. Long, angled wings and
deeply-forked tail streamers in adult;
streamers longer in male than female.
Spread tail shows row of white spots.
Upperparts dark metallic blue; face and
throat red, bordered below by narrow,
dark breast band.
Remaining
underparts vary
from pale cream to
rich pink.
Status: common
and widespread
summer visitor.
Similar Species:
House Martin
(p.171) and Sand Martin (p.169).

BARN SWALLOW

Type	swallow-like
Size	16–22cm (6½–8½in)
Habitat	gardens, freshwater marshes, moors, fields
Behaviour	aerial, takes off and lands on buildings
Flocking	1–100s
Flight	glides; flitting
Voice	high-pitched *vit-vit-vit*; song, a twittering trill

IDENTIFICATION

Adult

Crown	dark metallic blue
Upperparts	dark metallic blue
Rump	dark metallic blue
Tail	blue-black; long and forked
Throat	red
Breast	dark metallic blue; narrow band
Belly	pale cream to rich pink
Bill	black; short and thin
Legs	black; short
Juvenile	lacks tail streamers

BREEDING

Nest	mud cup inside outbuilding
Eggs	4–5; white with reddish spots
Incubation	14–16 days, ♀ alone?
Young	helpless; downy
Fledging	17–24 days
Broods	2–3; May–June
Food	insects
Population	500,000+ pairs

J	F	M	A	M	J	J	A	S	O	N	D
0	0	2	4	5	5	5	5	5	4	2	0

no breast band

white rump

C ompact, black and white, swallow-
like bird. Common summer visitor,
nesting mostly under eaves of buildings;
usually forms colonies. Requires nearby
source of soft mud to construct nearly
spherical nest, which is well known in
many small towns and villages. Blue-
black on crown and back; black wings
and tail; prominent white rump and pure
white underparts.
Usually gregarious
but does not join
communal roosts of
Barn Swallows and
Sand Martins in
reed beds. Often
seen feeding over
freshwater.
Status: common
and widespread summer visitor.
Similar Species: Barn Swallow (p.170)
and Sand Martin (p.169).

J	F	M	A	M	J	J	A	S	O	N	D
0	0	2	3	5	5	5	5	4	4	3	0

HOUSE MARTIN

Type	swallow-like
Size	12–13cm (4½–5in)
Habitat	towns, inland freshwater
Behaviour	aerial, takes off and lands on buildings
Flocking	1–100
Flight	glides; flitting
Voice	harsh *chirrup*, quite unlike other 'swallows'

IDENTIFICATION

Adult	
Crown	blue-black
Upperparts	blue black, wing black
Rump	white
Tail	black; short and forked
Throat	white
Breast	white
Belly	white
Bill	black; short and thin
Legs	white; short

BREEDING

Nest	mud dome under eaves; colonial
Eggs	4–5; white
Incubation	13–19 days ♂♀
Young	helpless; downy
Fledging	19–25 days
Broods	2–3; May–June
Food	insects
Population	300,000–600,000 pairs

171

Tree Pipit *Anthus trivialis*

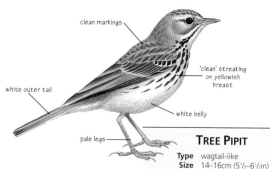

clean markings

'clean' streaking on yellowish breast

white outer tail

white belly

pale legs

Similar to more widespread and abundant Meadow Pipit but summer visitor only preferring open woodlands and overgrown heaths with plentiful perches. Brown streaks on buff upperparts, buffy yellow breast and white flanks; conspicuous buffy eyebrow. Voice distinct, frequently uttered in sing flight starting and terminating on perch.
Status: summer visitor to Britain; absent from Ireland except on passage.
Similar Species: Meadow Pipit (p.173) has (mostly) different habitat and call; streaking less clear and clean. See also Rock Pipit (p.174).

TREE PIPIT

Type	wagtail-like
Size	14–16cm (5½–6½in)
Habitat	heaths, woods
Behaviour	walks, perches openly, takes off from vegetation or ground
Flocking	solitary
Flight	direct; hovers
Voice	harsh *tees*; also a loud descending trill with drawn-out *see-see-see* ending

IDENTIFICATION

Adult	
Crown	buff, streaked brown
Upperparts	buff, streaked brown
Rump	buff, streaked brown
Tail	buff, streaked brown, white outer feathers; medium length, notched
Throat	buff
Breast	buffy yellow, streaked brown
Belly	white
Bill	brown; short and thin
Legs	pinkish; medium length
BREEDING	
Nest	cup on ground
Eggs	4–6; variable, speckled brown
Incubation	12–14 days ♀
Young	helpless; downy
Fledging	12–13 days
Broods	1–2; May–June
Food	insects
Population	50,000–100,000 pairs

J	F	M	A	M	J	J	A	S	O	N	D
0	0	2	3	3	3	3	3	3	3	2	0	0

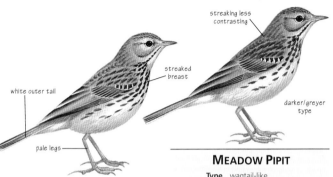

streaking less contrasting

streaked breast

white outer tail

pale legs

darker/greyer type

Widespread and numerous at all seasons and abundant among shoreline marshes and on beaches in winter. Olive-brown or greyish above with heavy, dark streaking. Buff breast and white belly with dense streaking on breast and flanks. Pinkish brown legs with long hind claw and white outer tail feathers. Forms flocks in favoured areas; usually gregarious on migration.

Status: widespread resident; abundant passage migrant and winter visitor.
Similar Species: in summer, Tree Pipit (p.172); along shorelines and in winter, Rock and Water Pipits (pp.174-175).

MEADOW PIPIT

Type	wagtail-like
Size	14–15cm (5½–6in)
Habitat	marshes, heaths, coasts, estuaries, fields
Behaviour	walks, perches openly, takes off and lands on ground
Flocking	1–50
Flight	direct; hovers
Voice	thin, high-pitched *tissip* or *eest*; also an accelerating trill in parachuting display flight

IDENTIFICATION

Adult

Crown	buff, streaked dark brown
Upperparts	olive-brown or greyish, streaked dark brown
Rump	buff, streaked dark brown
Tail	white outer feathers; medium length, notched
Throat	white
Breast	buff, streaked dark brown
Belly	white
Bill	brown; short and thin
Legs	pinkish; medium length

BREEDING

Nest	cup on ground
Eggs	3–5; variable, spotted brown
Incubation	11–15 days ♀
Young	helpless; downy
Fledging	10–14 days
Broods	2; Apr–June
Food	insects
Population	3,000,000+ pairs

J	F	M	A	M	J	J	A	S	O	N	D
5	5	5	5	5	5	5	5	5	5	5	5

Rock Pipit *Anthus petrosus*

darker than
Meadow Pipit

pale eyebrow
more prominent

grey outer tail

fewer streaks
on whiter belly

'littoralis' spring

dark legs

dark legs

'petrosus'

Two distinct sub-species occur. British Rock Pipit, *A.p. petrosus*, streaked black on olive above, streaked black on buff below; short supercilium; grey outer tail. Scandinavian Rock Pipit, *A. p. littoralis*, streaked brownish above with prominent supercilium. White belly; fine streaking on pinkish breast; grey outer tail. Both are coastal birds at all seasons. Darker and more uniformly coloured than Meadow Pipit at all seasons. *Status:* breeds mostly along rocky shorelines; also shingle beaches and gullies. Winters all types of shoreline.

Similar Species: nearer Meadow Pipit, though more closely related to Water Pipit and once regarded as conspecific.

ROCK PIPIT

Type	wagtail-like
Size	15–16.5cm (6–6½in)
Habitat	coasts, estuaries
Behaviour	walks, perches openly, takes off from ground
Flocking	1–15
Flight	direct, hovers
Voice	clear but harsh *weest*
IDENTIFICATION	
Crown	grey
Upperparts	grey, diffuse brown streaks
Rump	grey
Tail	black with grey outer feathers, medium, notched
Throat	buff
Breast	buff, diffuse brown streaks
Belly	buff
Bill	black, short and thin
Legs	dark, medium length
BREEDING	
Nest	cup hidden on ground
Eggs	4–6; grey, spotted brown
Incubation	14 days ♀
Young	helpless; downy
Fledging	16 days
Broods	2; Apr–May
Food	insects
Population	unknown

J	F	M	A	M	J	J	A	S	O	N	D
3	3	3	3	3	3	3	3	3	3	3	3

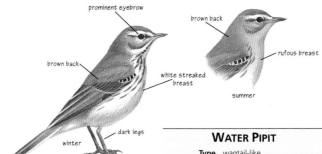

- prominent eyebrow
- brown back
- brown back
- white streaked breast
- rufous breast
- summer
- dark legs
- winter

H igh altitude breeder that is winter visitor to parts of southern England. The combination of unstreaked back, bold supercilium and white outer tail make for straightforward separation from other pipits at all times. Finely-streaked white breast in winter; unstreaked creamy buff in spring. Recently separated from Rock Pipit as distinct species.
Status: winters freshwater margins, marshes and especially watercress beds.
Similar Species: none with plain olive-brown back and bold supercilium.

WATER PIPIT

Type	wagtail-like
Size	15–16.5cm (6–6½in)
Habitat	freshwater marshes
Behaviour	walks, perches openly, takes off from ground
Flocking	1–15
Flight	direct, hovers
Voice	harsh *weest*

IDENTIFICATION

Crown	grey-brown
Upperparts	grey, diffuse brown streaks
Rump	grey-brown
Tail	black with white outer feathers, medium, notched
Throat	white
Breast	white, brown streaks
Belly	white
Bill	black, short and thin
Legs	dark, medium length

BREEDING

Nest	cup hidden on ground
Eggs	4–6; grey, spotted brown
Incubation	14 days ♀
Young	helpless; downy
Fledging	16 days
Broods	2; May–June
Food	insects
Population	unknown

J	F	M	A	M	J	J	A	S	O	N	D
3	3	3	3	3	3	3	3	3	3	3	3

Yellow Wagtail *Motacilla flava*

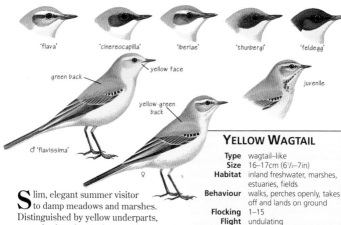

'flava'   'cinereocapilla'   'iberiae'   'thunbergi'   'feldegg'

green back — yellow face

yellow-green back

juvenile

♂ 'flavissima'   ♀

Slim, elegant summer visitor to damp meadows and marshes. Distinguished by yellow underparts, green back and typical wagtail bounce of its long, white-edge, black tail. Spends much time walking. Several different sub-species; main difference is head colour – most obvious in spring male. British breeders usually have yellow heads; others have blue, black, grey and black and even white heads. Blue-headed Wagtail regular passage migrant; gregarious on passage.
Status: widespread summer visitor to England, Wales and central Scotland.
Similar Species: Grey Wagtail (p.177) also has yellow underparts but grey back in all plumages.

YELLOW WAGTAIL

Type	wagtail–like
Size	16–17cm (6½–7in)
Habitat	inland freshwater, marshes, estuaries, fields
Behaviour	walks, perches openly, takes off and lands on ground
Flocking	1–15
Flight	undulating
Voice	loud *see-ip*; also a disjointed warble

IDENTIFICATION

Ad.*flavissima*

Crown	green
Upperparts	green, wings black and white
Rump	green
Tail	black, white-edged; long and notched
Throat	yellow
Breast	yellow
Belly	yellow
Bill	brown; short and thin
Legs	black; medium length
Other sub-sp.	adults vary in head colour

BREEDING

Nest	cup on ground
Eggs	5–6; greyish, speckled brown
Incubation	12–14 days, mainly ♀
Young	helpless; downy
Fledging	17 days
Broods	1–2; May–June
Food	insects
Population	c25,000 pairs

J	F	M	A	M	J	J	A	S	O	N	D
0	0	2	3	4	4	4	4	4	3	2	0	0

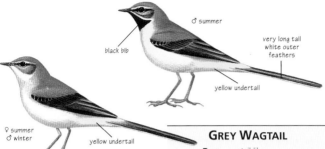

♂ summer

black bib

very long tail white outer feathers

yellow undertail

♀ summer
♂ winter

yellow undertail

Largest of the three British wagtails and the one most closely associated with water, especially fast-running streams. In winter also found near waterfalls, weirs and sometimes lakes, reservoirs, watercress beds and even farmyards. Upperparts grey with white eyebrow, black wings, yellow green rump, and long, white-edge black tail. Underparts white with yellow undertail coverts and variable amount of yellow on breast. In summer, male has prominent black bib.
Status: widespread, common resident, but only winter visitor to areas of eastern England; summer visitor to northern Scotland.
Similar Species: Yellow Wagtail (p.176) and Pied Wagtail (p.178).

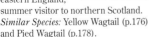

J	F	M	A	M	J	J	A	S	O	N	D
3	3	3	3	3	3	3	3	3	3	3	3

GREY WAGTAIL

Type	wagtail-like
Size	18–20cm (7–8in)
Habitat	inland freshwater, marshes
Behaviour	walks, perches openly, takes off from vegetation or ground
Flocking	1–2
Flight	undulating
Voice	metallic *tzitzi*; also a warble reminiscent of Blue Tit

IDENTIFICATION

Ad. ♂ summer	
Crown	grey, white eyebrow
Upperparts	grey, wings black
Rump	yellow-green
Tail	black, white-edged; long and notched
Throat	white; black bib
Breast	yellow
Belly	white
Bill	black; short and thin
Legs	pink; medium length
Ad. ♀, winter ♂	less yellow below; lacks black bib.

BREEDING

Nest	neat cup in crevice beside stream
Eggs	4–6; buffy, mottled greyish
Incubation	11–14 days, mainly ♀
Young	helpless; downy
Fledging	17 days
Broods	1, occasionally 2; Apr–May
Food	insects
Population	25,000–50,000 pairs

Pied Wagtail *Motacilla alba*

pied ♂ winter

white chin

white ♂ summer
grey back

black chin

white ♂ winter

black chin

white chin

black of chin never meets black of crown in white wagtail

white ♀ summer

pied ♂ summer

sooty back

pied ♀ summer

juvenile pied

Familiar black and white wagtail; widespread resident of open habitats with and without water. Common sub-species in British Isles is *M.a.yarrellii*. Male mainly black above with white face, white margins to flight feathers and white outer tail. Black bib terminates in broad black breast band; remaining underparts white. Female similar but with slate-grey back. Juveniles and first winter birds have grey backs and are similar to Continental sub-species *M.a.alba*, known as White Wagtails, regularly occur on migration and have uniform grey backs.

Status: widespread resident.
Similar Species: none.

PIED WAGTAIL

Type	wagtail-like
Size	17–18cm (6½–7in)
Habitat	inland freshwater, fields, gardens
Behaviour	walks, perches openly, takes off from ground
Flocking	1–10
Flight	undulating
Voice	harsh *chis-ick*; also a disjointed twitter

IDENTIFICATION

M.a.yarrellii

Crown	black, white face
Upperparts	black, white tipped flight feathers
Rump	black
Tail	white outer feathers; long
Throat	black bib in summer; white in winter
Breast	black band
Belly	white
Bill	black; medium length
Legs	black; medium length
M.a.alba	back pale grey at all times

BREEDING

Nest	cup on ground
Eggs	5–6; grey, speckled brown
Incubation	12–14 days; ♀ only ?
Young	helpless; downy
Fledging	13–16 days
Broods	2; Apr–June
Food	insects
Population	c500,000 pairs

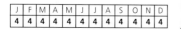

J	F	M	A	M	J	J	A	S	O	N	D
4	4	4	4	4	4	4	4	4	4	4	4

crest

black bib

yellow on wings
and tail

WAXWING

Type	unique/starling-like
Size	17–18.5cm (7in)
Habitat	gardens, heaths, hedgerows
Behaviour	perches openly, hops, takes off from vegetation or ground
Flocking	1–100
Flight	direct
Voice	tinkling trill

IDENTIFICATION

Adult	
Crown	pinkish brown; swept-back crest
Upperparts	pinkish brown; black wings spotted red and yellow
Rump	grey
Tail	grey, black banded, tipped yellow; short and square
Throat	pinkish brown, black bib
Breast	pinkish brown
Belly	pinkish brown
Bill	black; short and thin
Legs	black; medium length

BREEDING

Nest	cup in conifer
Eggs	5; pale blue, spotted black
Incubation	13–14 days ♀
Young	helpless; naked
Fledging	15–17 days
Broods	1; May–June
Food	berries
Population	variable, up to several hundred in autumn and winter

Decidedly starling-like in shape and size, but pinkish brown in colour. Swept-back crest, black lores and chin patch broken by white moustachial streak produce 'cross' expression. Black wings marked by tiny wax-like spots of red and yellow; black banded tail tipped yellow. Irrupts in numbers every five or six years; roams hedgerows and gardens in flocks, sometimes a hundred or more strong; otherwise no more than a rarity.
Status: irregular autumn and winter visitor from Scandinavia and northern Russia, mainly to east coast; numbers variable.
Similar Species: in flight can be mistaken for Common Starling (p.231).

J	F	M	A	M	J	J	A	S	O	N	D
2	2	2	0	0	0	0	0	0	0	1	2

179

Dipper *Cinclus cinclus*

white breast

scaly

juvenile

adult

Portly, short-tailed, blackish bird marked by bold white gorget; reminiscent of large, white breasted Wren. Confined to fast-running streams; most often seen from bridges or riverside paths. Spends much time searching for food among tumbling, rock-strewn waters where wades, swims and dives with complete mastery. Usually solitary, often perching openly on rocks; may be quite tame. Territory can be 2km or more long but only as wide as a river or stream across. *Status:* resident in northern and western hilly areas; some immigration of Continental birds in winter. *Similar Species:* none.

DIPPER

Type	wren-like
Size	17–18cm (7in)
Habitat	inland freshwater
Behaviour	swims, dives from surface, wades, walks, perches openly, takes off from water or ground
Flocking	solitary
Flight	direct
Voice	*zit-zit*

IDENTIFICATION

Adult	
Crown	chocolate-brown
Upperparts	black
Rump	black
Tail	black; short and notched
Throat	white
Breast	white
Belly	chestnut-brown
Bill	brown; short and thin
Legs	pinkish; medium length
Juvenile	slate-grey above, scaly patterning on whitish breast

BREEDING

Nest	dome in hole beside stream
Eggs	5; white
Incubation	15–18 days ♀
Young	helpless; downy
Fledging	19–25 days
Broods	2–3; Mar-June
Food	aquatic insects
Population	c30,000 pairs

J	F	M	A	M	J	J	A	S	O	N	D
3	3	3	3	3	3	3	3	3	3	3	3

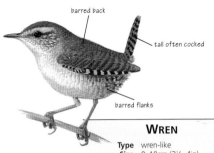

barred back

tall often cocked

barred flanks

WREN

Type	wren-like
Size	9–10cm (3½–4in)
Habitat	gardens, marshes, heaths, sea cliffs, woods, hedges
Behaviour	flits, hops, perches openly, takes off from vegetation or ground
Flocking	1–2
Flight	laboured; direct
Voice	repeated *tic-tic* and *clink*; also a loud ripping warble ending in wheezing *chur*

IDENTIFICATION

Adult	
Crown	chestnut brown
Upperparts	chestnut brown, darkly barred
Rump	chestnut brown
Tail	chestnut brown; short and square
Throat	buffy
Breast	buffy
Belly	buffy, flanks barred
Bill	brown; short and thin
Legs	brown; medium length
BREEDING	
Nest	dome in hole in bank
Eggs	5–8; white, speckled red
Incubation	14–17 days ♀
Young	helpless; downy
Fledging	15–20 days
Broods	1; Apr–May
Food	insects
Population	4–5,000,000 pairs

One of the most widespread and numerous birds of Britain and Ireland, easily recognized by small size and cocked tail. Chestnut above, with clear pale eyebrow and barred back and wings. Underparts buffy; some barring on flanks. Spends much time hunting through dense ground cover, where presence betrayed only by characteristic calls and loud, wheezing song. Quite tame in gardens.
Status: widespread and numerous.
Similar Species: none; wrens are New World birds and this is the only species to have colonized the Old World.

J	F	M	A	M	J	J	A	S	O	N	D
5	5	5	5	5	5	5	5	5	5	5	5

181

Hedge Accentor *Prunella modularis*

thin bill

grey face

streaked flanks

adult

Tame garden and woodland bird; spends most of its time crouched low on ground searching for food. Seldom moves far from cover; usually perches openly only when singing. Flicks wings more or less continuously. Flies low and briefly in undulating flight. Easily overlooked among House Sparrows but grey foreparts and thin bill separate easily. Back and wings brown, liberally streaked with black; brown streaking on flanks. Juvenile has less grey on head and entire underparts are streaked.

Status: common and widespread resident; some autumn migrants stay to winter.

Similar Species: extremely rare Alpine Accentor.

HEDGE ACCENTOR

Type	sparrow-like
Size	14–15cm (5½–6in)
Habitat	gardens, heaths, woods, fields and hedges
Behaviour	flits, perches openly, hops, takes off from vegetation and ground
Flocking	1–2
Flight	undulating
Voice	jingling, staccato warble

IDENTIFICATION

Adult	
Crown	grey-brown
Upperparts	brown, streaked black
Rump	dark grey
Tail	brown and black; medium length, notched
Throat	grey
Breast	grey
Belly	whitish grey; brown streaks on flanks
Bill	black; short and thin
Legs	flesh; medium length

BREEDING

Nest	cup in tree or bush
Eggs	4–5; bright blue
Incubation	12–13 days ♀
Young	helpless; downy
Fledging	12 days
Broods	2–3?; Apr–May
Food	insects, berries
Population	c5,000,000 pairs

J	F	M	A	M	J	J	A	S	O	N	D
5	5	5	5	5	5	5	5	5	5	5	5

scaled above
and below

juvenile

red face
and breast

adult

ROBIN

The most familiar and popular of garden and woodland birds; generally confiding with people. Upright, plump little bird; perches openly and hops on the ground. Adult warm olive-brown with red face, chin and breast. Sides of breast pale grey; belly white. Juvenile has brown head, wings and tail with brown barring on buffy back and breast; indistinguishable from adults after moult (June–August).

Status: widespread and numerous resident throughout year. Often influx of Continental birds in autumn; some northern females migrate southwards and to Continent in autumn.

Similar Species: Common Redstart (p.186), Stonechat (p.188), crossbills (pp.242-243), Bullfinch (p.244) all have 'red' breasts but none are orange-red.

Type	chat-like
Size	13–15cm (5–6in)
Habitat	towns and gardens, heaths, woods, hedges
Behaviour	flits, perches openly, hops, takes off from vegetation and ground
Flocking	solitary
Flight	undulating
Voice	thin *tic-tic-tic*, repeated; leisurely warble

IDENTIFICATION

Adult	
Crown	brown
Upperparts	brown
Rump	brown
Tail	brown; medium length, notched
Throat	orange-red
Breast	orange-red, sides pale grey
Belly	white
Bill	brown; short and pointed
Legs	brown; medium length
Juvenile	lacks red breast, scaly above and below

BREEDING

Nest	cup on ground, in tree stump or on bark
Eggs	5–6; white, speckled reddish
Incubation	12–15 days ♀
Young	helpless; downy
Fledging	12–15 days
Broods	2–3; Apr–June
Food	insects
Population	3,500,000 pairs

J	F	M	A	M	J	J	A	S	O	N	D
6	6	6	6	6	6	6	6	6	6	6	6

183

Nightingale *Luscinia megarhynchos*

warm brown

adult

rufous tail

juvenile

scaled

Fabulous songster more often heard than seen. Song a virtuoso performance of liquid trills ending in crescendo; commonly heard well after dark but also frequently during the day. When disturbed, dives into nearest cover showing characteristic rust-red, conspicuously rounded tail. Adult rufous brown above merging with creamy white underparts. Juvenile marked with scale-like crescents, as juvenile Robin. Rust-red tail remains characteristic. *Status:* summer visitor to south-eastern England from late April. *Similar Species:* rare Thrush Nightingale.

NIGHTINGALE

Type	chat-like
Size	16–17cm (6–6¹/₂in)
Habitat	heaths, woods
Behaviour	flits, takes off or lands on vegetation
Flocking	solitary
Flight	direct
Voice	long song of liquid trills with *peeoo* notes at beginning; also harsh *tchak* and *whooeet* contact notes

IDENTIFICATION

Adult	
Crown	rufous brown
Upperparts	rufous brown
Rump	rust-red
Tail	rust-red; longish and rounded
Throat	white
Breast	creamy white
Belly	white
Bill	brown; short and pointed
Legs	grey; medium length
Juvenile	paler above and below with scaly markings; rust-red tail

BREEDING

Nest	cup well hidden close to ground
Eggs	4–5; mottled reddish
Incubation	13–14 days ♀
Young	helpless; downy
Fledging	11–12 days
Broods	1; May–June
Food	insects
Population	10,000 pairs

J	F	M	A	M	J	J	A	S	O	N	D
0	0	0	2	3	3	2	2	1	0	0	0

white wing flash

red tail

♂ summer

♂ winter

dusky breast

♀

red tail

Colonizing summer visitor. Favours demolition sites, industrial complexes, power stations and railway sidings; also sea cliffs. Perches openly with rusty tail shimmering. Summer male has black head, back, breast and belly; bold white flash on wings. In winter, black areas become dark grey; black remains on throat; underparts dirty white. Female is brown, darker above, paler below; juvenile as female but lightly barred; both have rust-red tails.
Status: scarce summer visitor to southern and central England. Passage migrant; some stay through winter.
Similar Species: female and juvenile Common Redstart are lighter brown.

BLACK REDSTART

Type	chat-like
Size	14–15cm (5½–6in)
Habitat	cliffs, towns and cities
Behaviour	perches openly
Flocking	solitary
Flight	undulating; flitting
Voice	brief *sip* or *tissic*

IDENTIFICATION

Ad.♂ summer	
Crown	black
Upperparts	black; white flash on wings
Rump	rust-red
Tail	rust-red, medium, notched
Throat	black
Breast	black
Belly	grey-black
Bill	black; short and pointed
Legs	black; medium length
Ad.♂ winter	greyer above, throat remains black; underparts dirty white
Ad.♀	brown; rust-red tail
Juvenile	as ♀, lightly barred

BREEDING

Nest	cup hidden in hole or crevice
Eggs	4–6; white
Incubation	12–16 days ♀
Young	helpless; downy
Fledging	12–19 days
Broods	2–3; Apr–June
Food	insects
Population	c30-100 pairs

J	F	M	A	M	J	J	A	S	O	N	D
1	1	3	3	3	2	2	2	3	3	1	1

Common Redstart *Phoenicurus phoenicurus*

♂ winter

white forehead

buff brown

♂ red tail

grey back

buffy

♀

black face

red tail

red tail

♂ summer

Summer visitor to old woodlands and heaths with scattered trees. Perches on lower branches of trees and bushes and makes pouncing sallies to ground; also flits among vegetation. Orange-red tail frequently shimmered. Summer male has dove-grey crown and back; wings brown. White eyebrows meet on forehead; rest of face black. Underparts orange-red; tail orange-red with darker centre. Female also has orange-red tail but is buffy brown. Juvenile similar to female but speckled. *Status:* widespread summer visitor; more common in north and west. Also passage migrant. *Similar species:* Black Redstart (p.185) is darker and has different habitat.

COMMON REDSTART

Type	chat-like
Size	13.5–14.5cm (5¼–5¾in)
Habitat	woods, heaths, parks
Behaviour	flits, perches openly, hops, takes off from vegetation or ground
Flocking	solitary
Flight	direct; flitting
Voice	*hooeet*, brief warble

IDENTIFICATION

Ad.♂ summer

Crown	grey
Upperparts	grey; wings brown
Rump	rust-red
Tail	rust-red; medium length, notched
Throat	black
Breast	orange-red
Belly	creamy white
Bill	black; medium length, short and pointed
Legs	black; medium length

Ad.♀ summer

	buffy; rust-red tail

BREEDING

Nest	cup hidden in bank, tree roots or tree hole
Eggs	6–7; pale blue
Incubation	11–14 days ♀
Young	helpless; downy
Fledging	14–20 days
Broods	2; May–June
Food	insects
Population	c50,000–100,000 pairs

J	F	M	A	M	J	J	A	S	O	N	D
0	0	0	4	4	4	3	3	4	2	0	0

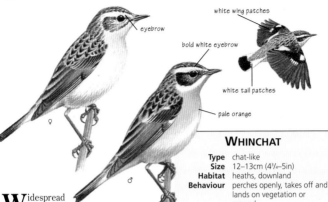

white wing patches

eyebrow

bold white eyebrow

white tail patches

pale orange

♀

♂

WHINCHAT

Type	chat-like
Size	12–13cm (4¾–5in)
Habitat	heaths, downland
Behaviour	perches openly, takes off and lands on vegetation or ground
Flocking	solitary
Flight	direct; flitting
Voice	metallic *tic-tic*; brief warble

IDENTIFICATION

Adult

Crown	brown, streaked black
Upperparts	brown, streaked black; white wing patches
Rump	brown, streaked black
Tail	brown centre, white patches on side, black band at tip; short and square
Throat	creamy orange
Breast	creamy orange
Belly	creamy orange
Bill	black; short and pointed
Legs	black; medium length

BREEDING

Nest	cup on ground at base of bush
Eggs	5–7; pale blue, finely speckled brown
Incubation	13–14 days ♀
Young	helpless; downy
Fledging	17 days
Broods	1–2; May–June
Food	insects
Population	20,000–40,000 pairs

Widespread summer visitor and passage migrant to open heaths and downland; most often seen perched atop a small bush. Pounces to ground to feed; often returns to same perch. In summer, adult has brown upperparts, heavily streaked black; white flash in closed wing. Prominent, creamy white eyebrow; dark ear coverts. Underparts pale creamy orange. In flight, shows white patch on inner wing and white patches either side of tail. Female more subdued version of male. *Status:* summer visitor April–Sept. Passage migrant.

S*imilar Species:* closely related Stonechat (p.188) lacks prominent eyebrow in all plumages.

J	F	M	A	M	J	J	A	S	O	N	D
0	0	0	2	4	4	4	4	4	2	0	0

187

Stonechat *Saxicola torquata*

black head, white half collar

grey brown head

♂

white rump

♀

Widespread chat, present throughout year; prefers gorse habitats. Perches prominently on tops of bushes and pounces to ground. Flies low, showing greyish white rump and white patches on wings. In summer, male has black head bordered by prominent white half collar. Back and wings dark brown, streaked black; tail dark brown. Breast orange-red. Female much paler than male with dark, not black, head. Eastern sub-species paler and greyer with little colour on breast.
Status: resident and winter visitor.
Similar Species:
Whinchat (p.187) is summer visitor, has prominent eyebrow and creamy, not reddish, breast.

STONECHAT

Type	chat-like
Size	12–13cm (4¾–5in)
Habitat	heaths, grassland
Behaviour	perches, hops, takes off and lands on ground
Flocking	solitary
Flight	direct; flitting
Voice	metallic *chak-chak* also jingling warble

IDENTIFICATION

Adult ♂	
Crown	black
Upperparts	dark brown, streaked black; white wing patches
Rump	greyish white
Tail	dark brown; medium length
Throat	black, white half collar
Breast	orange-red
Belly	white
Bill	black; short and pointed
Legs	black; medium length
Adult ♀	paler, orange-buff breast; lacks black head

BREEDING

Nest	cup at base of bush
Eggs	5–6; pale blue, lightly-speckled brown
Incubation	14-15 days ♀
Young	helpless; downy
Fledging	12–13 days
Broods	2–3; Apr–June
Food	insects, worms
Population	30,000–60,000 pairs

J	F	M	A	M	J	J	A	S	O	N	D
2	2	3	4	4	4	4	4	4	3	3	2

Oenanthe oenanthe **Northern Wheatear**

black wings

white rump and outer tail

grey crown and back

black mask

♂

pale eyebrow
dark ear coverts

hint of mask

♀

juvenile

Widespread summer visitor to open country; seldom perches higher than rock or fence post. Typical upright position with sudden darting movements; frequently 'bobs'. In flight, white rump and tail pattern distinctive. Adult male has grey crown and back with black 'mask'. Wings black; underparts creamy buff. Adult female grey-brown above with only hint of face mask. Juvenile has sandy crown and back with pale margins to dark wing feathers; only hint of mask. Greenland sub-species *O.o.leucorrhoa* larger with longer wings. *Status:* common summer visitor March–October; passage migrant. *Similar Species:* Three rare wheatears all have browner wings and different rump-tail patterns.

NORTHERN WHEATEAR

Type	chat-like
Size	14–15.5cm (5½–6in)
Habitat	moors, heaths, beaches
Behaviour	hops, perches openly, takes off from ground
Flocking	solitary
Flight	hovers; strong and powerful; direct; flitting
Voice	harsh *chak-chak*; brief warble

IDENTIFICATION

Adult ♂	
Crown	grey
Upperparts	grey; wings black
Rump	white
Tail	white with black tip; medium length, square
Throat	creamy buff
Breast	creamy buff
Belly	creamy buff
Bill	black; short and pointed
Legs	black; medium length
Ad. ♀ and juv.	browner above; hint of face mask

BREEDING

Nest	untidy cup in hole in rocks or bank
Eggs	5–6; pale blue, unmarked
Incubation	14 days, mainly ♀
Young	helpless; downy
Fledging	15 days
Broods	1–2; Apr–May
Food	insects
Population	c50,000–100,000 pairs

J	F	M	A	M	J	J	A	S	O	N	D
0	4	4	4	4	4	4	4	4	4	3	0	0

Ring Ouzel *Turdus torquatus*

silvery wings

white crescent

♂

♀

S ummer visitor to mountains and moorlands with screes and rocky outcrops. Behaviour much as Blackbird but much less confiding. Flies swift and low showing silvery wings. On passage, often skulks in dense cover. In summer, male black with brownish wash; distinctive white crescent across breast. Silvery wing margins form obvious pale panel on folded wing. In winter, male browner with scaly markings. Adult female like winter male. Juvenile with pale edges to wing feathers. *Status:* widespread summer visitor to north and west. Scarce passage migrant March-November. *Similar Species:* Blackbird (p.191) lacks white crescent and silver wings.

J	F	M	A	M	J	J	A	S	O	N	D
0	0	0	3	3	3	3	3	3	3	2	0	0

RING OUZEL

Type	thrush-like
Size	23–25cm (9–10in)
Habitat	mountains and moorlands
Behaviour	hops, runs, perches openly, takes off and lands on vegetation or ground
Flocking	solitary, small flocks
Flight	strong and powerful; direct
Voice	harsh *chak-chak*; also a loud *peu-u peu-u*

IDENTIFICATION

Adult ♂	
Crown	black-brown
Upperparts	black-brown; wings have silvery edges
Rump	black-brown
Tail	black-brown; medium length, square
Throat	black-brown
Breast	white crescent
Belly	black-brown
Bill	pale yellow; medium length
Legs	black, medium length
Adult ♀	subdued colours
Juvenile	scaley

BREEDING

Nest	cup on ground
Eggs	4–5; pale blue, blotched brown
Incubation	13–14 days ♂ ♀
Young	helpless, downy
Fledging	13–14 days
Broods	1–2; Apr–May
Food	worms, insects, berries
Population	8,000–16,000 pairs

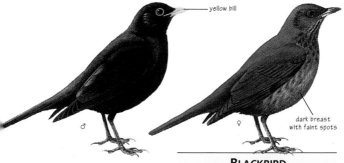

yellow bill

♂

dark breast
with faint spots

♀

BLACKBIRD

Type	thrush-like
Size	24–27cm (9½–11in)
Habitat	gardens, heaths, woods, hedges
Behaviour	perches openly, walks, hops
Flocking	1–15
Flight	strong and powerful; direct
Voice	loud harsh chatter of alarm; also a fluty warble

IDENTIFICATION

Adult ♂	
Crown	black
Upperparts	black
Rump	black
Tail	black; medium length
Throat	black
Breast	black
Belly	black
Bill	yellow; short and thin
Legs	black; medium length
Adult ♀	underparts mottled grey-brown or rufous brown; brownish bill

BREEDING

Nest	cup in tree or bush
Eggs	4–5; light blue, spotted red
Incubation	11–17 days ♀
Young	helpless; downy
Fledging	12–19 days
Broods	2–3; Mar–May
Food	insects, worms, berries
Population	7,000,000 pairs

O ne of the most familiar of British birds, common to woodlands, fields and gardens, as much at home in towns as countryside. All-black male has yellow bill and eye ring. Female browner, with subdued speckling on breast varying considerably from rufous brown to greyish brown. First winter males retain dark brown wing feathers; distinguishes from older, black-winged birds. Generally highly territorial, though Continental immigrants often arrive in large autumn flocks. *Status:* widespread and numerous resident; common passage migrant and winter visitor throughout Britain and Ireland.
Similar Species: Ring Ouzel (p.190).

J	F	M	A	M	J	J	A	S	O	N	D
6	6	6	6	6	6	6	6	6	6	6	6

Fieldfare *Turdus pilaris*

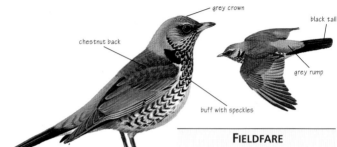

grey crown

chestnut back

black tail

grey rump

buff with speckles

L arge, typical thrush with densely speckled breast washed buffy yellow. Head, nape and rump dove-grey – latter particularly useful field mark in flight. Wings and back chestnut-brown; tail black. Pattern of head and face markings produces 'cross' expression. Generally gregarious, forming quite substantial flocks along hedgerows and in fields.
Status: scarce breeder in northern England and Scotland; abundant winter visitor throughout Britain and Ireland.
Similar Species: related Mistle and Song Thrush (pp.195, 193) and Redwing (p.194) have less densely speckled breasts and lack grey crown and rump.

FIELDFARE

Type	thrush-like
Size	24–27cm (9½–11in)
Habitat	heaths, woods, fields and hedges, gardens
Behaviour	perches openly, hops, walks, takes off from vegetation or ground
Flocking	1–100s
Voice	harsh *chak-chak*, normally in flight

IDENTIFICATION
Adult

Crown	dove-grey
Upperparts	chestnut-brown
Rump	dove-grey
Tail	black; medium length, notched
Throat	buffy yellow
Breast	buffy yellow, speckled black
Belly	white, speckled black
Bill	yellow; short and thin
Legs	black; medium length

BREEDING

Nest	cup in fork of tree
Eggs	5–6; pale blue, reddish markings
Incubation	11–14 days ♀
Young	helpless; downy
Fledging	12–16 days
Broods	1–2; Apr–June
Food	worms, insects, berries, fruit
Population	very rare breeder; 1,000,000 winter

J	F	M	A	M	J	J	A	S	O	N	D
5	5	5	3	3	2	2	2	2	2	3	4	5

Turdus philomelos **Song Thrush**

brown back

buff with speckles

N eat, medium-sized thrush found in woods, fields and gardens. Brown above; white neatly spotted with black below; creamy yellow wash on breast. Characteristic habit of repeating song phrase three or four times.
Status: widespread resident throughout Britain and Ireland; passage migrant and winter visitor.
Similar Species: can be confused with Redwing (p.194) in winter and Mistle Thrush (p.195) throughout year.

SONG THRUSH

Type	thrush-like
Size	22–24cm (8½–9½in)
Habitat	gardens, heaths, woods, fields
Behaviour	perches openly, hops, walks, takes off from vegetation or ground
Flocking	1–15
Flight	strong and powerful; direct
Voice	variety of repeated phrases; *chuk* alarm call

IDENTIFICATION

Adult	
Crown	brown
Upperparts	brown
Rump	brown
Tail	brown; medium length, square
Throat	creamy yellow, spotted black
Breast	white, spotted black
Bill	black; short and thin
Legs	pink; medium length

BREEDING

Nest	neat cup in tree or bush
Eggs	4–6; pale blue, speckled black
Incubation	11–15 days ♀
Young	helpless; downy
Fledging	12–16 days
Broods	2–3; Mar–June
Food	worms, snails, insects, berries
Population	1,000–3,500,000 pairs

J	F	M	A	M	J	J	A	S	O	N	D
6	6	6	6	6	6	6	6	6	6	6	6

193

Redwing *Turdus iliacus*

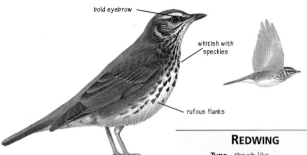

bold eyebrow

whitish with speckles

rufous flanks

Common winter visitor, forming flocks that roam through fields and hedgerows. Brown above, with brown ear coverts separating and accentuating bold eyebrow and double moustachial streak; face markings give distinctly 'cross' look. Whitish underparts spotted in clear streaks, with bold rust-red patch along flanks. Flight fast and direct like Song Thrush; unlike undulating flight of Mistle Thrush.

Status: widespread and abundant winter visitor; scarce breeder in northern Scotland.

Similar Species: smaller than Song and Mistle Thrushes (pp.193, 195), which lack rust-red on flanks and prominent face patterns.

REDWING

Type	thrush-like
Size	20–22cm (8–9in)
Habitat	gardens, heaths, woods, fields and hedges
Behaviour	perches openly, hops, walks, takes off from vegetation or ground
Flocking	1–100
Flight	strong and powerful; direct
Voice	soft *seeip* in flight

IDENTIFICATION

Adult	
Crown	brown
Upperparts	brown
Rump	brown
Tail	brown; medium length, square
Throat	whitish
Breast	whitish, streaked brown
Belly	whitish, streaked brown; rust-red flanks
Bill	black; short and thin
Legs	yellow; medium length

BREEDING

Nest	cup against tree trunk
Eggs	4–5; pale blue, speckled brownish
Incubation	11–15 days ♀
Young	helpless; downy
Fledging	10–15 days
Broods	2; Apr–June
Food	berries, worms, insects
Population	30–60 pairs; 1,000,000 winter

J	F	M	A	M	J	J	A	S	O	N	D
5	5	5	2	2	1	1	1	1	2	4	5

Turdus viscivorus **Mistle Thrush**

white tail margins

greyish-brown back

whitish with speckles

L argest of thrushes with distinctly greyer and paler appearance than Song Thrush. Upperparts buffy grey-brown with pale margins to flight feathers. Underparts white, heavily spotted black. In undulating flight, shows grey-brown rump and white corners to tail. Generally less gregarious than other thrushes; forms small, loose groups but seldom large flocks. Song similar to Blackbird but generally with faster delivery. *Status:* widespread resident. *Similar Species:* Song Thrush (p.193) is smaller and darker, has warm yellowish wash on breast and prominent eyebrow. See also Fieldfare (p.192).

MISTLE THRUSH

Type	thrush-like
Size	26–28cm (10–11in)
Habitat	gardens, heaths, woods, fields and hedges
Behaviour	perches openly, hops, walks, takes off from vegetation or ground
Flocking	1–15
Flight	strong and powerful; undulating
Voice	loud *tuk-tuk*; a dry, rattling chuckle, Blackbird-like, fluty song, but faster

IDENTIFICATION

Adult	
Crown	grey-brown
Upperparts	grey-brown
Rump	grey-brown
Tail	grey-brown, white corners; medium length, square
Throat	whitish, spotted black
Breast	whitish, spotted black
Belly	whitish, spotted black
Bill	black, short and thin
Legs	yellow; medium length
BREEDING	
Nest	cup in fork of tree
Eggs	4–5; blue, spotted reddish
Incubation	12–15 days ♀
Young	helpless; downy
Fledging	20 days
Broods	2; Mar–May
Food	berries, worms, insects
Population	300,000–600,000 pairs

J	F	M	A	M	J	J	A	S	O	N	D
5	5	5	5	5	5	5	5	5	5	5	5

195

Grasshopper Warbler *Locustella naevia*

streaked back

rounded tail

S ummer visitor to heaths, young conifer plantations, scrub and edges of reed beds. One of 'streaked-back' marshy warblers; upperparts buffy streaked with dark brown; short and inconspicuous pale eyebrow. Underparts buff with faint breast streaking. Most frequently observed at dawn or dusk when produces continuous reeling call – like rewinding of fishing reel.

Status: widespread summer visitor throughout Britain and Ireland.

Similar Species: Sedge Warbler (p.197) has more pronounced streaking above and bold creamy eyebrow.

GRASSHOPPER WARBLER

Type	warbler-like
Size	12–13cm (4½–5in)
Habitat	marshes, heaths, plantations
Behaviour	flits, takes off and lands on vegetation
Flocking	solitary
Flight	flitting
Voice	ventriloquial reeling
IDENTIFICATION	
Adult	
Crown	buffy brown, dark streaked
Upperparts	buffy brown, dark streaked
Rump	buffy brown, dark streaked
Tail	buffy brown; medium length, rounded
Throat	buff
Breast	buff, faint streaking
Belly	buff
Bill	black; short and thin
Legs	buff; medium length
BREEDING	
Nest	cup on or near ground
Eggs	6; white, speckled brownish
Incubation	13–15 days ♂♀
Young	helpless; downy
Fledging	10–12 days
Broods	2; May–June
Food	insects
Population	25,000 pairs

J	F	M	A	M	J	J	A	S	O	N	D
0	0	0	2	3	3	3	3	3	2	0	0

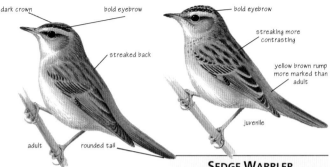

dark crown · bold eyebrow · bold eyebrow

streaking more contrasting

streaked back

yellow brown rump more marked than adult

juvenile

adult · rounded tail

Summer visitor to variety of wetland habitats including reed beds, bushy margins, ditches and dykes. Upperparts heavily streaked black on brown; streaked crown often quite dark, giving capped appearance. Broad, creamy eyebrow extends almost to nape; contrasts with narrow black eye stripe. Underparts buffy, especially on flanks. Often keeps well hidden among vegetation, but also perches openly. Has brief song flight.
Status: common and widespread summer visitor.
Similar Species: plumage similar to Grasshopper Warbler (p.196); Reed Warbler (p.198) has similar song but lacks melodic phrases; Marsh Warbler (p.199) is rarer and song much more melodic.

SEDGE WARBLER

Type	warbler-like
Size	12–13cm (4½–5in)
Habitat	freshwater and marshes
Behaviour	flits, takes off and lands on vegetation
Flocking	solitary
Flight	flitting
Voice	harsh grating notes mixed with melodic phrases and mimicry

IDENTIFICATION

Adult	
Crown	brown, streaked black
Upperparts	brown, streaked black
Rump	yellow-brown
Tail	brown, streaked black
Throat	buffy white
Breast	buffy white
Belly	white
Bill	black; short and thin
Legs	grey; medium length
Juvenile	yellower rump
BREEDING	
Nest	cup in vegetation, on or near ground
Eggs	5–6; pale green, speckled
Incubation	13–14 days, mainly ♀
Young	helpless; naked
Fledging	10–12 days
Broods	1; May–June
Food	insects
Population	c300,000 pairs

J	F	M	A	M	J	J	A	S	O	N	D
0	0	0	4	5	5	5	5	5	4	0	0

Reed Warbler *Acrocephalus scirpaceus*

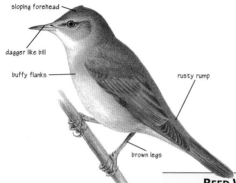

sloping forehead

dagger like bill

buffy flanks

rusty rump

brown legs

S ummer visitor to reed beds and other waterside vegetation. Tends to skulk in deep cover but will perch on reed-tops, especially while singing. Upperparts warm brown, with distinct rufous wash on rump. Underparts white with buffy flanks. Sloping forehead reaches peak at top of crown, accentuating length of bill.
Status: common summer visitor, mainly to southern England.
Similar Species: call similar to Sedge Warbler (p.197); plumage very similar to Marsh Warbler (p.199).

REED WARBLER

Type	warbler-like
Size	12–13cm (4½–5in)
Habitat	inland freshwater and marshes
Behaviour	flits, takes off and lands on vegetation
Flocking	solitary
Flight	flitting
Voice	series of harsh, grating notes – *jag-jag, chirrug-chirrug*

IDENTIFICATION

Adult	
Crown	brown
Upperparts	brown
Rump	rufous brown
Tail	brown; medium length, rounded
Throat	white
Breast	whitish
Belly	whitish, flanks buff
Bill	brown; short and thin
Legs	grey-brown, medium length
BREEDING	
Nest	deep cup in reeds
Eggs	4; pale green, spotted olive
Incubation	11–12 days ♂♀
Young	helpless; naked
Broods	1; Apr–June
Food	insects
Population	40,000–80,000 pairs

J	F	M	A	M	J	J	A	S	O	N	D
0	0	0	3	5	5	5	5	4	2	0	0

steep forehead

paler eyebrow than Reed

shorter bill

pale tips to tertials

uniform underparts

longer wings than Reed

pale legs

U ncommon and extremely elusive summer visitor to southern England. Uniform olive-brown upperparts and buff and white underparts. Very similar to more widespread Reed Warbler, but generally more olive above and whiter below, with flatter crown and slightly longer wings. Prefers areas of willows and rushes near water to stands of pure reed. Best identified by song – a remarkable mimic; harsher notes reminiscent of Greenfinch *Status:* breeds regularly only in West Midlands and south-east; elsewhere rare passage migrant.
Similar Species: Reed Warbler (p.198) as above.

MARSH WARBLER

Type	warbler-like
Size	12–13cm (4½–5in)
Habitat	inland freshwater, marshes, fields
Behaviour	flits, takes off and lands on vegetation
Flocking	solitary
Flight	flitting
Voice	rich phrases, loud trills, harsh notes; mimic
IDENTIFICATION	
Adult	
Crown	olive-brown
Upperparts	olive-brown
Rump	olive-brown
Tail	olive-brown; medium length, rounded
Throat	white
Breast	buffy white
Belly	white, flanks creamy
Bill	brown; short and thin
Legs	pinkish; medium length
BREEDING	
Nest	cup in dense vegetation near ground
Eggs	4–5; pale blue
Incubation	12 days ♂♀
Young	helpless; naked
Fledging	10–14 days
Broods	1; May–June
Food	insects
Population	10–32 pairs

J	F	M	A	M	J	J	A	S	O	N	D
0	0	0	0	2	2	2	2	2	2	0	0

Dartford Warbler *Sylvia undata*

often cocked

grey crown

pinker than ♂

very long tail

vinous brown

♂

♀

Tiny, elusive warbler generally well hidden in thick cover of dense stands of gorse and heather; most easily seen while singing in early spring. Upperparts grey-brown, greyer on head; underparts dark vinous brown with sparse white flecking on throat. Outstanding feature is long tail; often cocked when perching. Juveniles browner above and buffy below. Flies on rounded, whirring wings with long tail trailing.
Status: scarce resident, confined to few heathland areas in southern England; suffers population crashes during severe winters.
Similar Species: no other warbler has long tail and dark underparts.

DARTFORD WARBLER

Type	warbler-like
Size	12–13cm (4¹/₂–5in)
Habitat	heaths
Behaviour	flits, takes off and lands on vegetation
Flocking	solitary
Flight	flitting; undulating
Voice	harsh *chur* or *tic*; also a scratchy warble

IDENTIFICATION

Adult ♂	
Crown	grey
Upperparts	grey-brown
Rump	grey-brown
Tail	black; long and rounded
Throat	vinous brown, white flecked
Breast	vinous brown
Belly	white
Bill	black; short and thin
Legs	yellow; medium length
Adult ♀	underparts pinker
Juvenile	browner above, buffy below

BREEDING

Nest	cup near ground in thick vegetation
Eggs	3–4; white, spotted reddish
Incubation	12–13 days, mainly ♀
Young	helpless; naked
Fledging	11–13 days
Broods	2–3; Apr–June
Food	insects
Population	100–700 pairs

J	F	M	A	M	J	J	A	S	O	N	D
2	2	2	2	2	2	2	2	2	2	2	2

short, thickish bill

plain face

greyish-brown

buffy

Compact summer visitor, virtually devoid of field marks. Upperparts greyish brown, underparts buffy white. Short, stubby bill is best identification feature. Frequents open deciduous and mixed woodland with plenty of undergrowth, as well as scrub, overgrown hedgerows and young plantations. Mostly skulks, even when singing.
Status: summer visitor to England, Wales, southern Scotland and central Ireland; double passage migrant.
Similar Species: nondescript appearance could confuse with variety of warblers; song similar to Blackcap (p.204), but more subdued and usually longer lasting.

GARDEN WARBLER

Type	warbler-like
Size	13–15cm (5–6in)
Habitat	gardens, heaths, woods, hedges
Behaviour	flits, takes off and lands on vegetation
Flocking	solitary
Flight	flitting
Voice	fine but quiet warbling

IDENTIFICATION

Adult	
Crown	grey-brown
Upperparts	grey-brown
Rump	grey-brown
Tail	brown; medium length, notched
Throat	buffy white
Breast	buffy white
Belly	buffy white
Bill	black; short and stubby
Legs	grey; medium length

BREEDING

Nest	cup in bush
Eggs	4–5; white, blotched brown
Incubation	11–12 days ♂ ♀
Young	helpless, naked
Fledging	9–10 days
Broods	2; May–June
Food	insects, berries
Population	60,000–100,000 pairs

J	F	M	A	M	J	J	A	S	O	N	D
0	0	0	3	4	4	4	4	4	2	1	0

Lesser Whitethroat *Sylvia curruca*

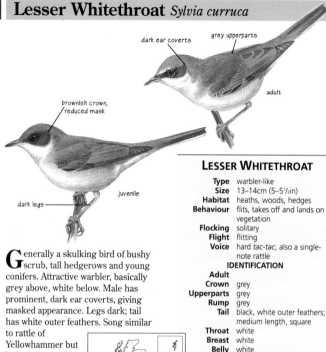

dark ear coverts

grey upperparts

adult

brownish crown, reduced mask

juvenile

dark legs

Generally a skulking bird of bushy scrub, tall hedgerows and young conifers. Attractive warbler, basically grey above, white below. Male has prominent, dark ear coverts, giving masked appearance. Legs dark; tail has white outer feathers. Song similar to rattle of Yellowhammer but lacking final flourish.

Status: summer visitor mostly to southern England; passage migrant especially to south and east coasts.

Similar Species: Common Whitethroat (p.203) is slightly larger, rusty brown above and pinkish below.

LESSER WHITETHROAT

Type	warbler-like
Size	13–14cm (5–5½in)
Habitat	heaths, woods, hedges
Behaviour	flits, takes off and lands on vegetation
Flocking	solitary
Flight	flitting
Voice	hard *tac-tac*; also a single-note rattle

IDENTIFICATION

Adult

Crown	grey
Upperparts	grey
Rump	grey
Tail	black, white outer feathers; medium length, square
Throat	white
Breast	white
Belly	white
Bill	black; short and thin
Legs	grey; medium length

BREEDING

Nest	neat cup in low bush
Eggs	4–6; white, blotched olive
Incubation	10–14 days ♂ ♀
Young	helpless; naked
Fledging	10–11 days
Broods	1–2?; May–June
Food	insects
Population	25,000–50,000 pairs

J	F	M	A	M	J	J	A	S	O	N	D
0	0	0	3	4	4	4	4	4	3	1	0

Sylvia communis **Common Whitethroat**

brownish crown

grey crown

prominent rusty wings

white throat

buffy legs

♂

♀

Summer visitor to heaths, commons, scrub and hedgerows. Marked by white throat; particularly obvious in singing male. Upperparts greyish brown; broad rusty margins to wing feathers immediately identify. Head grey in male, buffy brown in female and juvenile. Breast pinkish, belly white, legs pale. Though often skulks in dense cover, in spring will sit atop bushes to sing. Has short, dancing song flight.
Status: widespread summer visitor to all but Scottish Highlands; decline in 1970s and 1980s associated with extension of Sahara southwards into Sahel wintering grounds.
Similar Species: Lesser Whitethroat (p.202) differs in colour and size.

COMMON WHITETHROAT

Type	warbler-like
Size	13–15cm (5–6in)
Habitat	gardens, heaths, woods, hedges
Behaviour	flits, takes off and lands on vegetation
Flocking	solitary
Flight	undulating; flitting
Voice	hard *tac-tac;* song, a brief scratch warble

IDENTIFICATION

Adult ♂	
Crown	grey
Upperparts	greyish brown, wings brown with rusty margins
Rump	greyish brown
Tail	greyish brown; medium length, square
Throat	white
Breast	pinkish
Belly	white
Bill	buff short and thin
Legs	buff; medium length
Ad. ♀ and juv.	buffy brown head

BREEDING

Nest	cup near ground
Eggs	4–5; pale blue, speckled olive
Incubation	11–13 days ♂♀
Young	helpless; naked
Fledging	10–12 days
Broods	2; May–June
Food	insects, berries
Population	500,000–700,000 pairs

J	F	M	A	M	J	J	A	S	O	N	D
0	0	0	4	5	5	5	5	5	1	0	0

Blackcap *Sylvia atricapilla*

black cap

grey back

rust cap

♀

♂

BLACKCAP

Type	warbler-like
Size	13–15cm (5–6in)
Habitat	gardens, heaths, woods, hedges
Behaviour	flits, takes off and lands on vegetation
Flocking	solitary
Flight	flitting
Voice	a varied warble

IDENTIFICATION

Adult ♂	
Crown	sooty black cap
Upperparts	grey
Rump	grey
Tail	grey; medium length, notched
Throat	greyish white
Breast	greyish white
Belly	white
Bill	black; short and thin
Legs	black; medium length
Adult♀	rusty cap; browner above, buffy below

BREEDING

Nest	cup in bush or tree
Eggs	5; white, blotched reddish
Incubation	12–13 days ♂♀
Young	helpless, naked
Fledging	10–14 days
Broods	2; May–June
Food	insects, berries
Population	c200,000 pairs; 3000 winter

Best known for its delightful song, which some compare to Nightingale; has greater variety of notes and phrases than Garden Warbler. Male has sooty black cap and grey back; greyish white below. Female has rusty cap; browner above and buffy below. Frequents open deciduous or mixed woodland with well-developed undergrowth; generally hides among vegetation.
Status: widespread summer visitor, except to extreme north and west; passage migrant; scarce winter visitor to southern England and south-eastern Ireland.
Similar Species: male could be confused with Marsh Tit (p.214) and Willow Tit (p.215) but is larger and slimmer.

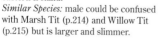

J	F	M	A	M	J	J	A	S	O	N	D
1	1	2	5	5	5	5	5	4	3	1	1

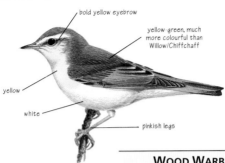

- bold yellow eyebrow
- yellow-green, much more colourful than Willow/Chiffchaff
- yellow
- white
- pinkish legs

S ummer visitor to dense deciduous
woods with scant undergrowth.
Larger than closely related Willow
Warbler, but greener above, with more
yellow on wing and head, and pure white
below. Pronounced yellowish eyebrow
with dark eye stripe. Legs pale. Song
flight on fluttering wings below tree
canopy quite distinctive.
Status: summer visitor; more numerous
in west than east, though almost absent
from Ireland;
decidedly scarce
on migration.
Similar Species:
Chiffchaff (p.206)
and especially
Willow Warbler
(p.207) can be quite
yellow, particularly
in first winter
plumage; neither are white on breast
and belly, or green above.

WOOD WARBLER

Type	warbler-like
Size	12–13cm (4½–5in)
Habitat	heaths, woods
Behaviour	flits, takes off and lands on vegetation
Flocking	solitary
Flight	flitting
Voice	*peu;* flight song starts *peu-peu,* accelerates into rapid trill

IDENTIFICATION

Adult	
Crown	greeny yellow
Upperparts	greeny yellow
Rump	greeny yellow
Tail	greeny yellow; medium length, notched
Throat	yellow
Breast	yellow
Belly	white
Bill	black; short and thin
Legs	pinkish; medium length
BREEDING	
Nest	dome on ground
Eggs	6–7; white, speckled reddish
Incubation	13 days ♀
Young	helpless; downy
Fledging	11–12 days
Broods	1; May–June
Food	insects
Population	30,000–60,000 pairs

J	F	M	A	M	J	J	A	S	O	N	D
0	0	0	2	4	4	4	4	1	0	0	0

205

Chiffchaff *Phylloscopus collybita*

short, less marked eyebrow than Willow Warbler

autumn

yellowish

adult spring

buffy white

dark legs

Widespread summer visitor; named after its characteristic call. Inhabits open woodland but occurs in gardens and scrub on passage. Olive-brown above, dull buffy white below. Eyebrow and eye stripe less distinct than very similar Willow Warbler. Always appears as less well marked and less clean-cut version of Willow Warbler, with shorter eyebrow and (usually) dark legs. Active little bird; flits about foliage in non-stop feeding. Sometimes feeds on ground; continuously flicks wings.
Status: common summer visitor; passage migrant; winter visitor to south-west England.
Similar Species: Willow Warbler (p.207) and Wood Warbler (p.205).

CHIFFCHAFF

Type	warbler-like
Size	10.5–11.5 cm (4–4¹⁄₂in)
Habitat	heaths, woods, hedges
Behaviour	flits, takes off and lands on vegetation
Flocking	solitary
Flight	flitting
Voice	distinct *chiff-chaff-chiff-chaff*, repeated; also *hueet*, especially on passage

IDENTIFICATION

Adult	
Crown	olive-brown
Upperparts	olive-brown
Rump	olive-brown
Tail	olive-brown; medium length, notched
Throat	buffy white
Breast	buffy white
Belly	buffy white
Bill	black; short and thin
Legs	black; medium length
Juvenile	yellower below
BREEDING	
Nest	dome on ground
Eggs	4–9; white, speckled purple
Incubation	13–14 days ♀
Young	helpless; downy
Fledging	12–15 days
Broods	1–2; Apr–May
Food	insects
Population	300,000 pairs; 300–1000 winter

J	F	M	A	M	J	J	A	S	O	N	D
1	1	2	5	6	6	6	5	4	4	3	1

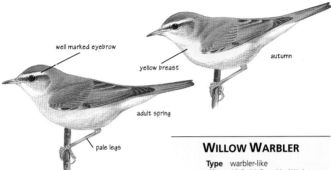

well marked eyebrow

yellow breast

autumn

adult spring

pale legs

Most common and widespread warbler; summer visitor to wide variety of wooded habitats, from forests to bushy commons. Very similar to Chiffchaff – olive-brown above; buffy yellow below. Clear eyebrow extends well beyond eye. Always cleaner-cut than Chiffchaff with pale (not dark) legs. *Status:* abundant and widespread summer visitor.
Similar Species:
Chiffchaff (p.206);
Wood Warbler
(p.205).

WILLOW WARBLER

Type	warbler-like
Size	10.5–11.5cm (4–4½in)
Habitat	heaths, woods, hedges
Behaviour	flits, takes off and lands on vegetation
Flocking	solitary
Flight	flitting
Voice	weak *hoo-eet*; also a descending warbled trill, repeated

IDENTIFICATION

Adult	
Crown	olive-brown
Upperparts	olive-brown
Rump	olive-brown
Tail	olive-brown; medium length, notched
Throat	buffy yellow
Breast	buffy yellow
Belly	buffy white
Bill	black; short and thin
Legs	pale brown; medium length
Juvenile	yellower below

BREEDING

Nest	dome on ground
Eggs	6–7; white, speckled
Incubation	13 days ♀
Young	helpless; downy
Fledging	13–16 days
Broods	1–2; Apr–June
Food	insects
Population	3,000,000 pairs

J	F	M	A	M	J	J	A	S	O	N	D
0	0	1	4	6	6	6	6	5	4	1	0	0

Goldcrest *Regulus regulus*

golden crest

♀

moustache

plain head

juvenile

plain face, no eyebrow, no eye stripe

olive-green

♂

Smallest British bird; tiny but decidedly rotund, with shortish tail. Crown has distinctive golden-orange blaze bordered by black. Face remarkably plain with large, dark eye and fine moustachial streak. Back olive-green; wings black with broad white margins and clear, single (sometimes double) wingbar. Underparts buffy white. Ever-active; flicks wings continuously during non-stop search for food among trees. Shows marked preference for conifers. In winter often associated with tit flocks.
Status: common and widespread resident.
Similar Species: closely related Firecrest (p.209) also has orange crown stripe bordered by black, but has distinctive face pattern.

GOLDCREST

Type	warbler-like
Size	8.5–9cm (3½in)
Habitat	gardens, heaths, woods
Behaviour	flits, takes off and lands on vegetation
Flocking	1–10
Flight	hovers; undulating; flitting
Voice	high-pitched *zi-zi-zi-zi*, repeated; song similar but ending in flourish

IDENTIFICATION

Adult	
Crown	golden blaze, bordered black; lacks eye stripe and eyebrow
Upperparts	olive-green; wings black with white margins, wingbar
Rump	olive-green
Tail	black; medium length, notched
Throat	white
Breast	buffy white
Belly	buffy white
Bill	black; short and thin
Legs	black; medium length

BREEDING

Nest	cup high in tree
Eggs	7–10; white, speckled brown
Incubation	14–17 days ♀
Young	helpless; downy
Fledging	16–21 days
Broods	2; Apr–May
Food	insects, spiders
Population	1,000,000–1,500,000 pairs; 3,000,000–5,000,000 wint.

J	F	M	A	M	J	J	A	S	O	N	D
5	5	5	5	5	5	5	5	5	5	5	5

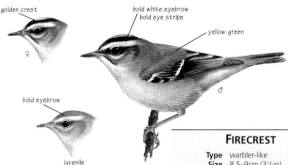

golden crest

♀

bold white eyebrow
bold eye stripe

yellow-green

♂

bold eyebrow

juvenile

Similar to Goldcrest with similar high-pitched call and active, non-stop search for food among conifers. Firecrest is much rarer. Greener on back with distinctive face pattern of bold white stripe. Easily identified if seen clearly. Different call and song; both stronger than Goldcrest, song often ends abruptly.
Status: rare breeding bird in south-east England (often overlooked). Scarce winter visitor to southern England; regular late autumn migrant.
Similar Species: Goldcrest (p.208).

FIRECREST

Type	warbler-like
Size	8.5–9cm (3½in)
Habitat	gardens, heaths, woods, hedges
Behaviour	flits, takes off and lands on vegetation
Flocking	1–2
Flight	hovers; undulating; flitting
Voice	*zit-zit-zit*; song similar, often ending abruptly

IDENTIFICATION

Adult Crown	golden blaze, bordered black; prominent eye stripe and eyebrow
Upperparts	yellow-green; wings black with white margins, wingbar
Rump	yellow-green
Tail	black; medium length, notched
Throat	white
Breast	white
Belly	white
Bill	black; short and thin
Legs	black; medium length

BREEDING

Nest	cup high in tree
Eggs	7–11; pale buffy, speckled brown
Incubation	14–15 days ♀
Young	helpless; downy
Fledging	19–20 days
Broods	2; May–June
Food	insects, spiders
Population	10–40 pairs; 200–400 winter

J	F	M	A	M	J	J	A	S	O	N	D
1	1	2	2	2	2	2	2	2	3	3	2	1

Spotted Flycatcher *Muscicapa striata*

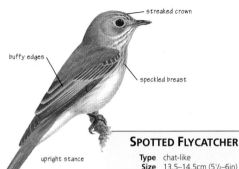

streaked crown

buffy edges

speckled breast

upright stance

M ost frequently seen perched upright on fence or twig, flying out to catch passing insects and returning to original or nearby perch. Agile flight on large wings; snap of bill audible at close range. Solitary or in pairs. Upperparts greyish brown; narrow, pale edges to inner flight feathers and wing coverts. Crown streaked brown and buff. Underparts white; buff-brown streaking on breast. Short, broad black bill. First winter birds differ only in having broader buff margins to wing feathers. *Status:* widespread summer visitor. *Similar Species:* female and first winter Pied Flycatcher (p.211) also brownish, but with extensive white wing.

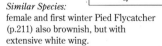

SPOTTED FLYCATCHER

Type	chat-like
Size	13.5–14.5cm (5½–6in)
Habitat	gardens, heaths, woods, hedges
Behaviour	perches openly, takes off and lands on vegetation
Flocking	1 or 2
Flight	strong and powerful; flitting
Voice	weak *tzee*
IDENTIFICATION	
Adult	
Crown	brown and buff
Upperparts	greyish brown; wings pale-edged
Rump	greyish brown
Tail	greyish brown; medium length, notched
Throat	buffy
Breast	white, streaked buff-brown
Belly	white
Bill	black; short and broad
Legs	black; short
BREEDING	
Nest	cup against wall or tree trunk, often near ground
Eggs	4–5; pale blue, blotched reddish
Incubation	11–15 days ♀
Young	helpless; downy
Fledging	12–14 days
Broods	1-2; May–June
Food	insects
Population	100,000–200,000 pairs

J	F	M	A	M	J	J	A	S	O	N	D
0	0	0	1	4	4	4	4	4	3	0	0

white forehead

white in wing

white in wing

♂

♀

cocked tail

S tout little bird with tiny bill. Like Spotted Flycatcher perches openly watching for passing insects, but returns to same perch less frequently. Summer male black above with white forehead and bold area of white in wing; underparts white. Female, winter male and first winter birds similar, but brown above with smaller white area in wing. Takes readily to nest boxes in open oak and birch woods.

Status: summer visitor to north and west Britain; passage migrant elsewhere, including eastern Ireland; sometimes numerous; usually regarded as important element of Scandinavian migration.

Similar Species: Spotted Flycatcher (p.210) has streaked breast.

PIED FLYCATCHER

Type	chat-like
Size	12–13cm (4½–5in)
Habitat	woods
Behaviour	perches openly, takes off and lands on vegetation
Flocking	solitary
Flight	strong and powerful; flitting
Voice	*whit* or *tic*; also a repeated *zee-chi* ending in flourish

IDENTIFICATION

Adult	
Crown	black and white
Upperparts	black, with white in wing
Rump	black
Tail	black, white outer feathers; medium length, square
Throat	white
Breast	white
Belly	white
Bill	black; tiny
Legs	black; short
Ad. ♀, winter ♂	
	brown above; less white in wing

BREEDING

Nest	cup in tree hole or nest box
Eggs	4–7; pale blue
Incubation	12–13 days ♀
Young	helpless; downy
Fledging	13–16 days
Broods	1; May–June
Food	insects
Population	20,000 pairs

J	F	M	A	M	J	J	A	S	O	N	D
0	0	0	3	4	4	4	4	4	4	2	0	0

Bearded Tit *Panurus biarmicus*

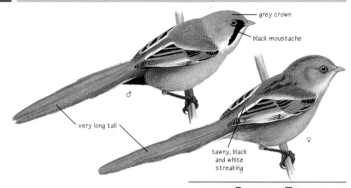

grey crown

black moustache

very long tail

tawny, black and white streaking

♂

♀

Small buff-brown bird with inordinately long tail. As alternative name Bearded Reedling implies, confined to extensive stands of reeds where most often seen flying low on short whirring wings, long tail streaming out behind. Also perches on reed-tops, especially in early mornings and during autumn. Male rich orange-brown above, with bold black and white margins to wings. Head blue-grey marked by droopy black moustache; both lacking in female. *Status:* highly local; breeders confined to reed beds in East Anglia and south-east England; irrupts across southern England in autumn. *Similar Species:* none.

BEARDED TIT

Type	tit-like
Size	16–17cm (6–6¹/₂in)
Habitat	reed beds
Behaviour	flits, takes off and lands on vegetation
Flocking	1–15
Flight	laboured; direct
Voice	loud *pting,* repeated in flight

IDENTIFICATION

Adult ♂	
Crown	blue-grey
Upperparts	orange-brown; black and white wing margins
Rump	orange-brown
Tail	orange-brown; long
Throat	white
Breast	orange-buff
Belly	orange-buff
Bill	yellow; short and thin
Legs	black; medium length
Adult ♀	head orange-brown

BREEDING

Nest	cup near ground, over water
Eggs	5–7; white, speckled brown
Incubation	12–13 days ♂ ♀
Young	helpless; naked
Fledging	9–12 days
Broods	2–3; Apr–May
Food	insects, seeds
Population	c600 pairs

J	F	M	A	M	J	J	A	S	O	N	D
2	2	2	2	2	2	2	2	2	2	2	2

bold eyebrow

northern
sub-species

pink

very long tail

juvenile

Small, active bird with tail longer than body – no other woodland bird has such a long tail. Crown white with bold black stripe over eye extending to black back; tiny black bill. Wing black and white with broad pink band across upper edge; tail black with white outer feathers. Underparts white with pink undertail coverts. Juveniles lack pink and have sooty black heads. Rare northern sub-species has all-white head. Usually found throughout year in small flocks up to twenty strong. Prefers hedgerows and woods with plentiful secondary growth, as well as bushy heaths and commons.
Status: widespread resident.
Similar Species: none.

J	F	M	A	M	J	J	A	S	O	N	D
4	4	4	4	4	4	4	4	4	4	4	4

LONG-TAILED TIT

Type	tit-like
Size	13.5–14.5cm (5¹⁄₂–6in)
Habitat	heaths, woods, gardens, hedges
Behaviour	flits, takes off and lands on vegetation
Flocking	1–15
Flight	laboured, flitting
Voice	continuous *zee-zee-zee* contact call among flock

IDENTIFICATION

Adult	
Crown	white, black eye stripe
Upperparts	black and white, wings pink-banded
Rump	black and white
Tail	black, white outer feathers; long and rounded
Throat	white
Breast	white
Belly	white, pink undertail
Bill	black; tiny
Legs	black; medium length
Juvenile	lacks pink; head sooty black

BREEDING

Nest	dome in bush
Eggs	8–12; white
Incubation	12–14 days, mainly ♀
Young	helpless; naked
Fledging	14–18 days
Broods	1–2; Mar–Apr
Food	insects, seeds
Population	50,000 pairs

Marsh Tit *Parus palustris*

glossy cap

small bib

Name misleading as haunts deciduous woods and hedgerows. Typical tit with round head, short bill, black cap and uniform buff-brown upperparts. Behaviour also typical – ever-active forager through tree canopy, often in company of related species. Great care needed to distinguish from very similar Willow Tit; Marsh Tit cap shiny (not dull), bib small (not large and diffuse); lacks pale panel in wing. Marsh Tit is neat and elegant little bird; Willow Tit decidedly scruffy. Calls quite different.
Status: widespread resident in England, Wales and southern Scotland.
Similar Species: Willow Tit (p.215) as above.

MARSH TIT

Type	tit-like
Size	11–12cm (4½–5in)
Habitat	heaths, woods, hedges, gardens
Behaviour	flits, takes off and lands on vegetation
Flocking	1–5
Flight	undulating; flitting
Voice	distinctive repeated *pitchoo-pitchoo-pitchoo*, also repeated *chip-chip*

IDENTIFICATION

Adult	
Crown	shiny black cap
Upperparts	buff-brown
Rump	buff-brown
Tail	buff-brown; medium length, notched
Throat	black bib
Breast	white
Belly	white
Bill	black; short and stubby
Legs	black; medium length
BREEDING	
Nest	cup in hole in rotten wood
Eggs	6–9; white, spotted reddish
Incubation	13–17 days ♀
Young	helpless; downy
Fledging	16–21 days
Broods	1–2; Apr–May
Food	insects, seeds
Population	50,000–110,000 pairs

J	F	M	A	M	J	J	A	S	O	N	D
4	4	4	4	4	4	4	4	4	4	4	4

dull, sooty cap

pale wing edges

large bib

WILLOW TIT

Type	tit-like
Size	11–12cm (4½–5in)
Habitat	heaths, woods, hedges, gardens
Behaviour	flits, takes off and lands on vegetation
Flocking	1–2
Flight	undulating; flitting
Voice	buzzing *erz-erz-erz*; also high-pitched *zi-zi-zi*

IDENTIFICATION

Adult	
Crown	dull black cap
Upperparts	buff-brown, pale wing edges
Rump	buff-brown
Tail	buff-brown; medium length, notched
Throat	black bib
Breast	white
Belly	white
Bill	black; short and stubby
Legs	black; medium length
BREEDING	
Nest	self-excavated cavity, thinly lined
Eggs	6–9; white, speckled reddish
Incubation	13–15 days ♀
Young	helpless; downy
Fledging	17–19 days
Broods	1; Apr–May
Food	insects, seeds
Population	50,000–100,000 pairs

V ery like closely related Marsh Tit and found in similar habitats, especially damp alder and birch woods. Somewhat ill-kempt appearance. Distinguished from Marsh Tit by dull black cap, larger white cheeks, larger and more diffuse black bib and (especially in winter) pale wing panel. In summer, must have dead rotting trees in which to excavate nest hole.

Status: widespread resident in England, Wales and southern Scotland.

Similar Species: Marsh Tit (p.214).

J	F	M	A	M	J	J	A	S	O	N	D
4	4	4	4	4	4	4	4	4	4	4	4

Crested Tit *Parus cristatus*

crest streaked

black line
surrounds face

Typically active, often associated with other tits but confined to areas of old Scots Pine with broken tree stumps and scattered birches. Grey-brown upperparts with prominent black and white streaked crest. Face white with clearly marked black eye stripe, black ear coverts. Underparts whitish.
Status: scarce, confined to central Scottish Highlands.
Similar Species:
only 'crested' tit.

CRESTED TIT

Type	tit-like
Size	11–12cm (4½–5in)
Habitat	forests and woods
Behaviour	flits, takes off and lands on vegetation
Flocking	1–15
Flight	undulating; flitting
Voice	trilled *chirr-chirr-rr*
IDENTIFICATION	
Adult	
Crown	black and white, crest
Upperparts	grey-brown
Rump	grey-brown
Tail	grey-brown; medium length, notched
Throat	black bib
Breast	whitish
Belly	whitish
Bill	black; short and stubby
Legs	black; medium length
BREEDING	
Nest	cup in excavated hole in old stump
Eggs	4–8; white, speckled purple
Incubation	13–18 days ♀
Young	helpless; downy
Fledging	17–21 days
Broods	1; Apr–May
Food	insects, seeds
Population	c900 pairs

J	F	M	A	M	J	J	A	S	O	N	D
3	3	3	3	3	3	3	3	3	3	3	3

white nape patch

grey back

bold double wingbar

COAL TIT

Type	tit-like
Size	10.5–11.5cm (4¹/₂in)
Habitat	woods, hedges, heaths, gardens
Behaviour	flits, takes off and lands on vegetation
Flocking	1–15
Flight	undulating; flitting
Voice	high-pitched *zee-zee-zee*; also a repeated *weecho-weecho-weecho*

IDENTIFICATION

Adult	
Crown	black, white nape
Upperparts	grey-blue, white wingbars
Rump	grey-blue
Tail	grey-blue; medium length, notched
Throat	black bib
Breast	greyish white
Belly	greyish white
Bill	black; short and stubby
Legs	black; medium length

BREEDING

Nest	cup in tree hole
Eggs	7–9; white, speckled reddish
Incubation	14–18 days ♀
Young	helpless; downy
Fledging	16–19 days
Broods	2; Apr–May
Food	insects, seeds
Population	1,000,000 pairs

Smallest tit, most often found among conifers, but also visits mature deciduous and mixed woodland, gardens and bird tables. Grey-blue above, with double white wingbar; underparts greyish white. Crown and substantial bib glossy black; white patch on nape distinguishes from other woodland tits. Gregarious, often associating with other tits, particularly outside breeding season. *Status:* widespread and common resident except in extreme northern and north-western isles. *Similar Species:* white nape patch unique. Call similar to Goldcrest (p.208); song to a similar phrase of Great Tit (p.219).

J	F	M	A	M	J	J	A	S	O	N	D
5	5	5	5	5	5	5	5	5	5	5	5

Blue Tit *Parus caeruleus*

greenish crown

blue crown

eyebrow and eye stripe

blue wings

juvenile

adult

Most common and familiar of tits; comes readily to bird tables and other feeders; will also occupy nest boxes and use bird baths. Wings pale blue with single white wingbar; back greenish. Underparts yellow with neat dividing line on centre of breast. White cheeks enclosed by dark line from eye to chin.
Status: abundant and widespread resident of Britain and Ireland.
Similar Species: Great Tit (p.219) larger with black cap and face pattern, and bold black line down breast.

BLUE TIT

Type	tit-like
Size	11–12cm (4½–5in)
Habitat	gardens, marshes, heaths, woods, hedges
Behaviour	flits, takes off and lands on vegetation
Flocking	1–30
Flight	undulating; flitting
Voice	*tsee-tsee-tsee;* also harsh *churr*

IDENTIFICATION

Adult	
Crown	pale blue
Upperparts	greenish, wings pale blue
Rump	greenish
Tail	blue; medium length, notched
Throat	blue bib
Breast	yellow
Belly	yellow, dark dividing line
Bill	black; short and stubby
Legs	black; medium length
Juvenile	crown greyish

BREEDING

Nest	cup in tree hole or nest box
Eggs	7–12; white, speckled reddish
Incubation	12–16 days ♀
Young	helpless; downy
Fledging	15–23 days
Broods	1; Apr–May
Food	insects, seeds, nuts
Population	4,500,000 pairs

J	F	M	A	M	J	J	A	S	O	N	D
6	6	6	6	6	6	6	6	6	6	6	6

black crown

white cheeks

greyish crown

bold belly stripe

yellow cheeks

juvenile

adult

GREAT TIT

Type	tit-like
Size	13.5–14.5cm (5½in)
Habitat	gardens, marshes, heaths, woods, hedges
Behaviour	flits, takes off and lands on vegetation
Flocking	1–30
Flight	undulating; flitting
Voice	*see-saw* and *teecha-teecha-teecha* most common

IDENTIFICATION

Adult	
Crown	black
Upperparts	green; wings pale blue, white outer feathers
Rump	pale blue
Tail	pale blue; medium length, notched
Throat	black bib
Breast	yellow; black centre stripe
Belly	yellow; black centre stripe
Bill	black; short and stubby
Legs	black; medium length
Juvenile	crown greyish black

BREEDING

Nest	cup in tree or nest box
Eggs	8–13; white, spotted reddish
Incubation	13–13 days ♀
Young	helpless; downy
Fledging	16–22 days
Broods	1; Mar–May
Food	insects, seeds
Population	3,030,000 pairs

L argest and most clearly marked of all the tits, with shiny black cap and bib joined by bold black line enclosing white cheeks; black stripe down yellow bib and belly (wider in male than female). Back green, wings and tail pale blue; latter with white outer feathers. Common in all types of woods, including pure conifer stands where often most abundant bird. Comes readily to gardens where aggressive at feeders. Joins mixed tit flocks outside breeding season. Has wide variety of calls and songs – fifty-seven distinct forms described.
Status: common and widespread resident.
Similar Species: Blue Tit (p.218) is much smaller and has fainter belly line.

J	F	M	A	M	J	J	A	S	O	N	D
6	6	6	6	6	6	6	6	6	6	6	6

European Nuthatch *Sitta europaea*

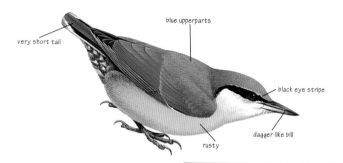

very short tail

blue upperparts

black eye stripe

dagger-like bill

rusty

A gile tree-climber, similar to woodpeckers but with ability to climb up and down trees. Does not undulate in flight like woodpecker. Upperparts pale blue with bold black eye stripe and black wingtips. Throat white; remaining underparts warm buff, with chestnut on flanks. Tail short and square. Produces sounds by hacking at nuts wedged in tree crevice with sharply pointed bill.
Status: widespread resident of England and Wales.
Similar Species: none.

EUROPEAN NUTHATCH

Type	woodpecker-like
Size	13.5–14.5cm (5½in)
Habitat	woods, hedges, heaths, gardens
Behaviour	climbs, takes off and lands on vegetation
Flocking	1–2
Flight	strong and powerful; direct
Voice	high-pitched *chwit-chwit*; also a repeated *kee-kee-kee*

IDENTIFICATION

Adult

Crown	pale blue
Upperparts	pale blue, black wingtips
Rump	pale blue
Tail	pale blue; short and square
Throat	white
Breast	warm buff
Belly	warm buff
Bill	black; short and thin
Legs	buff; medium length

BREEDING

Nest	tree hole, plastered mud
Eggs	6–9; white, spotted reddish
Incubation	14–18 days ♀
Young	helpless; downy
Fledging	23-25 days
Broods	1; Apr–May
Food	seeds, nuts, insects
Population	20,000 pairs

J	F	M	A	M	J	J	A	S	O	N	D
4	4	4	4	4	4	4	4	4	4	4	4

Certhia familiaris **Eurasian Treecreeper**

long decurved bill

streaked upperparts

white

pointed tail

EURASIAN TREECREEPER

Type	woodpecker-like
Size	12–13cm (4¹/₂–5in)
Habitat	woods, heaths, hedges, gardens
Behaviour	climbs, takes off and lands on vegetation
Flocking	solitary
Flight	undulating
Voice	Goldcrest-like *tsee-tsee*

IDENTIFICATION

Adult	
Crown	buff and brown, streaked
Upperparts	buff and brown, streaked
Rump	rusty brown
Tail	brown; medium length, pointed
Throat	white
Breast	white
Belly	white
Bill	black; long and thin, decurved
Legs	grey; medium length

BREEDING

Nest	cup behind bark
Eggs	6; white, speckled reddish
Incubation	14–15 days ♀
Young	helpless; downy
Fledging	14–16 days
Broods	1–2; Apr–June
Food	insects
Population	150,000–300,000 pairs

S mall tree-climber that uses long, decurved bill to search bark for food. Well camouflaged and easily overlooked; streaked brown and buff above with rusty rump. White eyebrow; double wingbar; tail feathers have protruding shafts. Underparts white. Frequently shy, climbing out of view of watcher; call often attracts attention. Joins mixed tit flocks in winter.
Status: widespread resident of Britain and Ireland.
Similar Species: none.

J	F	M	A	M	J	J	A	S	O	N	D
4	4	4	4	4	4	4	4	4	4	4	4

Red-backed Shrike *Lanius collurio*

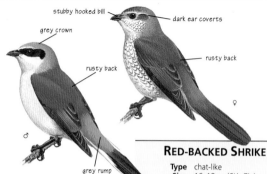

stubby hooked bill

grey crown

rusty back

dark ear coverts

rusty back

♀

grey rump

♂

F ast-declining summer visitor to
open heaths in east England.
Spends much time sitting on top or side
of low bush waiting for prey – large
insects and small birds. Male has grey
crown and broad, black eye patch; back
rust-red; tail black with partially white
outer feathers; underparts white. Female
sandy brown above with dark mark
through eye and barred underparts;
outer tail feathers
white. Juvenile
similar to female,
but barred above as
well as below.
Status: scarce
summer visitor to
eastern England;
probably migrant
elsewhere.
Similar Species: Great Grey Shrike
(p.223) has grey and black plumage.

RED-BACKED SHRIKE

Type	chat-like
Size	16–18cm (6½–7in)
Habitat	heaths
Behaviour	perches openly, takes off and lands on vegetation
Flocking	solitary
Flight	direct
Voice	harsh *chak-chak*

IDENTIFICATION

Adult ♂	
Crown	grey
Upperparts	rest-red
Rump	grey
Tail	black and white; medium length, square
Throat	white
Breast	white
Belly	white
Bill	black; short and stubby
Legs	black; medium length
Adult ♀	lacks grey head and rump, paler brown above; barred underparts
Juvenile	as ♀ but heavily barred

BREEDING

Nest	cup in dense thicket
Eggs	5–6; highly variable, spotted shades of brown
Incubation	14–16 days ♀
Young	helpless; naked
Fledging	12–16 days
Broods	1; May–June
Food	insects, small birds
Population	1–4 pairs

J	F	M	A	M	J	J	A	S	O	N	D
0	0	0	0	2	2	2	2	2	0	0	0

grey back

black mask

black wings

long tail

Medium-sized, grey and black winter visitor, generally in small numbers. Crown, back and rump grey; wings and long tail black, marked with white patches. Bold black mask through eye. Underparts white. Often sits openly on top of bush or telegraph post, where glistening white breast visible at considerable distances. Like other shrikes, pounced on prey. Invariably solitary.
Status: scarce winter visitor to eastern Scotland and England.
Similar Species: Red-backed Shrike (p.222).

GREAT GREY SHRIKE

Type	chat-like
Size	23–25cm (9–10in)
Habitat	heaths, hedges
Behaviour	perches openly, takes off and lands on vegetation
Flocking	solitary
Flight	direct
Voice	harsh *chek-chek*
IDENTIFICATION	
Adult	
Crown	grey
Upperparts	grey, black wings with white patches
Rump	grey
Tail	black with white patches; long and rounded
Throat	white
Breast	white
Belly	white
Bill	black; short and stubby
Legs	black; medium length
BREEDING	
Nest	cup in bush
Eggs	5–7; white, spotted reddish
Incubation	15 days ♂, mainly ♀
Young	helpless; naked
Fledging	19–20 days
Broods	1; Apr–May
Food	birds, voles
Population	150+ winter

J	F	M	A	M	J	J	A	S	O	N	D
2	2	2	1	0	0	0	0	0	1	2	2

blue-black wings

long, rounded,
green-black tail

Large black and white crow, with distinctive long, wedge-shaped, green-glossed tail. Black head, breast and back; wings black with glossy blue wash and bold, white oval patches. Belly white. Mainly scavenger and robber, often seen in early morning picking at corpses along roads. Usually solitary or in small groups.
Status: widespread resident; has moved into city-centres in present century.
Similar Species: only large black and white bird of the countryside.

MAGPIE

Type	crow-like
Size	42–50cm (16½–20in)
Habitat	heaths, woods, hedges, gardens
Behaviour	perches openly, hops, takes off from vegetation or ground
Flocking	1–15
Flight	laboured; direct
Voice	harsh *chak-chak-chak*

IDENTIFICATION

Adult	
Crown	black
Upperparts	black, blue-black wings with white patches
Rump	black
Tail	green-black, long and wedge-shaped
Throat	black
Breast	black
Belly	white
Bill	black; short and thin
Legs	black; medium length

BREEDING

Nest	dome of twigs in bush or tree
Eggs	5–8; pale blue, blotched olive
Incubation	17–18 days ♀
Young	helpless, naked
Fledging	22–28 days
Broods	1; Apr–May
Food	nestlings, eggs, carrion, seeds, insects
Population	250,000+ pairs

J	F	M	A	M	J	J	A	S	O	N	D
6	6	6	6	6	6	6	6	6	6	6	6

decurved red bill

square wingtips with fingers

square tail

red legs

B lack, crow-like bird with thin, decurved, red bill and red legs. Wings broad and square, with deep fingering at tips. Found only along cliff-lined shores and in mountain gorges and quarries, where masterful flight involves diving, soaring and aerobatics. Gregarious, forming flocks where numbers sufficient.
Status: scarce and highly localized resident in Islay, Scotland and west Wales and Ireland.
Similar Species: Jackdaw (p.226) is similar size and colour and shares habitat and behaviour, but wings more rounded and lacks red bill and legs.

RED-BILLED CHOUGH

Type	crow-like
Size	36–41cm (14–16in)
Habitat	moors, sea cliffs
Behaviour	walks, perches openly, takes off and lands on ground
Flocking	1–15
Flight	soars, glides, aerial dive; strong and powerful
Voice	ringing *keear*, repeated

IDENTIFICATION

Adult	
Crown	black
Upperparts	black; wingtips deep-fingered
Rump	black
Tail	black; medium length, square
Throat	black
Breast	black
Belly	black
Bill	red; decurved, long and thin
Legs	red; medium length

BREEDING

Nest	cup on ledge in cave or crevice
Eggs	3–4; pale green, blotched brown
Incubation	17–23 days ♀
Young	helpless; downy
Fledging	38 days
Broods	1; Apr–May
Food	insects, worms, seeds
Population	c1000 pairs

J	F	M	A	M	J	J	A	S	O	N	D
2	2	2	2	2	2	2	2	2	2	2	2

Jackdaw *Corvus monedula*

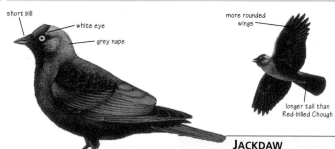

short bill

white eye

grey nape

more rounded wings

longer tail than Red-billed Chough

Smallest crow; typical black plumage broken by grey nape, often not visible at distance. Short, stubby bill distinguishes from Crow and Rook. Gregarious, forming flocks in wide variety of habitats. Performs aerobatics (like much rarer and more localized Red-billed Chough) along cliff-lined shores, gorges and, in towns, cathedrals, and so on. Feeds mostly on farmland, often in company with Rooks.

Status: widespread and common resident of Britain and Ireland.

Similar Species: Rook (p.227) and Carrion Crow (p.228) are bigger with larger bills; Red-billed Chough (p.225) is rare, with red bill and legs.

JACKDAW

Type	crow-like
Size	32–34cm (12½–13½in)
Habitat	towns, heaths, sea cliffs, woods, hedges
Behaviour	walks, takes off from vegetation or ground
Flocking	1–200
Flight	soars, glides, aerial dive; laboured; direct
Voice	high-pitched *kya*; distinctive *chak*

IDENTIFICATION

Adult	
Crown	black, grey nape
Upperparts	black
Rump	black
Tail	black; medium length, square
Throat	black
Breast	black
Belly	black
Bill	black; short and stubby
Legs	black; medium length
BREEDING	
Nest	tree or cliff hole; also holes in buildings, chimneys
Eggs	4–6; pale blue, spotted brown
Incubation	17–18 days ♀
Young	helpless; downy
Fledging	28–32 days
Broods	1; Apr–May
Food	worms, nestlings, eggs, small mammals, grain
Population	c500,000 pairs

J	F	M	A	M	J	J	A	S	O	N	D
6	6	6	6	6	6	6	6	6	6	6	6

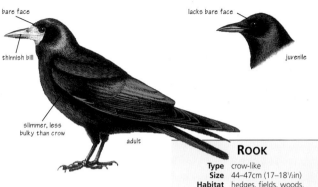

bare face

thinnish bill

slimmer, less bulky than crow

adult

lacks bare face

juvenile

H ighly gregarious crow, forming large flocks, roosts, and colonial nesting groups, called rookeries, in tall clumps of tress. Crown has distinct peak above eye. Bare skin around base of bill main distinguishing feature; absent in juvenile. Similar to Carrion Crow, but slimmer and more angular, especially in flight. Feeds mostly on arable land, taking more pests than crops.
Status: widespread and common resident, but more numerous in east than west.
Similar Species: Carrion Crow (p.228) as above.

ROOK

Type	crow-like
Size	44–47cm (17–18¹/₂in)
Habitat	hedges, fields, woods, heaths
Behaviour	perches openly, hops, walks, takes off from vegetation or ground
Flocking	1–200
Flight	laboured; direct
Voice	cawing *kaah*

IDENTIFICATION

Adult	
Crown	black
Upperparts	black
Rump	black
Tail	black; medium length, square
Throat	black
Breast	black
Belly	black
Bill	grey; short and thin
Legs	black; medium length
Juvenile	lacks bare face patch

BREEDING

Nest	cup of twigs high in tree; colonial
Eggs	3–5; pale blue-green, blotched brown
Incubation	16–20 days ♀
Young	helpless; downy
Fledging	29–30 days
Broods	1; Mar–Apr
Food	worms, insects, seeds
Population	1,500,000 pairs

J	F	M	A	M	J	J	A	S	O	N	D
6	6	6	6	6	6	6	6	6	6	6	6

Carrion Crow *Corvus corone*

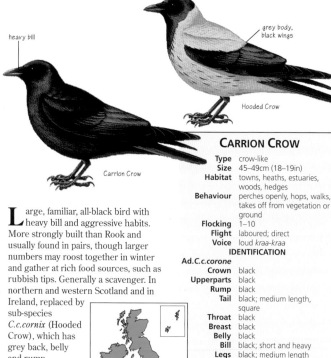

heavy bill

grey body, black wings

Hooded Crow

Carrion Crow

Large, familiar, all-black bird with heavy bill and aggressive habits. More strongly built than Rook and usually found in pairs, though larger numbers may roost together in winter and gather at rich food sources, such as rubbish tips. Generally a scavenger. In northern and western Scotland and in Ireland, replaced by sub-species *C.c.cornix* (Hooded Crow), which has grey back, belly and rump. *Status:* widespread in Britain and Ireland. *Similar Species:* Rook (p.227) and Common Raven (p.229).

CARRION CROW

Type	crow-like
Size	45–49cm (18–19in)
Habitat	towns, heaths, estuaries, woods, hedges
Behaviour	perches openly, hops, walks, takes off from vegetation or ground
Flocking	1–10
Flight	laboured; direct
Voice	loud *kraa-kraa*

IDENTIFICATION

Ad.*C.c.corone*

Crown	black
Upperparts	black
Rump	black
Tail	black; medium length, square
Throat	black
Breast	black
Belly	black
Bill	black; short and heavy
Legs	black; medium length

Ad.*C.c.cornix* grey back, belly and rump

BREEDING

Near	cup near top of tree
Eggs	4–6; greenish blue, speckled brown
Incubation	18–20 days ♀
Young	helpless; downy
Fledging	4–5 weeks
Broods	1; Mar–May
Food	carrion, birds, eggs, insects, worms, grain
Population	1,000,000 pairs

J	F	M	A	M	J	J	A	S	O	N	D
6	6	6	6	6	6	6	6	6	6	6	6

thick, heavy bill

beard

wedge-shaped tail

L argest crow, similar to Carrion Crow, but considerably bigger with more powerful head and bill, shaggy beard and large wedge-shaped tail. Found in mountainous and hilly areas, and along cliff-lined coasts; frequently soars like bird of prey. Mainly a scavenger, but also kills small birds and mammals.

Status: widespread in hilly districts of north and west.

Similar Species: Carrion Crow (p.228) smaller with less massive head and bill.

COMMON RAVEN

Type	crow-like
Size	60–67cm (23½–26½in)
Habitat	moors, heaths, sea cliffs
Behaviour	hops, walks, perches openly, takes off from vegetation or ground
Flocking	1–15
Flight	soars, glides; laboured; direct
Voice	hollow *pruk-pruk*

IDENTIFICATION

Adult

Crown	black
Upperparts	black
Rump	black
Tail	black; long and wedge-shaped
Throat	black, shaggy beard
Breast	black
Belly	black
Bill	black; short and heavy
Legs	black; medium length

BREEDING

Nest	large cup on ledge or fork in tree
Eggs	4–6; pale greenish blue, spotted brown
Incubation	20–21 days ♀
Young	helpless; downy
Fledging	5–6 weeks
Broods	1; Feb–Mar
Food	carrion, birds, mammals, eggs, snails, grain
Population	5000 pairs

J	F	M	A	M	J	J	A	S	O	N	D
5	5	5	5	5	5	5	5	5	5	5	5

229

Eurasian Jay *Garrulus glandarius*

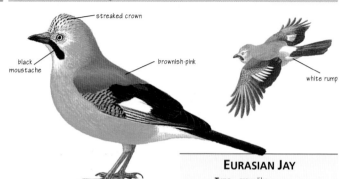

streaked crown

black moustache

brownish-pink

white rump

Large woodland bird with distinctive plumage, rounded wings and long tail. Crown streaked black and white; black moustachial streak. Back buff-brown; underparts pinkish buff. Wings and tail black; in flight shows bold white rump and white patches on inner wing. Small but distinctive blue and white barred patch on primary coverts. Generally secretive; presence often detected by harsh cries. Gregarious only in early spring. *Status:* widespread resident of wooded areas, except northern Scotland. *Similar Species:* none.

EURASIAN JAY

Type	crow-like
Size	33–36cm (13–14in)
Habitat	forests, hedges, heaths, gardens
Behaviour	perches openly, hops, flits, takes off from vegetation or ground
Flocking	1–10
Flight	laboured; direct
Voice	harsh *kaaa*

IDENTIFICATION

Adult	
Crown	black and white, streaked
Upperparts	buff-brown, black wings
Rump	white
Tail	black; medium length, square
Throat	white
Breast	pinkish buff
Belly	pinkish buff
Bill	black; short and thin
Legs	buff; medium length
BREEDING	
Nest	cup in tree fork
Eggs	5-7; pale green, speckled buff
Incubation	16–17 days ♂♀
Young	helpless; naked
Fledging	19–20 days
Broods	1; Apr–May
Food	nuts, nestlings, worms, insects
Population	100,000 pairs

J	F	M	A	M	J	J	A	S	O	N	D
5	5	5	5	5	5	5	5	5	5	5	5

yellow

glossy black

summer

grey brown

heavily speckled breast

winter

juvenile

COMMON STARLING

Type	unique
Size	20.5–22.5cm (8–9in)
Habitat	ubiquitous
Behaviour	flits, perches openly, walks, takes off from vegetation or ground
Flocking	1–100,000
Flight	strong and powerful; direct
Voice	variety of wheezing calls; much mimicry

IDENTIFICATION

Ad.summer	
Crown	black
Upperparts	black, wings tipped brown
Rump	black
Tail	black; short and square
Throat	black
Breast	black
Belly	black
Bill	yellow; short and thin
Legs	red; medium length
Ad.winter	head and underparts spotted white
Juvenile	grey-buff with white chin

BREEDING

Nest	untidy; in hole in tree, cliff, building, nest box
Eggs	5–7; pale blue
Incubation	12–15 days ♂ ♀
Young	helpless; downy
Fledging	20–22 days
Broods	1–2; Apr–May
Food	insects, seeds, fruit
Population	4,000,000–7,000,000 pairs

Noisy and aggressive bird; walks with a waddling swagger. Highly successful and abundant species; gregarious outside breeding season forming huge flocks, particularly at favoured roosts. Upperparts glossy black with brown margins to wing feathers. Head, back and underparts glossy black in summer; spotted white in winter. Bill yellow, legs red. Juveniles grey-buff with white chin. Pointed wings and short tail give characteristic flight silhouette. *Status:* abundant and widespread resident and winter visitor. *Similar Species:* none.

J	F	M	A	M	J	J	A	S	O	N	D
6	6	6	6	6	6	6	6	6	6	6	6

House Sparrow *Passer domesticus*

grey crown

large bib

pale eyebrow

♂

♀

Most familiar of British birds, found everywhere permanently inhabited by people. Male streaked brown and black above, with chocolate nape and grey crown; black bib widens out across breast. Female buffy and brown with streaked back, prominent pale eyebrow and double wingbar; lacks bib. Usually gregarious; forms huge post-harvest flocks in late summer. Nests in holes in houses, but also in bushes when these not available.
Status: widespread but declining resident.
Similar Species: Tree Sparrow (p.233).

HOUSE SPARROW

Type	sparrow-like
Size	14–15.5cm (5½–6in)
Habitat	ubiquitous
Behaviour	flits, perches openly, hops, takes off from vegetation or ground
Flocking	1–500
Flight	direct
Voice	*chirrup*; various twitters

IDENTIFICATION

Adult ♂	
Crown	grey
Upperparts	brown and black, streaked
Rump	grey
Tail	brown and black; medium length, notched
Throat	black bib
Breast	black and white
Belly	white
Bill	brown; short and stubby
Legs	pinkish; medium length
Ad. ♀ and juv.	buff and brown above; lack bib

BREEDING

Nest	dome in hole in building, sometimes tree; colonial
Eggs	3–5; grey, blotched black
Incubation	11–14 days, mainly ♀
Young	helpless; naked
Fledging	15 days
Broods	3; Apr–June
Food	seeds, insects, bread
Population	11,000,000–12,000,000 pairs

J	F	M	A	M	J	J	A	S	O	N	D
6	6	6	6	6	6	6	6	6	6	6	6

brown crown

white half collar

small neat bib

TREE SPARROW

Both sexes resemble male House
Sparrow, but slightly smaller with
upperparts more clearly streaked black
and brown. Crown chocolate-brown; tiny
black bib; black comma on white
cheeks. White half-collar visible at
considerable distance – best field mark.
Underparts white. Prefers parkland and
gardens, but often associates with flocks
of House Sparrows. Colonial nester,
often in boxes erected for tits.
Status: widespread resident, but
curiously absent
from some
western areas.
Similar Species:
House Sparrow
(p.232).

Type	sparrow-like
Size	13.5–14.5cm (5½–6in)
Habitat	gardens, heaths, woods, fields and hedges
Behaviour	flits, perches openly, hops, takes off from vegetation or ground
Flocking	1–15
Flight	direct
Voice	distinct *chup-chup;* also *tek-tek*

IDENTIFICATION

Adult	
Crown	chocolate-brown
Upperparts	brown and black; streaked
Rump	buff
Tail	brown; medium length, notched
Throat	black bib
Breast	white
Belly	white
Bill	black; short and stubby
Legs	red; medium length
BREEDING	
Nest	dome in tree hole, among rocks or against walls
Eggs	4–6; pale grey, spotted brown
Incubation	11–14 days ♂ ♀
Young	helpless; naked
Fledging	12–14 days
Broods	2–3; Apr–June
Food	seeds, insects
Population	250,000 pairs

J	F	M	A	M	J	J	A	S	O	N	D
4	4	4	4	4	4	4	4	4	4	4	4

233

Chaffinch *Fringilla coelebs*

buffy crown

blue-grey crown

creamy breast

broad wingbar

pinkish breast

♂

♀

Most common finch, found in wide variety of habitats. Often seen beside roads, where may fly up showing white outer tail feathers and bold, white, double wingbar (in both sexes). Male has blue-grey crown and pinkish breast. Female duller, in shades of buff. Forms large winter flocks.

Status: numerous and widespread resident; winter visitor.

Similar Species: female similar to female House Sparrow (p.232) but Chaffinch distinguished by bold, white, double wingbar.

CHAFFINCH

Type	finch-like
Size	14.5–16cm (5½–6¼in)
Habitat	gardens, heaths, woods, fields and hedges
Behaviour	flits, hops, perches openly, takes off from vegetation or ground
Flocking	1–200
Flight	undulating
Voice	loud *pink-pink;* delicate song ending in flourish

IDENTIFICATION

Adult ♂

Crown	blue-grey
Upperparts	brown, wings black and with
Rump	buff
Tail	black and white; medium length, notched
Throat	pinkish
Belly	pinkish
Breast	pinkish
Bill	blue-grey; short and stubby
Legs	brown; medium length
Adult ♀	buff-brown above; buffy cream below

BREEDING

Nest	neat cup in low vegetation
Eggs	4–5; pale blue, scrawled red
Incubation	11–13 days ♀
Young	helpless; downy
Fledging	12–15 days
Broods	1–2; Apr–May
Food	seeds, fruit
Population	7,000,000 pairs

J	F	M	A	M	J	J	A	S	O	N	D
6	6	6	6	6	6	6	6	6	6	6	6

black head and back with scaling

black crown and back

♂ summer

scaled black on buff

white rump

♀

bright orange breast

♂ winter

BRAMBLING

Type	finch-like
Size	14–15cm (5½–6in)
Habitat	heaths, woods, fields and hedges
Behaviour	flits, hops, takes off and lands on vegetation or ground
Flocking	1–100
Flight	undulating
Voice	hard *tswick* and *chik*

IDENTIFICATION

Ad. ♂ winter	
Crown	black and buff
Upperparts	black and buff
Rump	white
Tail	black; medium length
Throat	orange
Breast	orange
Belly	white
Bill	yellow; short and stubby
Legs	red; medium length
Ad. ♂ summer	
Crown	cap black
Adult ♀	paler than winter ♂

BREEDING

Nest	cup in pine tree, near trunk
Eggs	5–7; pale blue, blotched red
Incubation	11-12 days ♀
Young	helpless; downy
Fledging	11–13 days
Broods	1; May–June
Food	seeds, berries
Population	2–10 pairs breed; 50,000–2,000,000 winter

Similar and closely related to Chaffinch, often associating in winter flocks, where may be overlooked. Winter male has blackish upperparts, liberally edged buff on crown and back. Tail black; shows square white rump in flight. Breast bright orange; belly white. Buff margins lost in summer; head and back become pure black with broad orange band below. Female more heavily edged buff at all seasons.
Status: regular and numerous winter visitor, although more abundant in east; 2–10 pairs breed in north.
Similar Species: Chaffinch (p.234).

J	F	M	A	M	J	J	A	S	O	N	D
4	4	4	2	1	1	1	1	2	4	4	4

Greenfinch *Carduelis chloris*

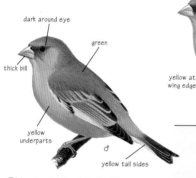

dark around eye

green

thick bill

yellow underparts

♂

yellow tail sides

yellow at wing edge

♀

C hunky, thick-set finch with substantial white bill. Male green above, with bold yellow margin to folded grey wing; yellowish below. Female paler and browner. In flight, shows yellow at base of primaries and incomplete yellow edges to tail. Largest and most common of green-yellow finches; found in range of habitats, but most at home in parkland and gardens.
Status: widespread and numerous resident of Britain and Ireland.
Similar Species: female similar to female House Sparrow (p.232) but Greenfinch has narrow yellow edge to folded wing.

GREENFINCH

Type	finch-like
Size	14–15cm (5½–6in)
Habitat	gardens, marshes, heaths, woods, hedges
Behaviour	flits, perches openly, hops, takes off from vegetation or ground
Flocking	1–100
Flight	undulating
Voice	nasal *skeer*, *chup-chup* flight call

IDENTIFICATION

Adult ♂	
Crown	green
Upperparts	green; grey wings yellow-edged
Rump	green
Tail	black; medium length, notched
Throat	yellowish
Breast	yellowish
Belly	yellowish
Bill	white; short and stubby
Legs	pink; medium length
Adult ♀	paler and browner

BREEDING

Nest	cup in bush
Eggs	4–6; pale blue, spotted black
Incubation	12-14 days ♀
Young	helpless; downy
Fledging	13–16 days
Broods	2–3; Apr–June
Food	seeds, berries
Population	1,000,000–1,750,000 pairs

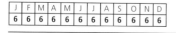

J	F	M	A	M	J	J	A	S	O	N	D
6	6	6	6	6	6	6	6	6	6	6	6

crimson face

lacks face pattern

juvenile

yellow wingbar

white rump

bright yellow in black wing

adult

A ttractive, easily identified finch with distinctive face pattern of crimson, white and black. Back warm brown; wings black with broad yellow band apparent both at rest and in flight. Shows bold white rump in flight. Feeds on teazles; prefers gardens and overgrown areas. Mostly gregarious.
Status: widespread resident except in north.
Similar Species: none.

GOLDFINCH

Type	finch-like
Size	11.5–12.5cm (4 ½in)
Habitat	gardens, heaths, woods, fields and hedges
Behaviour	flits, perches openly, hops, takes off from vegetation or ground
Flocking	1–100
Flight	undulating
Voice	sweet tinkling

IDENTIFICATION

Adult	
Crown	crimson, black and white
Upperparts	brown; wings black, yellow bars
Rump	white
Tail	black; medium length, notched
Throat	crimson
Breast	buff
Belly	white
Bill	white; short and stubby
Legs	buff; medium length
Juvenile	lacks head pattern; more buffy

BREEDING

Nest	cup in bush
Eggs	4–7; blue, spotted blackish
Incubation	12–14 days ♀
Young	helpless; downy
Fledging	13–16 days
Broods	2; Apr–May
Food	seeds
Population	300,000 pairs

J	F	M	A	M	J	J	A	S	O	N	D
6	6	6	6	6	6	6	6	6	6	6	6

237

Siskin *Carduelis spinus*

dark crown

bib

yellow

streaked flanks

♂

yellow tail patches

yellow in wing

♀

Small woodland finch found mostly near damp areas; has particular liking for alder. Male greenish above, yellowish below with streaked flanks. Crown black, forming distinct cap; small black bib. Wings black with bold yellow wingbars; yellow rump. Female much duller with yellow only in wings and tail; upperparts grey-green, underparts buffy with streaking above and below. Agile feeder, hanging upside down, tit-like, to extract seeds; comes to red-peanut feeding nets in late winter. *Status:* winter visitor; breeds in many parts of Britain and Ireland, especially north and west.
Similar Species: Greenfinch and Common Redpoll (pp.236 and 241).

SISKIN

Type	finch-like
Size	11.5–12.5cm (4³⁄₄in)
Habitat	woods, hedges, heaths, gardens
Behaviour	flits, perches openly, takes off and lands on vegetation
Flocking	1–50
Flight	undulating
Voice	*tsu, tsu-weet*, various twitterings

IDENTIFICATION

Adult ♂	
Crown	black cap
Upperparts	green; black wings, yellow wingbars
Rump	yellow
Tail	black and yellow; medium
Throat	black bib
Breast	yellow
Belly	white
Bill	white; short and stubby
Legs	brown; medium length
Adult ♀	greyish green above; buffy and streaked below

BREEDING

Nest	cup high in conifer
Eggs	3-5; pale blue, speckled reddish
Incubation	11–14 days ♀
Young	helpless; downy
Fledging	13–15 days
Broods	2; Apr–May
Food	seeds
Population	20,000–40,000 pairs; 150,000–500,000 winter

J	F	M	A	M	J	J	A	S	O	N	D
3	3	3	3	2	2	2	2	3	3	3	3

red forehead

white wing flashes

brown back

♀

white in tail

red breast

♂ summer

Small finch abundant in open areas, especially coastal marshes and shingle in winter. Summer male distinguished by red forehead and breast; grey head, brown back. Female lacks red; streaked above and below. Male loses red in winter. Both sexes show white in tail and wings in flight. Gregarious, often forming huge flocks, sometimes with smaller numbers of Twite.
Status: widespread and numerous resident.
Similar Species: Twite (p.240) very similar to female Linnet but much more heavily streaked.

LINNET

Type	finch-like
Size	13–14cm (5–5½in)
Habitat	heaths, estuaries, woods, hedges, gardens
Behaviour	flits, perches openly, hops, takes off from vegetation or ground
Flocking	1–500
Flight	undulating
Voice	high-pitched twittering in flight

IDENTIFICATION

Ad. ♂ summer	
Crown	red
Upperparts	brown
Rump	buff
Tail	black and white; medium
Throat	buff
Breast	red
Belly	buff
Bill	grey; short and stubby
Legs	grey; medium length
Ad. ♂ winter	lacks red
Adult ♀	lacks red; streaked

BREEDING

Nest	cup in bush
Eggs	4–6; pale blue, speckled reddish
Incubation	10–14 days ♀
Young	helpless; downy
Fledging	14–17 days
Broods	2–3; Apr–June
Food	seeds
Population	less than 1,000,000 pairs

J	F	M	A	M	J	J	A	S	O	N	D
6	6	6	6	6	6	6	6	6	6	6	6

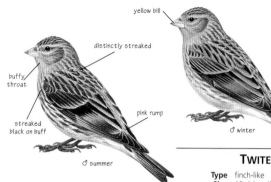

yellow bill

distinctly streaked

buffy throat

streaked black on buff

pink rump

♂ summer

♂ winter

Northern upland equivalent of Linnet. Regularly winters along coasts, often in association with large flocks of Linnets; shows similar markings in flight. In all seasons and plumages, Twite warm, buffy brown bird, heavily streaked black above and below. Linnet never as heavily streaked, even in juvenile plumage. Twite has pink rump but difficult to see. Juvenile and winter birds have yellow, not grey, bills.
Status: resident in northern and hilly areas; winter visitor to coast, except in south-west.
Similar Species:
Linnet (p.239) as above.

TWITE

Type	finch-like
Size	13–14cm (5–5¹/₂in)
Habitat	moors, estuaries, woods, fields, gardens
Behaviour	hops, perches openly, takes off and lands on ground
Flocking	1–500
Flight	undulating
Voice	similar to Linnet, but harder

IDENTIFICATION

Ad.summer

Crown	brown, streaked black
Upperparts	brown, streaked black
Rump	pink
Tail	black; medium length, notched
Throat	buff
Breast	buff, streaked black
Belly	white
Bill	grey; short and stubby
Legs	black; medium length

Ad.winter and juvenile

	bill yellow

BREEDING

Nest	cup on ground
Eggs	5–6; pale blue, speckled reddish
Incubation	12–13 days ♀
Young	helpless; downy
Fledging	15 days
Broods	1–2; Apr–May
Food	seeds
Population	100,000–150,000 pairs

J	F	M	A	M	J	J	A	S	O	N	D
3	3	3	3	4	4	4	4	3	3	3	3

red forehead

streaked back

tiny black bib

pink breast

♂ summer

♀

S mall, streaked finch; arboreal, hangs tit-like among trees when feeding. As name suggests, forehead red. Small black bib. Heavily streaked buff and brown above; lighter streaking below, confined to flanks in summer male. Best identified by buzzing flight note. Forms large flocks, particularly among conifers.

Status: widespread resident.

Similar Species: Siskin (p.238) similar size; also forms feeding flocks among tree-tops.

COMMON REDPOLL

Type	finch-like
Size	11.5–13cm (4½–5in)
Habitat	heaths, woods, hedges, gardens
Behaviour	flits, perches openly, takes off and lands on vegetation
Flocking	1–50
Flight	undulating
Voice	buzzing nasal trill in flight

IDENTIFICATION

Adult	
Crown	red
Upperparts	buff, streaked brown
Rump	buff, streaked brown
Tail	black; medium length, notched
Throat	black bib
Breast	pink, streaked buff
Belly	white
Bill	buff; short and stubby
Legs	black; medium length
Ad. ♂ summer	loses streaking below, apart from on flanks

BREEDING

Nest	cup in tree
Eggs	4–5; pale blue, speckled reddish
Incubation	10–13 days ♀
Young	helpless; downy
Fledging	11–14 days
Broods	1–2; Apr–June
Food	seeds
Population	300,000+ pairs

J	F	M	A	M	J	J	A	S	O	N	D
4	4	4	4	4	4	4	4	4	4	4	4

Common Crossbill *Loxia curvirostra*

chunky crossed bill

♂

♀

C hunky, thick-set finch with large head and substantial bill. Name derives from distinctive crossed mandibles, visible at close range. Male dirty reddish on crown and underparts; wings dark brown. Female grey-green with light streaking above and below. Large head and shortish tail useful in flight. Mostly gregarious. Regularly irrupts from the Continent; confined to mature conifers and now breeds in various parts of country when new plantations mature to provide food. *Status:* widespread but localized resident; irregular autumn and winter immigrant. *Similar Species:* Scottish Crossbill (p.243).

COMMON CROSSBILL

Type	finch-like
Size	16–17cm (6–6½in)
Habitat	forests
Behaviour	flits, perches openly, takes off and lands on vegetation
Flocking	1–15
Flight	undulating
Voice	distinctive *jip-jip*
IDENTIFICATION	
Adult ♂	
Crown	reddish
Upperparts	brown
Rump	reddish
Tail	black; medium length, notched
Throat	reddish
Breast	reddish
Belly	reddish
Bill	grey; short and stubby
Legs	black; medium length
Adult ♀	grey-green, lightly streaked
BREEDING	
Nest	twiggy cup high in conifer
Eggs	3–4; pale blue, spotted purple
Incubation	13–16 days ♀
Young	helpless; downy
Fledging	17–22 days
Broods	1; Jan–Apr
Food	pine seeds
Population	1000–2000 pairs

J	F	M	A	M	J	J	A	S	O	N	D
2	2	2	2	2	2	2	2	2	2	3	3	3

larger crossed bill than
Common Crossbill

♀

♂

A lmost identical to Common
Crossbill; recognized as separate
species (and Britain's sole endemic bird)
only in 1970s. Differs in larger bill and
habitat; restricted to old Caledonian
forests of Scottish Highlands.
Status: resident Scottish Highlands.
Similar Species: Common Crossbill
(p.242).

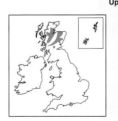

SCOTTISH CROSSBILL

Type	finch-like
Size	16–17cm (6–6¹/₂in)
Habitat	forests
Behaviour	flits, perches openly, takes off and lands on vegetation
Flocking	1–15
Flight	undulating
Voice	distinctive *jip-jip*, as Common Crossbill

IDENTIFICATION

Adult ♂	
Crown	reddish
Upperparts	brown
Rump	reddish
Tail	black; medium length, notched
Throat	reddish
Breast	reddish
Belly	reddish
Bill	grey; short and stubby
Legs	black; medium length
Adult ♀	grey-green, lightly streaked

BREEDING

Nest	twiggy cup high in conifer
Eggs	3–4; pale blue, spotted purple
Incubation	13–16 days ♀
Young	helpless; downy
Fledging	17–22 days
Broods	1; Jan–Apr
Food	pine seeds
Population	c750 pairs

J	F	M	A	M	J	J	A	S	O	N	D
2	2	2	2	2	2	2	2	2	2	2	2

243

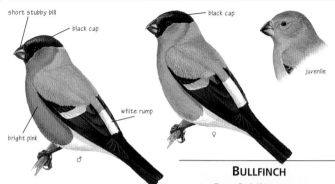

Bullfinch *Pyrrhula pyrrhula*

short stubby bill

black cap

black cap

juvenile

white rump

bright pink

♂

♀

Portly, buff-necked finch of gardens and hedgerows, most often seen singly or in pairs. Male has black crown with thick black conical bill and bright pink breast; upperparts blue-grey. Female similar but with pale buffy breast. Both sexes have black wings with broad white wingbar, black tail and square white rump.
Status: widespread resident.
Similar Species: none.

BULLFINCH

Type	finch-like
Size	14–15cm (5½–6in)
Habitat	gardens, heaths, woods, hedges
Behaviour	flits, perches openly, takes off and lands on vegetation
Flocking	1–2
Flight	undulating
Voice	soft *heu*

IDENTIFICATION

Adult ♂	
Crown	black
Upperparts	blue-grey
Rump	white
Tail	black; medium length, notched
Throat	bright pink with black bib
Breast	bright pink
Belly	bright pink
Bill	black; short and stubby
Legs	black; medium length
Adult ♀	buffy below

BREEDING

Nest	twig platform in bush
Eggs	4–5; pale blue, spotted purple
Incubation	12–14 days ♀
Young	helpless; downy
Fledging	12–18 days
Broods	1–2; Apr–May
Food	buds, seeds
Population	600,000 pairs

J	F	M	A	M	J	J	A	S	O	N	D
4	4	4	4	4	4	4	4	4	4	4	4

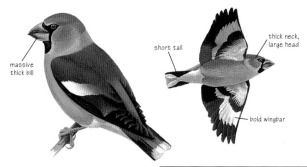

massive
thick bill

short tail

thick neck,
large head

bold wingbar

S tout finch with huge, thick, grey bill. Large head and bill, thick-set body and short tail obvious in flight; broad wingbars above and below diagnostic. Crown rufous, back brown, wings black, rump and underparts buff. Generally elusive and difficult to find; inhabits old woods and parks, often perching immobile for long periods. Forms communal roosts in winter.
Status: widespread resident; absent northern Scotland and Ireland.
Similar Species: none.

HAWFINCH

Type	finch-like
Size	16–17cm (6–6½in)
Habitat	woods, gardens, parks
Behaviour	flits, perches openly, takes off and lands on vegetation
Flocking	1–15
Flight	strong and powerful; direct
Voice	Robin-like *zic* or *tic*

IDENTIFICATION

Adult	
Crown	rufous
Upperparts	brown, wings black and white
Rump	buff
Tail	buff with white tip; short and notched
Throat	black bib
Breast	buff
Belly	buff
Bill	grey; short and stubby
Legs	red; medium length

BREEDING

Nest	twiggy cup in tree
Eggs	5; pale blue, spotted blackish
Incubation	9–14 days ♀, occasionally ♂
Young	helpless; downy
Fledging	10–14 days
Broods	1; Apr–May
Food	seeds, nuts
Population	5000–10,000 pairs

J	F	M	A	M	J	J	A	S	O	N	D
2	2	2	2	3	2	2	2	2	2	2	2

245

Lapland Bunting *Calcarius lapponicus*

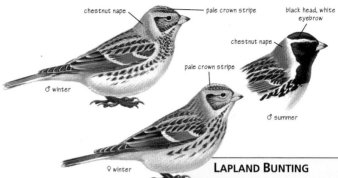

chestnut nape

pale crown stripe

black head, white eyebrow

chestnut nape

♂ winter

pale crown stripe

♂ summer

♀ winter

S carce, ground-dwelling bunting that
usually perches on large stone or
similar object. Summer male has black
head with rich chestnut nape and
prominent creamy eyebrow extending
behind eye. Back streaked black and
white; wings rufous; underparts white.
Female, juvenile and winter male similar
to female Reed Bunting and often found
in same areas; but with pale central
stripe on crown,
rusty wings and (in
male) rusty nape.
Status: scarce
winter visitor
mainly to low-lying
east coast; rare
breeder in Scotland.
Similar Species:
female, juvenile and
winter male similar to female Reed
Bunting (p.250).

LAPLAND BUNTING

Type	bunting-like
Size	14–16cm (5½–6½in)
Habitat	marshes, estuaries, moors
Behaviour	hops, perches openly, takes off and lands on ground
Flocking	strong and powerful; direct
Voice	rolling *rrrp*

IDENTIFICATION

Ad. ♀, ♂ winter

Crown	black and white with stripe
Upperparts	rusty and black, streaked
Rump	rusty and black, streaked
Tail	black and white; medium length, notched
Throat	white
Breast	streaked buff
Belly	white
Bill	yellow; short and stubby
Legs	black; medium length

Ad. ♂ summer

	black head with bold, creamy eyebrow

BREEDING

Nest	cup on ground
Eggs	5-6; greenish, mottled reddish
Incubation	10–14 days mainly ♀
Young	helpless; downy
Fledging	11–15 days
Broods	1; May–June
Food	seeds
Population	has bred; 200–500 winter

J	F	M	A	M	J	J	A	S	O	N	D
2	2	2	1	1	1	1	1	1	1	2	2

buffy marks on head

white in wing

white in tail

♂ winter

buffy marks on head

♀ winter

white head

♂ summer

Breeds on high mountain tops; winters along shorelines where forms large flocks. Flies like pieces of white paper blowing in wind. At all times shows much white in wing and tail. Summer male mainly white with black back; wings black and white. Female, juvenile and winter male have mottled upperparts and variable amount of streaking or buff on head. Feeds on shingle and among dunes, keeping low on ground. *Status:* scarce breeder in Scottish mountains; regular but local visitor to east coast. *Similar Species:* none.

SNOW BUNTING

Type	bunting-like
Size	16–17cm (6–6½in)
Habitat	moors, shorelines
Behaviour	hops, perches openly, takes off and lands on ground
Flocking	1–500
Flight	strong and powerful; direct; flitting
Voice	loud *tsweep*

IDENTIFICATION

Ad. ♂ summer

Crown	white
Upperparts	black and white
Rump	white
Tail	black and white; medium length, notched
Throat	white
Breast	white
Belly	white
Bill	black; short and stubby
Legs	black; medium length

Ad. ♂ winter

white below, mottled

Ad. ♀ and juv.

above; buffy head markings

BREEDING

Nest	cup on ground in rocks
Eggs	4–6; pale blue, spotted
Incubation	10–15 days ♀
Young	helpless; downy
Fledging	15–20 days
Broods	2; May–July
Food	seeds
Population	6–17 pairs; 10,000–15,000 winter

J	F	M	A	M	J	J	A	S	O	N	D
3	3	2	1	1	1	1	1	1	1	3	3	3

Yellowhammer *Emberiza citrinella*

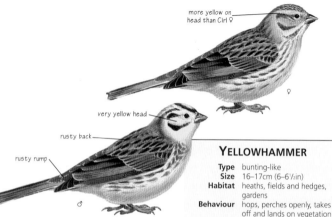

more yellow on head than Cirl ♀

♀

very yellow head

rusty back

rusty rump

♂

Yellow bunting most often seen perched on wire or top of bush. Male has bright yellow head and underparts, brown wings and prominent rusty rump. Female similar but with less yellow; more extensive and darker head markings. Generally solitary, but forms winter flocks. Prefers fields, hedgerows and heaths. *Status:* widespread resident. *Similar Species:* female could be confused with rarer female Cirl Bunting (p.249).

YELLOWHAMMER

Type	bunting-like
Size	16–17cm (6–6½in)
Habitat	heaths, fields and hedges, gardens
Behaviour	hops, perches openly, takes off and lands on vegetation or ground
Flocking	1–50
Flight	direct
Voice	familiar 'little-bit-of-bread-and-no-cheese'

IDENTIFICATION

Adult ♂	
Crown	yellow
Upperparts	rust-brown and black
Rump	rusty
Tail	black and white; medium length, notched
Throat	yellow
Breast	yellow
Belly	yellow
Bill	grey; short an stubby
Legs	buff; medium length
Adult ♀	less yellow, darker head markings

BREEDING

Nest	cup in low bush
Eggs	3–5; white, blotched purplish
Incubation	11–14 days ♀
Young	helpless; downy
Fledging	16 days
Broods	2–3; Apr-June
Food	seeds, berries
Population	1,000,000 pairs

J	F	M	A	M	J	J	A	S	O	N	D
5	5	5	5	5	5	5	5	5	5	5	5

black and pale yellow head

rusty back

black chin

buffy rather than yellow

♂

♀

Male distinguished by bold head pattern of black and pale yellow; greenish breast band, pale yellow underparts and rusty, streaked back. Female rufous buff above, creamy buff below – heavily streaked. Decidedly local and declining resident; inhabits bushy slopes, old hedgerows, parks and gardens – often near sea.
Status: scarce resident in south-west England.
Similar Species: female confusable with female Yellowhammer (p.248), but Cirl never yellow and lacks rusty rump.

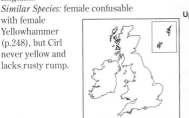

CIRL BUNTING

Type	bunting-like
Size	15.5–16.5cm (6–6½in)
Habitat	fields and hedges, heaths
Behaviour	perches openly, hops, takes off and lands on vegetation or ground
Flocking	1–2
Flight	direct
Voice	*sip*, also a quick rattle

IDENTIFICATION

Adult ♂	
Crown	black
Upperparts	rust and black
Rump	olive
Tail	rust and black; medium
Throat	black
Breast	pale yellow; greenish band
Belly	pale yellow
Bill	buff; short and stubby
Legs	buff; medium length
Adult ♀	streaked rufous buff above, creamy buff below

BREEDING

Nest	cup low among bushes
Eggs	3–4; white, speckled black
Incubation	11–13 days ♀
Young	helpless; downy
Fledging	11-13 days
Broods	2–3; May-June
Food	seeds, berries
Population	100–250 pairs

J	F	M	A	M	J	J	A	S	O	N	D
2	2	2	2	2	2	2	2	2	2	2	2

Reed Bunting *Emberiza schoeniclus*

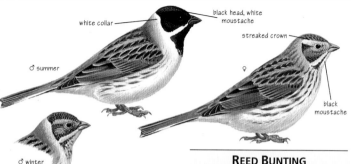

white collar

black head, white moustache

streaked crown

♂ summer

♀

black moustache

♂ winter

Common resident of marshland; has spread to drier habitats, including gardens. Male has black head marked by white moustache and collar; upperparts streaked black and brown. Female similar to other female buntings; heavily streaked buff and brown above, buffy below. Bold eyebrow and smudgy black moustache helpful distinguishing features. Both sexes have white outer tail feathers. Song unappealing and boring. *Status:* widespread and numerous resident. *Similar Species:* female similar to other female buntings (pp.246-251).

REED BUNTING

Type	bunting-like
Size	14–16cm (5½–6½in)
Habitat	marshes, heaths, fields
Behaviour	flits, perches openly, takes off from vegetation
Flocking	1–10
Flight	direct
Voice	several deliberate notes ending in a hurry

IDENTIFICATION

Adult ♂	
Crown	black
Upperparts	streaked brown and black; white collar
Rump	grey
Tail	black and white, medium
Throat	black
Breast	white
Belly	white
Bill	black; short and stubby
Legs	black; medium length
Adult ♀	heavily streaked brown and buff above, buffy below; eyebrow and moustache

BREEDING

Nest	cup on or near ground
Eggs	4–5; pale grey and black
Incubation	12–14 days, mainly ♀
Young	helpless; downy
Fledging	10–13 days
Broods	2–3; Apr–June
Food	seeds
Population	c300,000 pairs

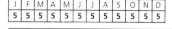

J	F	M	A	M	J	J	A	S	O	N	D
5	5	5	5	5	5	5	5	5	5	5	5

short thick neck

stubby bill

both sexes
streaked

pink legs

Chunky, thick-set bunting that
appears almost neckless. Streaked
buff and brown above and below; both
sexes similar to other female buntings.
No white in tail. Perches openly, usually
near ground in fields and open bushy
areas. Sings with head thrown back;
legs trail in fluttering flight. Gregarious
in winter.

Status: locally abundant resident; absent
from many areas
especially north
and west.
Similar Species: all
female buntings
(pp.246-251), but
Corn Bunting
larger and plumper.

CORN BUNTING

Type	bunting-like
Size	17–18.5cm (6¹⁄₂–7¹⁄₂in)
Habitat	heaths, fields and hedges, gardens
Behaviour	perches openly, hops, takes off and lands on vegetation or ground
Flocking	1–2
Flight	direct
Voice	jingling rattle

IDENTIFICATION

Adult

Crown	streaked buff and brown
Upperparts	streaked buff and brown
Rump	buff
Tail	brown; medium length, notched
Throat	white
Breast	streaked buff and brown
Belly	streaked buff and brown
Bill	buff; short and stubby
Legs	pink; medium length

BREEDING

Nest	cup on ground or in bush
Eggs	4–6; white, spotted grey
Incubation	12–14 days ♀
Young	helpless; downy
Fledging	12+ days
Broods	1–2; Apr–May
Food	seeds, berries
Population	30,000 pairs

J	F	M	A	M	J	J	A	S	O	N	D
4	4	4	4	4	4	4	4	4	4	4	4

Checklist

- Red-throated Diver
- Black-throated Diver
- Great Northern Diver
- Little Grebe
- Great Crested Grebe
- Red-necked Grebe
- Slavonian Grebe
- Black-necked Grebe
- Little Grebe
- Fulmar
- Manx Shearwater
- European Storm-petrel
- Leach's Storm-petrel
- Great Cormorant
- Shag
- Northern Gannet
- Bittern
- Grey Heron
- Spoonbill
- Mute Swan
- Bewick's Swan
- Whooper Swan
- Bean Goose
- Pink-footed Goose
- White-fronted Goose
- Greylag Goose

- Canada Goose
- Barnacle Goose
- Brent Goose
- Common Shelduck
- Eurasian Wigeon
- Northern Pintail
- Common Teal
- Garganey
- Gadwall
- Mallard
- Northern Shoveler
- Common Pochard
- Tufted Duck
- Greater Scaup
- Common Eider
- Long-tailed Duck
- Common Scoter
- Velvet Scoter
- Goldeneye
- Smew
- Red-breasted Merganser
- Goosander
- Ruddy Duck
- Honey Buzzard
- Red Kite
- White-tailed Eagle
- Marsh Harrier
- Hen Harrier
- Montagu's Harrier

- Marsh Harrier
- Golden Eagle
- Northern Goshawk
- European Sparrowhawk
- Common Buzzard
- Rough-legged Buzzard
- Common Kestrel
- Merlin
- Hobby
- Peregrine Falcon
- Osprey
- Common Quail
- Red Grouse
- Ptarmigan
- Black Grouse
- Capercaillie
- Red-legged Partridge
- Grey Partridge
- Common Pheasant
- Water Rail
- Corn Crake
- Moorhen
- Common Coot
- Oystercatcher
- Avocet
- Stone-curlew
- Little Ringed Plover
- Ringed Plover
- Dotterel
- European Golden Plover

- Grey Plover
- Lapwing
- Knot
- Sanderling
- Little Stint
- Temminck's Stint
- Curlew Sandpiper
- Purple Sandpiper
- Dunlin
- Ruff
- Jack Snipe
- Common Snipe
- Woodcock
- Black-tailed Godwit
- Bar-tailed Godwit
- Whimbrel
- Eurasian Curlew
- Spotted Redshank
- Common Redshank
- Greenshank
- Green Sandpiper
- Wood Sandpiper
- Common Sandpiper
- Turnstone
- Red-necked Phalarope
- Grey Phalarope
- Pomarine Skua
- Arctic Skua

- [ ] Great Skua
- [ ] Mediterranean Gull
- [ ] Common Gull
- [ ] Little Gull
- [ ] Black-headed Gull
- [ ] Herring Gull
- [ ] Lesser Black-backed Gull
- [ ] Great Black-backed Gull
- [ ] Kittiwake
- [ ] Sandwich Tern
- [ ] Roseate Tern
- [ ] Common Tern
- [ ] Arctic Tern
- [ ] Little Tern
- [ ] Black Tern
- [ ] Common Guillemot
- [ ] Razorbill
- [ ] Puffin
- [ ] Black Guillemot
- [ ] Rock Dove
- [ ] Stock Dove
- [ ] Wood Pigeon
- [ ] Collared Dove
- [ ] Turtle Dove
- [ ] Common Cuckoo
- [ ] Barn Owl
- [ ] Little Owl
- [ ] Short-eared Owl
- [ ] Long-eared Owl
- [ ] Tawny Owl

- [ ] European Nightjar
- [ ] Common Swift
- [ ] Common Kingfisher
- [ ] Wryneck
- [ ] Green Woodpecker
- [ ] Great Spotted Woodpecker
- [ ] Lesser Spotted Woodpecker
- [ ] Wood Lark
- [ ] Sky Lark
- [ ] Shore Lark
- [ ] Sand Martin
- [ ] Barn Swallow
- [ ] House Martin
- [ ] Tree Pipit
- [ ] Meadow Pipit
- [ ] Rock Pipit
- [ ] Water Pipit
- [ ] Yellow Wagtail
- [ ] Grey Wagtail
- [ ] Pied Wagtail
- [ ] Waxwing
- [ ] Dipper
- [ ] Wren
- [ ] Hedge Accentor
- [ ] Robin
- [ ] Nightingale
- [ ] Black Redstart
- [ ] Common Redstart
- [ ] Whinchat
- [ ] Stonechat
- [ ] Northern Wheatear
- [ ] Ring Ouzel

- [ ] Blackbird
- [ ] Fieldfare
- [ ] Song Thrush
- [ ] Redwing
- [ ] Mistle Thrush
- [ ] Grasshopper Warbler
- [ ] Sedge Warbler
- [ ] Reed Warbler
- [ ] Marsh Warbler
- [ ] Dartford Warbler
- [ ] Garden Warbler
- [ ] Lesser Whitethroat
- [ ] Common Whitethroat
- [ ] Blackcap
- [ ] Wood Warbler
- [ ] Chiffchaff
- [ ] Willow Warbler
- [ ] Goldcrest
- [ ] Firecrest
- [ ] Spotted Flycatcher
- [ ] Pied Flycatcher
- [ ] Bearded Tit
- [ ] Long-tailed Tit
- [ ] Marsh Tit
- [ ] Willow Tit
- [ ] Crested Tit
- [ ] Coal Tit
- [ ] Blue Tit
- [ ] Great Tit
- [ ] European Nuthatch
- [ ] Eurasian Treecreeper

- [ ] Red-backed Shrike
- [ ] Great Grey Shrike
- [ ] Magpie
- [ ] Red-billed Chough
- [ ] Jackdaw
- [ ] Rook
- [ ] Carrion Crow
- [ ] Common Raven
- [ ] Eurasian Jay
- [ ] Common Starling
- [ ] House Sparrow
- [ ] Tree Sparrow
- [ ] Chaffinch
- [ ] Brambling
- [ ] Greenfinch
- [ ] Goldfinch
- [ ] Siskin
- [ ] Linnet
- [ ] Twite
- [ ] Common Redpoll
- [ ] Common Crossbill
- [ ] Scottish Crossbill
- [ ] Bullfinch
- [ ] Hawfinch
- [ ] Lapland Bunting
- [ ] Snow Bunting
- [ ] Yellowhammer
- [ ] Cirl Bunting
- [ ] Reed Bunting
- [ ] Corn Bunting

Index

254

Index